PRINCIPLES OF DIGITAL COMPUTER OPERATION

PRINCIPLES OF DIGITAL COMPUTER OPERATION

M. DAVID FREEDMAN
BENDIX RESEARCH LABORATORIES
SOUTHFIELD, MICHIGAN

JOHN WILEY & SONS, INC.
NEW YORK LONDON SYDNEY TORONTO

Library of Congress Catalog Card Number: 71–37953

ISBN 0–471–27731–2

Printed in the United States of America.

10 9 8 7 6 5 4 3 2 1

PREFACE

In this book, I have presented the details of how a digital computer works. I have written the book so that no prior knowledge of computers is required. Of course, previous exposure to computers via BASIC or FORTRAN programming might be helpful, but I believe that for most college students, this book can adequately serve as an introduction to digital computing. Others, for whom this book should prove valuable, include the computer professional or programmer seeking an overview of the subject; the student or professional seeking to pass the Computer Society Examinations in England or Australia; and in fact, anyone who is interested in how a computer works.

I have organized the material presented as follows: The first chapter develops the organization of the computer in a step-by-step manner. By the end of Chapter 1, a fairly sophisticated computer organization has been presented, and the functional interaction of the major computer subsystems has been discussed. The concept of a stored program is introduced midway through Chapter 1.

In Chapter 2, I introduce the binary number system and also show how sequences of bits are interpreted as instructions, numbers, or addresses. I refrain from using mnemonics for instructions, since I feel that descriptive phrases are less likely to confuse the reader. Moreover, a universal set of mnemonics does not exist, although similar instructions are found in most machines.

Chapters 3 and 4 deal with arithmetic and number representations, topics relating to the arithmetic unit of the computer. Because of the combined length of the two chapters, it may be advisable for the reader to merely skim the material presented in Chapter 4 on a first reading.

Chapter 5 describes the registers of the computer and the role they play in its operation. In this chapter, the multi-accumulator machine which is currently very popular is introduced.

In Chapter 6, I present concepts which relate to the memory subsystem. Block transfers, input–output buffering, multiprocessing, and other topics involving the memory are presented.

Chapters 7 and 8 describe the input–output subsystem and many of the devices used for communicating with the computer. Auxiliary memory devices, such as magnetic tape and disk which operate as if they were input–output devices, are also described in Chapter 8.

Chapter 9 deals with the interrupt system, and justification for using interrupts is presented.

Time-sharing is covered in Chapter 10, which includes a discussion of how a multiprogramming system operates.

The software used routinely in a computer system is described in Chapter 11. It is in this chapter that I present a brief description of the higher-level algorithmic language FORTRAN and compare it to machine language and assembly language programming.

Since many computers are designed using microprogramming techniques, I have included Chapter 12, which deals with both fixed and dynamic microprogramming.

Chapter 13 presents a survey of applications for which computers are used, which will help the reader gain an insight into their vast potential.

Finally, Chapter 14 describes several computer organizations which are either being designed and are under construction, or are being contemplated for the future.

In summary, I have attempted to present a broad perspective of the computer field from which the reader will be able to branch out into more advanced disciplines such as programming, computer design, systems programming, etc.

As with any undertaking, there are several people who helped to make this book a reality. The encouragement of Professor Heinz von Foerster of the University of Illinois, Department of Electrical Engineering, when the book was still in its early stages of preparation is gratefully acknowledged. Discussions with Bendix colleagues Ed Johnson and Frank Russo were always helpful. I also appreciate the efforts of Professor Charles Freedman of the University of Minnesota, Department of Economics, Sid Freedman of the Psychology Department, Dalhousie University, Halifax, Nova Scotia, and Mark Ephron, a mathematics and computer science student at the University of Illinois, all of whom read preliminary versions of the manuscript and made significant comments. Finally, I want to express my appreciation to my wife Roberta, who not only read the manuscript at each stage of preparation and was my severest critic, but also typed it and helped to proofread the copy.

Southfield, Michigan
December 1971

M. David Freedman

CONTENTS

PRINCIPLES OF DIGITAL COMPUTER OPERATION

1

THE ORGANIZATION OF THE DIGITAL COMPUTER

In recent years, computers have increased in importance to the point that we come in contact with them almost every day. They are used to prepare paychecks, and tax and utility bills; to control sports scoreboards and traffic lights; to provide stock market and traffic violation information; and even to arrange timetables for college students. Certainly they have an overwhelming impact on our daily lives.

This book is about the digital computer and how it works. After a brief introduction to digital computation in Section 1.1, we proceed to describe the organization of the computer in an evolutionary fashion. Toward the end of this chapter, a fairly elaborate block diagram of the computer is presented (Figure 1-10). The operation of each of the subsystems contained in the block diagram will have been described in sufficient detail so that the reader has a working knowledge of the system. Subsequent chapters then elaborate on these subsystems and how they operate.

1.1 DIGITAL COMPUTATION

From the time we first learned to associate a number composed of a string of digits with a physical or monetary quantity, we have been using **digital quantities.** Ten feet, fifty-one miles per hour, and five dollars are all examples of digital quantities. Any string of digits such as that associated with a digital quantity is called a **digital number.** If we add or subtract digital quantities of similar units, or if we multiply or divide a digital quantity by a digital number, the arithmetic operation being performed is called a **digital computation**. Since the result of a digital computation is independent of the type of quantities involved and depends only on the numbers, it is customary to define a digital computation as being an arithmetic operation performed on digital numbers. For example, ten added to seven is equal to seventeen regardless of the physical or monetary quantities involved. Man has devised many means, ranging from counting on his fingers to inventing the electronic digital computer, to simplify the task of carrying out digital computations.

Digital computation began when early man learned to count by associating physical quantities in the world about him with his fingers. Some years later, a tablet was used to record larger numbers than can be represented by the fingers, and methods evolved for adding without counting. Subtraction, multiplication, and division followed naturally from these early concepts.

The first example of a semiautomatic device which was used in digital computation is the oriental abacus. In this device the positions of beads denote numerical magnitudes, and arithmetic is performed by manipulating the beads according to a fixed set of rules. It is possible for an experienced person to carry out computations more rapidly on an abacus than by using pencil and paper. More recently, mechanical adding machines and desk calculators have helped to automate digital computation. On these machines, the numbers to be manipulated are entered via a numeric keyboard and other keys are activated to carry out the desired computations. All these devices are examples of digital computers. Another example is the high-speed electronic digital computer. This machine is composed of a number of subsystems, one of them being an **arithmetic unit** whose purpose is to perform the digital computations. The other subsystems perform ancillary functions which allow the machine as a whole to operate completely automatically.

1.2 THE ARITHMETIC UNIT

The arithmetic unit is the workhorse of the electronic digital computer. It is capable of performing millions of operations per second and therefore must be fed its instructions and data automatically in order to take full advantage of its speed. We now examine how the arithmetic unit and the other subsystems of the digital computer operate.

In Figure 1-1, the arithmetic unit is represented by a box with lines drawn to it to represent the flow of information to and from the unit. Data is transmitted to the device through lines I and J and from it through line O. Instructions are transmitted to it as commands via lines A, S, M, and D, which represent ADD, SUBTRACT, MULTIPLY, and DIVIDE, respectively.* The actual mechanism

* In this section, we consider only the arithmetic operations performed by the arithmetic unit. Its other capabilities are deferred to Chapter 2.

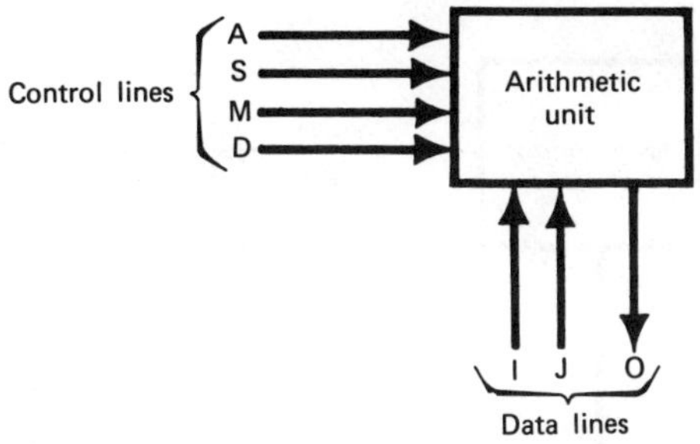

FIGURE 1-1. The arithmetic unit of an electronic digital computer showing the control and data lines.

whereby these lines represent the data or instructions is relatively unimportant at this stage; what is important is that a flow of information does take place and that we can represent it pictorially in a simplified block diagram form using lines and arrowheads as in Figure 1-1. The operation of the arithmetic unit can now be described with the aid of the block diagram.

To add two numbers together, line A is activated and the numbers, or **operands**, which we shall call i and j, are transmitted to the unit via lines I and J. After the arithmetic unit has completed the addition, the output, which in this case is the sum $i + j$, is put onto line O and is transmitted to a suitable destination in the computer via this line. For subtraction, line S is activated and the result on O is the difference $i - j$ between the operands. Similarly, if M is activated, the product $i \times j$ is formed, and if D is activated, the quotient $i \div j$ is formed.

The ultimate speed of the arithmetic unit is therefore restricted by its own operating rate, by the rate at which it is supplied with data and instructions, and by the rate at which results are transmitted to their destinations. It is the task of the **main control** subsystem to activate the control lines and to control the transmission of data to and from the arithmetic unit.

1.3 THE MAIN CONTROL

In Figure 1-2, the relationship between the main control and the arithmetic unit is illustrated in block diagram form. The control lines and the input data lines have been redrawn as single lines. This does not mean that single lines are used in practice, but merely serves to simplify the block diagram. The third block represents a "data bank" whose function is both to store data for transmission to the arithmetic unit and also to store results which are computed by the arithmetic unit and transmitted back to the data bank.

In operation, the main control transmits suitable control information to the data bank via line B, instructing the data bank to transmit two operands to the

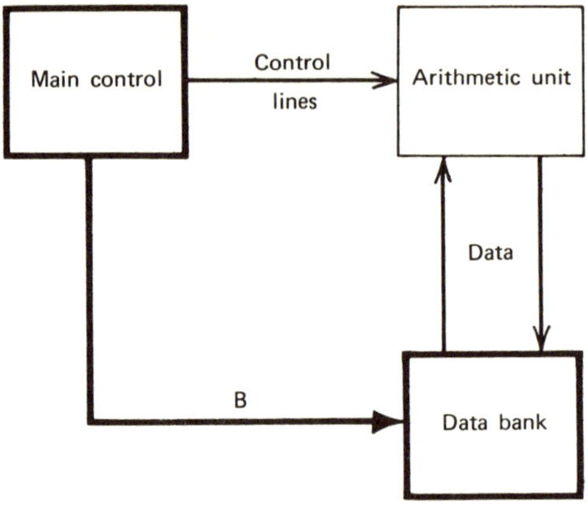

FIGURE 1-2. Computer block diagram showing the interconnections between the main control, data bank, and arithmetic unit.

arithmetic unit. Simultaneously, the arithmetic unit is commanded to perform a specific operation, such as addition, on the data. After the operation is performed by the arithmetic unit, the result of the computation is transmitted to the data bank which stores it according to further instructions furnished on line B by the main control. Assuming that the data bank is able to send data to and receive data from the arithmetic unit at a sufficiently rapid rate, the arithmetic unit can be operated efficiently, at least until the data bank is exhausted.

Therefore, the main control acts as a supervisor which sends commands to the various subsystems instructing them of their respective tasks. It also coordinates the data flow between subsystems, ensuring that the desired data is available when needed by each subsystem. To perform in this manner, the main control must have access to an instruction list which keeps it informed of the tasks to be done, their correct sequence, where to find the data required to carry out these tasks, and finally, where to store the results generated by each task as it is performed. This instruction list is stored in an "instruction bank" in much the same way that the data is stored in the data bank. The instruction bank is shown in Figure 1-3 which also illustrates its relation to the main control unit. Line C is used to transmit the instructions from the bank to the main control.

The two storage banks which are used to supply the instructions and data to the other subsystems and which store the computed results can be classified under the general heading of **computer memory**. Let us therefore take a closer look at the organization of the memory and how information is stored in and retrieved from the computer memory subsystem.

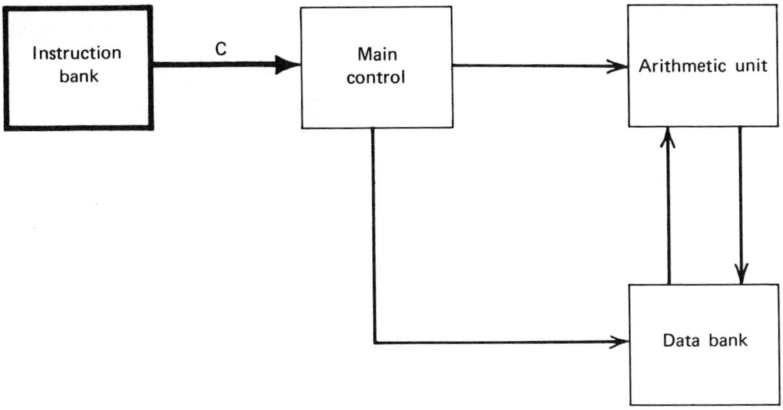

FIGURE 1-3. Computer block diagram which includes the instruction bank.

1.4 THE MEMORY

The computer memory can be compared to a blackboard which is divided into sections as shown in Figure 1-4. Information can be written into any section and can remain unaltered for any desired length of time. Whenever the information contained in a particular section is no longer required, it can be erased and new information written into the same space. To keep track of where a given piece of information is recorded, each blackboard section is assigned a number, called an **address**, as shown in the figure. In this example, the spaces, or memory locations, are numbered from 1 to 24. The instruction ADD is stored in location 6; other instructions are stored in locations 7, 8, and 9. The numbers 262, 101, and 297, which are examples of data, are stored in locations 19, 20, and 23. All other locations are blank. Note that any memory location can be used to store either instructions or data. This important feature allows the instruction and data banks of Figure 1-3 to be combined into a single device which is simply called the **memory**. The resulting block diagram is illustrated in Figure 1-5.

Instructions are usually stored in successive memory locations, as in the example of Figure 1-4, thus simplifying the task of determining where each instruction is located. The instructions are then transmitted via line C to the main control in the sequence in which they occur. When an instruction calls for an operand, the main control sends the address of the required operand to the memory. It also instructs the memory to transmit the operand to the arithmetic unit from the specified memory location. In this manner, both data and instructions are stored in a single memory system, thereby eliminating the need for separate storage banks.

1	2	3	4
5	6 ADD	7 STORE	8 ADD
9 STORE	10	11	12
13	14	15	16
17	18	19 262	20 101
21	22	23 297	24

FIGURE 1-4. Example illustrating the analogy between a partitioned blackboard and a computer memory.

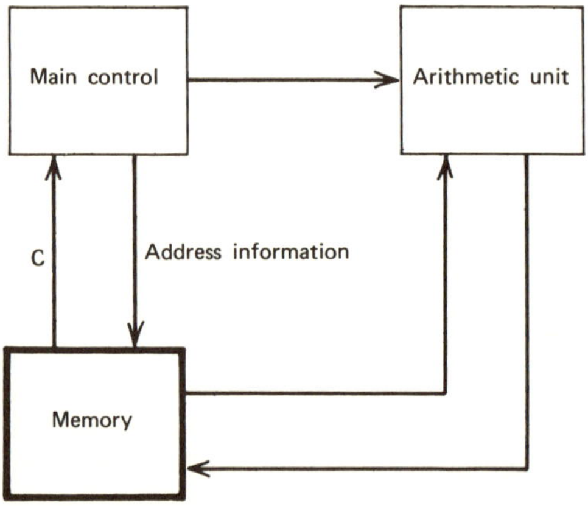

FIGURE 1-5. Computer block diagram showing the consolidation of the instruction and data banks into a single memory device.

A machine which is composed of a main control, an arithmetic unit, and a memory is called a **stored-program** digital computer. This differs from other digital computers because of its ability to obey a sequence of instructions, called a **program**, which is stored in the memory. Although stored-program computers are usually more elaborate than the one shown in Figure 1-5, nevertheless, all the intricacies of the stored-program concept can be illustrated using this configuration as an example. The programs which we shall use as examples throughout this book are composed of functional instructions such as ADD and STORE. Although every stored-program computer can execute such instructions, they are often given other names or differ slightly in the way they are executed, since no universal set of instructions exists for all computers. With this in mind, let us now examine how a stored program is executed by our hypothetical machine.

1.5 THE STORED PROGRAM

Figure 1-4, which is reproduced below in a compact form, illustrates how instructions and data are stored in a computer memory:

6	ADD
7	STORE
8	ADD
9	STORE
19	262
20	101
23	297

Only the memory locations which are not blank are shown. The numbers on the left are the memory addresses, and the contents of each memory location are shown on the right. The set of instructions which is stored in locations 6–9 is an example of a stored program.

If the computer were to attempt to execute the program, it would immediately find itself in difficulty. The first instruction is an ADD order, but no information is available to enable the computer to determine where the operands to be added are located. Similarly, the STORE order which follows is devoid of information which would instruct the computer where to store the results of the addition. The difficulty can be surmounted by including address information along with the instructions. For example, if the operands to be used in the first addition are stored in locations 19 and 20 in the memory, then the ADD instruction can be written as

ADD, 19, 20

Commas are used to separate the three parts of the instruction to prevent confusion. Thus, the complete program with its associated data can be rewritten to include the address information, as shown below:

6	ADD, 19, 20
7	STORE, 22
8	ADD, 22, 23
9	STORE, 21
19	262
20	101
23	297

During execution of the program, the following sequence of events takes place within the computer: The first instruction is sent to the main control from location 6 in the memory. The main control examines it and determines that it is an ADD instruction and that the operands to be used are stored in locations 19 and 20. It therefore commands the memory to transfer the contents of these locations to the arithmetic unit. Simultaneously, the main control sends a command to the arithmetic unit instructing it to add the two operands together when they are received. The main control is now prepared to receive the next instruction and so informs the memory. When the instruction is received from location 7, the main control examines it and determines that it is a STORE instruction and that memory location 22 is to be the destination. It therefore commands the arithmetic unit to transmit the results of the addition to the memory and instructs the memory to store the sum in location 22. After these first two instructions have been executed, the memory locations which are not blank will have the following contents:

6	ADD, 19, 20
7	STORE, 22
8	ADD, 22, 23
9	STORE, 21
19	262
20	101
22	363
23	297

Note that the contents of locations 19 and 20 remain unchanged. Only the contents of location 22, which now contains the number 363 has been changed.

The computer continues to operate, and executes the next two instructions in a similar manner. In this case, the contents of memory locations 22 and 23 are added together and stored in location 21. Therefore, after completing the execution of the instruction in location 9, the contents of the memory will be

6	ADD, 19, 20
7	STORE, 22
8	ADD, 22, 23
9	STORE, 21
19	262
20	101
21	660
22	363
23	297

The only change has been to store 660, which is the sum of 363 and 297, in location 21. The computer will now attempt to execute the "instruction" in memory location 10, but finding only a blank space in the memory, it will terminate its operation, since a blank instruction is considered illegal.

1.6 THE ACCUMULATOR

Let us examine the sample program more carefully. Its purpose is to add together the three numbers which are stored in locations 19, 20, and 23, and to store the results in location 21. Location 22 is used to store the interim results obtained by adding the first two numbers. A storage location used to store interim results produced by the arithmetic unit is called an **accumulator**. It is very convenient to designate a fixed location in the computer for use as an accumulator. As illustrated in Figure 1-6, the accumulator is not usually associated with the main memory.

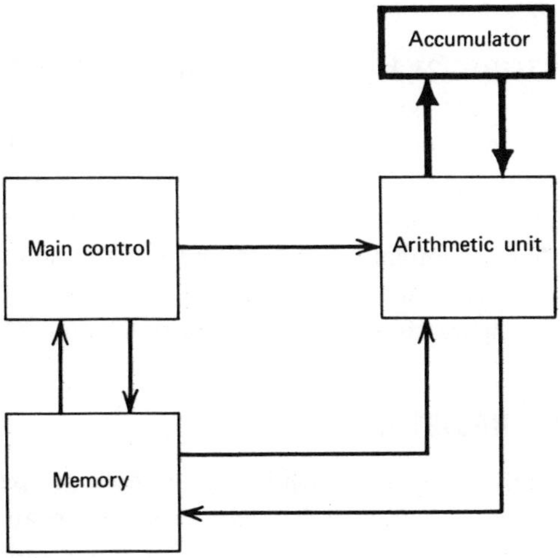

FIGURE 1-6. Block diagram showing how the accumulator is related to the computer.

Program	Accumulator	Location 19	Location 20	Location 21	Location 23
LOAD ACC, 19	262	262	101	–	297
ADD, 20	363	262	101	–	297
ADD, 23	660	262	101	–	297
STORE ACC, 21	660	262	101	660	297

FIGURE 1-7. Contents of memory locations 19–21 and 23, and the accumulator at the completion of the execution of each instruction of the sample program.

In order for the accumulator to be used efficiently, its contents should be employed as one of the operands in every arithmetic operation. This allows a simplification of the instruction format, since ADD, 23 can then be automatically interpreted to mean: Add the contents of memory location 23 to the contents of the accumulator and store the results in the accumulator. When we use the accumulator in this manner, we must be careful to avoid adding its previous contents to the current sum. This is ensured by using the instruction LOAD ACC, 19 at the beginning of the program to set the accumulator equal to the number stored in memory location 19. The program to add the three numbers together then becomes

```
6   LOAD ACC, 19
7   ADD, 20
8   ADD, 23
9   STORE ACC, 21
```

The instruction STORE, 21 has been changed to STORE ACC, 21 to indicate that the contents of the accumulator are to be stored in location 21. The contents of the accumulator and of memory locations 19, 20, 21, and 23, at the completion of the execution of each instruction, are shown in Figure 1-7. As expected, the contents of locations 19, 20, and 23, which contain the operands, are not altered. The accumulator is set to 262 initially and thereafter contains the correct partial sums. Finally, after the complete program has been executed, the sum of the three operands is stored in memory location 21.

1.7 THE INDEX REGISTER

Let us consider another program which is slightly more complex. In this case, we want to add together 80 operands, stored in memory locations 101–180, and store the result in memory location 100. A program which carries out the operations required to solve this problem is

```
LOAD ACC, 101
ADD, 102
ADD, 103
ADD, 104
  .   .
  .   .
  .   .
ADD, 179
ADD, 180
STORE ACC, 100
```

The difficulty associated with this program is that 79 memory locations are required to store the ADD instructions. Consider what would happen if one thousand operands were to be added together!

What we require is a program to execute the additions

```
ADD, 102
ADD, 103
  .   .
  .   .
  .   .
ADD, 179
ADD, 180
```

without the need to specify each ADD instruction explicitly. One method of accomplishing this makes use of a special location called an **index register**. Just as the accumulator is not usually associated with the main memory, neither is the index register. Its relationship to the computer is shown in Figure 1-8. All references to the index register are made by using the word INDEX. Consider, for example, the instruction, ADD, 181+INDEX. In place of the address, the formula, 181+INDEX, appears. When the main control encounters this formula in place of the address, it calculates the address of the operand from the formula

$$\textbf{Address} = \textbf{181} + \textbf{Contents of index register} \qquad (1\text{-}1)$$

Let us assume that the index register is initially set to −79 so that 102 will be the first address calculated from this formula. Then, let us repeat the execution of the ADD instruction and increase the contents of the index register by one, or **increment** it, each time an addition is performed. The address of the operand will automatically be incremented, since it is computed from the index register using (1-1). As a result, successive ADD instructions use operands which are stored in consecutive memory locations starting with location 102. The instruction INCREMENT INDEX is used to increment the contents of the index register.

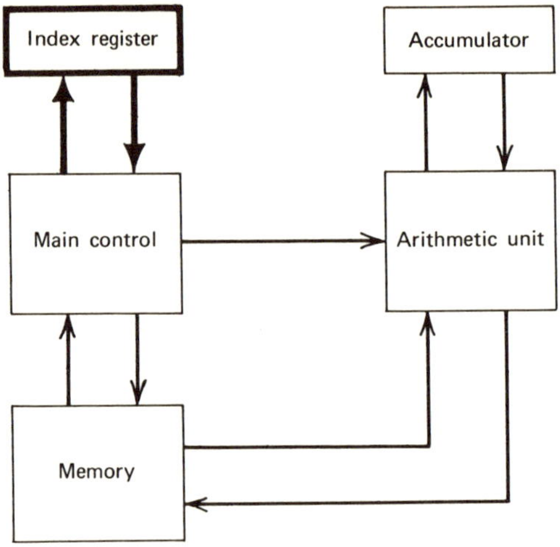

FIGURE 1-8. Block diagram of the computer showing the index register.

We now have a means for changing the operand address by using an index register. To be able to repeat the execution of an instruction, we need a command which alters the normal sequence in which instructions are executed. For example, if at any time we want the instruction stored in location n to be executed, we can insert the command TRANSFER TO n into the program. This instruction informs the main control that the next instruction to be executed is stored in memory location n, and this should be followed by executing the instruction stored in location n + 1, and so on. Thus, we can now replace the long string of ADD instructions by the simple program

```
1   LOAD ACC, 101
2   LOAD INDEX, (−79)
3   ADD, 181+INDEX
4   INCREMENT INDEX
5   TRANSFER TO 3
```

The instruction LOAD INDEX, (−79) sets the contents of the index register to −79. The brackets are used to prevent the number from being interpreted as an address. The instructions in locations 3, 4, and 5 instruct the computer to execute the desired sequence of ADD instructions starting with ADD, 102.

The action of repeatedly executing a sequence of instructions is called **looping**, and the instructions themselves are called a **loop**. The loop described above has a serious drawback. There is no provision for terminating the execution of the instructions in the loop after the 79 additions have been performed. Fortunately, an examination of the contents of the index register reveals how many times the loop has been executed, and this information can be used to terminate execution of the loop. An instruction for this purpose has been inserted into the loop in location 5, as shown below:

```
1  LOAD ACC, 101
2  LOAD INDEX, (−79)
3  ADD, 181+INDEX
4  INCREMENT INDEX
5  IF INDEX=0, TRANSFER TO 7
6  TRANSFER TO 3
7  STORE ACC, 100
```

If, when the computer encounters the instruction stored in location 5, the index register does not contain zero, it proceeds to instruction 6 and continues to execute the instructions in the loop. If the index register contains exactly zero, the main control then obeys the TRANSFER TO 7 instruction, thereby terminating the execution of the loop. Details of the execution of the last few steps of the loop are shown in Figure 1-9, verifying that the loop is correctly terminated.

Instruction	Contents of index register	Address of ADD instruction
. .	.	
. .	.	
. .	.	
6 TRANSFER TO 3	−2	
3 ADD, 181+INDEX	−2	181 + (−2) = 179
4 INCREMENT INDEX	−1	
5 IF INDEX=0, TRANSFER TO 7	−1	
6 TRANSFER TO 3	−1	
3 ADD, 181+INDEX	−1	181 + (−1) = 180
4 INCREMENT INDEX	0	
5 IF INDEX=0, TRANSFER TO 7	0	
7 STORE ACC, 100	0	
. .	.	
. .	.	
. .	.	

FIGURE 1-9. Details of the last steps of the example of a loop verifying that it is correctly terminated.

An alternate method of testing the index register, which simplifies the loop, is

```
1  LOAD ACC, 101
2  LOAD INDEX, (–79)
3  ADD, 181+INDEX
4  INCREMENT INDEX
5  IF INDEX=–, TRANSFER TO 3
6  STORE ACC, 100
```

In this case, as long as the index register is negative, the loop is continued; as soon as it becomes zero, the instruction stored in location 6 is executed. The reader can substitute this alternate loop in Figure 1-9 to verify for himself that the loop is terminated correctly.

By using the index register, we are able to condense a long string of repetitive instructions into a short program. This is one of the features of a stored-program computer which enhances its ability to operate at high speed for a prolonged period of time. The computer configuration shown in Figure 1-8, however, has no provision for communication between the machine and its environment. We must provide a method for feeding instructions and data into the memory initially, and for extracting results from the machine after they are calculated. These tasks are the responsibility of the **input–output** subsystems.

1.8 INPUT–OUTPUT SYSTEMS

Although there are many input–output (I/O) devices which are used for communication between the computer and its environment, the typewriter can be used to illustrate the principles involved. The I/O control and typewriter subsystems are illustrated in Figure 1-10, which also shows their interconnections with the rest of the machine. The I/O control supervises all input and output operations in the same manner that the main control supervises all internal operations. As shown in Figure 1-10, typewriter data is transmitted via the accumulator. An alternate scheme which is used for high-speed I/O devices and which causes data to be transmitted via the memory is described in Chapters 2 and 6.

The instruction which is used to transmit data from the accumulator to the typewriter is OUTPUT ACC, TYPE. If this instruction is encountered by the main control, it sends the instruction directly to the I/O control. The I/O control then instructs the accumulator to transmit the character which has been stored in it to the typewriter and also instructs the typewriter to print the character when it is received. An example of a program which instructs the computer to print the expression X=52 is

```
 49  LOAD ACC, 101
 50  OUTPUT ACC, TYPE
 51  LOAD ACC, 102
 52  OUTPUT ACC, TYPE
 53  LOAD ACC, 103
 54  OUTPUT ACC, TYPE
 55  LOAD ACC, 104
 56  OUTPUT ACC, TYPE
  .   .
  .   .
  .   .
101  X
102  =
103  5
104  2
```

In order to describe the transmission of input data from the typewriter to the computer, let us assume that the input data is punched one character at a time as a set of holes in a strip of paper tape, and that the typewriter has an attached device for reading this tape. The instruction which causes a character to be read from the tape and transmitted to the accumulator is INPUT ACC, TYPE. In operation, the I/O control receives the instruction from the main control and then instructs the typewriter to read one character from the tape and to transmit

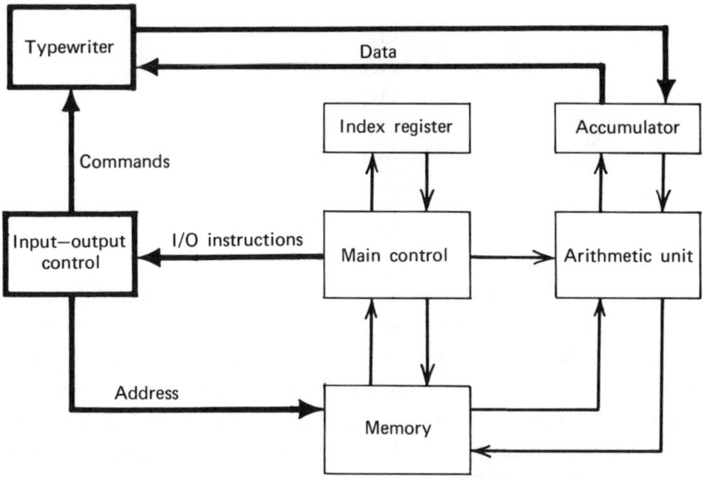

FIGURE 1-10. Computer block diagram illustrating the input–output control and typewriter subsystems.

this character to the accumulator. The accumulator is simultaneously instructed to store the character when it is received. An example of a program which commands the computer to read 13 characters from tape into the accumulator and to store them in memory locations 111–123 is

```
30   LOAD INDEX, (–13)
31   INPUT ACC, TYPE
32   STORE ACC, 124+INDEX
33   INCREMENT INDEX
34   IF INDEX=–, TRANSFER TO 31
35   – – – –
.    .
.    .
.    .
```

If the 13 characters on the tape are X=20,Y=51,Z=2, then after the program is executed, the contents of memory locations 111–123 will be

111	X
112	=
113	2
114	0
115	,
116	Y
117	=
118	5
119	1
120	,
121	Z
122	=
123	2

Thus far, we have described the operation of an automatic digital computer system which executes programs stored in its memory. It is able to perform high-speed arithmetic and to carry out input–output operations via a typewriter. We have shown that information in the form of commands and data is transmitted from subsystem to subsystem during the execution of a program. To simplify the description of how the computer operates, we used natural language phrases, such as ADD, STORE, and TRANSFER TO. However, the "language" which is used internally in the machine, called **machine language**, is quite unlike natural language. In Chapter 2 we show how information is encoded in machine language for transmission and storage in the machine.

EXERCISES

1.1 What is the function of the arithmetic unit of a digital computer?

1.2 What is the function of the main control system of a digital computer?

1.3 Why is it possible to store instructions and data in a single computer memory system?

1.4 What advantages does a digital computer with an accumulator have?

1.5 What is the index register of a digital computer used for?

1.6 Write a program to compute the function $y = x^2 + x$. Assume that the value of the variable x is stored in memory location 101 and that the calculated result is to be stored in location 151.

1.7 Write a program to compute the function $y = x^2 + x$ for each number stored in locations 101–150. Store the result corresponding to the number in location 101 in location 151, for 102 in 152, and so on.

[Hint: Use the index register and modify the program of Exercise 1.6 so that it becomes a loop. Do not forget to make sure that the loop is terminated correctly.]

1.8 Write a program which adds together the numbers stored in locations 101–140, and subtracts from this sum the sum of the numbers stored in locations 141–180.

1.9 Solve Exercise 1.8 using a single loop. [Hint: Write a program to add the number in location 101 to the accumulator and then subtract the number in location 141 from the accumulator. Modify the program into a loop using the index register, and be careful that the loop is correctly initiated and terminated.]

2

THE LANGUAGE OF THE COMPUTER

In Chapter 1 it was shown that, in order to command the arithmetic unit to perform addition, the main control activates a suitable control line, A. For subtraction, multiplication, and division, it activates control lines S, M, and D, respectively. Although this is an oversimplification of how the computer works, it is nevertheless true that all commands are transmitted by the presence or absence of electrical signals on control lines. If a line is inactive, that is, if no signal is present, we say that it is in the ZERO state. However, if a signal is present on the line, we say that it is in the ONE state. In this chapter, we show how all the information in the computer, whether in the form of instructions or data, can be represented by sequences of ZERO's and ONE's. Information represented in this way is easily transmitted and stored by the two-state elements used in the machine.

2.1 BINARY NUMBERS

In Chapter 1 we used the decimal number system to represent digital numbers. In the decimal system, each digit assumes a value from 0 to 9. Moreover, each digit position corresponds to a specific value. The first digit to the left of the decimal point denotes the number of **units**, the next digit, the number of **tens**, then **hundreds**, and so forth. In general, the first digit is weighted by 10^0, the second by 10^1, then 10^2, and the nth digit is weighted by 10^{n-1}, for any n. For example, the number 3297, in which the decimal point is understood to lie to the extreme right, denotes the value, $3 \times 10^3 + 2 \times 10^2 + 9 \times 10^1 + 7 \times 10^0$, or three thousand two hundred ninety-seven.

Digital computers, however, are composed of two-state elements which can represent only the values ZERO and ONE. Therefore we must encode all numbers as sequences of these two values. The **binary number system** provides us with one method of representing numbers using only ZERO's and ONE's. In this sytem, the first digit to the left of the "binary point" denotes the number of **units**, the next digit, the number of **twos**, then **fours**, **eights**, and so on. In general, the nth binary digit, or **bit**, is weighted by 2^{n-1}. For example, the binary number 110010 denotes the value

$$1 \times 2^5 + 1 \times 2^4 + 0 \times 2^3 + 0 \times 2^2 + 1 \times 2^1 + 0 \times 2^0 = 1 \times 32 + 1 \times 16 + 1 \times 2 = 50$$

Binary numbers can be used to represent negative numbers as well as positive numbers. For negative numbers, the **twos complement** representation is commonly used. In this representation, the left-hand, or Nth bit, is assigned the value $-(2^{N-1})$. For example, if eight bits are used, they are weighted by the values −128, 64, 32, 16, 8, 4, 2, and 1. Thus, the number, 10010100, is −128 + 16 + 4 or −108, whereas 01101100 is 64 + 32 + 8 + 4 or +108. Therefore, numbers from −128 (10000000) to +127 (01111111) can be represented by eight-bit numbers using the twos complement representation. It should be noted that whenever the left-hand bit of a twos complement number is a ONE, the number is negative; if it is a ZERO, the number is positive. Because the left-hand bit denotes the sign of the number, it is called the **sign bit.** However, in the special case where it is known in advance that the number is to be positive only, the left-hand bit is weighted by +128, and numbers from 0 to +255 can be represented by the eight bits. More will be said about the twos complement representation in Chapter 3.

Using the binary number system, numerical data and address information are easily represented in the computer and require only the storage and transmission of ZERO's and ONE's. However, the computer must also be able to interpret as instructions sequences of ZERO's and ONE's which are stored in the memory. We see how this is accomplished in Section 2.2.

2.2 MACHINE LANGUAGE INSTRUCTIONS*

Let us assume that each instruction stored in the memory is composed of a sequence of sixteen bits, which constitutes a **word** in the memory. Let us further assume that the leftmost eight bits of each word are used to define the

* As pointed out in Chapter 1, the instructions used in this book are functional in nature and are not intended to be identical to those used in an actual computer.

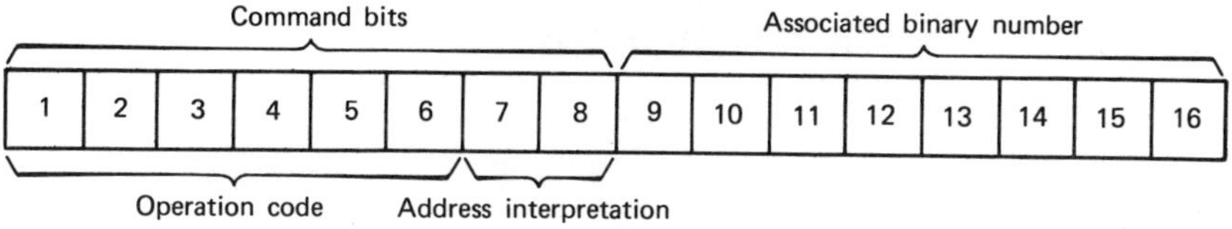

FIGURE 2-1. Machine language instruction format.

command, while the rightmost eight bits are interpreted as an **associated binary number**, which is usually used to represent an address. The command is further subdivided into two groups. Bits 1–6 then identify the **operation code** of the instruction, whereas bits 7 and 8 are used for **address interpretation**. Figure 2-1 illustrates this format. Figure 2-5, at the end of the chapter, contains a complete summary of the instructions and can be used as a reference by the reader throughout the chapter.

Before proceeding with the general interpretation of the instruction codes, let us consider the following example of an instruction:

001 000 00 0001 0011

Bits 1–6, which are 001 000, indicate that it is an ADD instruction, and bits 7 and 8, which are 00, indicate that the associated binary number defined by bits 9–16 is to be used as the address. Therefore, the instruction is ADD, 19, since the binary number 0001 0011 is equivalent to the decimal number 19.

Let us now examine how the command bits are used to represent instructions. The first three bits of the operation code define the type of operation to be executed according to the rules shown in Figure 2-2. In this chapter, we deal with each instruction group in order and describe the options given by bits 4–6 as they are encountered. We begin with the **arithmetic** instructions.

0 0 1	ARITHMETIC
0 1 0	LOGIC
0 1 1	LOAD AND STORE
1 0 0	TEST
1 0 1	SHIFT
1 1 0	INPUT–OUTPUT
1 1 1	MISCELLANEOUS

FIGURE 2-2. The interpretation of the first three operation code bits.

2.3 THE ARITHMETIC INSTRUCTIONS

We have already encountered the arithmetic instructions in Chapter 1. In each case, the number in the accumulator forms one of the operands and the second operand is usually located in the memory. Thus, for example, SUBTRACT, 46 causes the number in memory location 46 to be subtracted from the accumulator, and DIVIDE, 46 causes the number in the accumulator to be divided by the number in location 46.

In the operation code of an arithmetic instruction, bits 4 and 5 are used to differentiate between the four types of arithmetic operations, as follows:

Bit 4	Bit 5	Type of operation
0	0	ADD
0	1	SUBTRACT
1	0	MULTIPLY
1	1	DIVIDE

If bit 6 is a ONE, the associated binary number is not used as an address but is interpreted literally as the operand. For example,

001 001 00 0001 0011

is the instruction ADD, (19), where the parentheses indicate that the number 19 is to be used as the operand. Thus, when this instruction is executed, the number in the accumulator is increased by 19.

If bits 6, 7, and 8 are all ZERO, then the associated binary number is interpreted directly as an address. If, however, bit 7 is a ONE, then the index register is used to determine the address. For example, the instruction

001 000 10 0001 0011

is equivalent to ADD, 19+INDEX. Examples of indexing have been given in Chapter 1 in connection with the description of the index register.

In our sixteen-bit machine, an eight-bit associated binary number is available for specifying the address of an operand. Thus, only addresses from 0 to 255 can be specified directly. Most large computers have a longer word length which allows every address in the computer to be specified directly. In the smaller computers which have short word lengths, a technique called **indirect addressing** is commonly used to specify large addresses in the memory. In our computer, when bit 8 is a ONE, the associated binary number is interpreted as an indirect address.

2.4 INDIRECT ADDRESSING

Indirect addressing is a method for storing the address of an operand by using a full word in the memory, thereby allowing a large number of locations to be specified. When indirect addressing is used, the main control interprets the associated binary number of an instruction as an **indirect address.** The memory location specified by the indirect address contains the **actual address** of the operand to be used. Let us illustrate this concept with an example. A typical instruction which specifies an indirect address is ADD*, 19 where the asterisk is used to designate that the address, 19, is an indirect address. If memory location 19 contains a number equivalent to the decimal number 4081, for example, then the following sequence of events takes place: the main control, having received and interpreted the instruction as ADD*, 19, requests the memory to send it the contents of location 19. It receives a number which is equivalent to the decimal number 4081 and further instructs the memory to send the contents of location 4081 to the arithmetic unit. The latter is instructed to add this number to the accumulator when it is received from the memory. Thus we see that indirect addressing requires the execution of one additional step – that of obtaining the actual address from the location specified by the indirect address of the instruction.

An indirect address can be indexed. We will illustrate the concept of an indexed indirect address by an example using instructions which have been described in Chapter 1. If 80 numbers which are stored in locations 4001–4080 are to be added together and the sum stored in location 4081, the program written without indirect addressing would take the form*

```
1   LOAD ACC, (0)
2   LOAD INDEX, (–80)
3   ADD, 4081+INDEX
4   INCREMENT INDEX
5   IF INDEX=–, TRANSFER TO 3
6   STORE ACC, 4081
```

However, if the address 4081 is too large to be stored as the associated binary number in the instruction, it can be stored in another memory location whose address can be specified as an indirect address. The program then becomes

* The instruction LOAD ACC, (0) causes the accumulator to be set to zero initially. This prevents the previous contents of the accumulator from influencing the current sum.

```
1    LOAD ACC, (0)
2    LOAD INDEX, (—80)
3    ADD*, 19+INDEX
4    INCREMENT INDEX
5    IF INDEX=—, TRANSFER TO 3
6    STORE ACC*, 19
.        .
.        .
.        .
19   4081
```

which causes the instructions to be executed as if 4081 were written in place of 19. In operation, the main control first requests the memory to send it the contents of location 19. It then adds the contents of the index register to the contents of location 19 to determine the actual address of the operand for each ADD instruction. Note, therefore, that a memory location can be used to store an address, an instruction, or an operand. In the above example, location 19 contains an address, locations 1–6 contain instructions, and locations 4001–4080 contain operands.

Indirect addressing is sometimes provided in a computer which has a long word length even though direct addressing can specify every location in the memory. In this type of machine, the availability of the indirect addressing feature merely provides greater programming flexibility. For example, to change an operand address which is used by a large number of instructions, it is only necessary to change the contents of a single memory location. In the program described above, changing the contents of location 19 changes the actual address used by every instruction which specifies the indirect address 19.

This completes the description of the arithmetic instructions and some of the addressing options. The arithmetic unit is also capable of executing several types of nonarithmetic operations. We describe the **logic** instructions next.

2.5 THE LOGIC INSTRUCTIONS

The four logic instructions, COMPLEMENT, AND, OR, and EXCLUSIVE OR, are specified by bits 4 and 5:

Bit 4	Bit 5	Type of operation
0	0	COMPLEMENT
0	1	AND
1	0	OR
1	1	EXCLUSIVE OR

These instructions are executed by the arithmetic unit in conjunction with the accumulator in the same manner as the arithmetic instructions. When the COMPLEMENT instruction is encountered, each bit in the accumulator which is a ONE is converted to a ZERO, and each ZERO is converted to a ONE. Thus, if the accumulator contains 0000 1011 0101 1110 prior to the execution of COMPLEMENT, it will contain 1111 0100 1010 0001 after.

The OR and AND instructions cause each bit of an operand stored in the memory to be combined with the bit located in the corresponding position in the accumulator according to the following rules:

OR — If either or both bits of each pair is a ONE, the corresponding bit in the accumulator is set to ONE; otherwise, it is set to ZERO.

AND — If both bits of each pair are ONE, the corresponding bit in the accumulator is set to ONE; otherwise, it is set to ZERO.

As an example, assume that the accumulator initially contains 0000 1011 0101 1110 and the operand in memory location 15 is 0000 0000 1111 1111. The instruction OR, 15 causes the accumulator contents to be changed to 0000 1011 1111 1111, as shown in detail below:

Initial contents of accumulator	0000 1011 0101 1110
Contents of memory location 15	0000 0000 1111 1111
Final contents of accumulator	0000 1011 1111 1111

If the instruction AND, 15 were executed in the above example, the result in the accumulator would be 0000 0000 0101 1110.

The EXCLUSIVE OR instruction is a variation of the OR instruction. The rule used in this case is as follows:

EXCLUSIVE OR — If either but not both bits of each pair is a ONE, the corresponding bit in the accumulator is set to ONE; otherwise, it is set to ZERO.

If the instruction EXCLUSIVE OR, 15 were executed in the above example, the accumulator contents would become 0000 1011 1010 0001.

The rules governing the use of bits 6, 7, and 8 are the same as for the arithmetic instructions. Thus, the address can be indexed or determined indirectly, or both. If bit 6, the literal bit, is a ONE, however, bits 9–16 are used as the right half of the operand. Since the operand is sixteen bits long, the left-hand eight bits of the operand are set to ZERO's.

Let us examine how the logic instructions can be used to manipulate data. Let us assume that we wish to separate a sixteen-bit word into eight-bit segments called **bytes**, to manipulate each byte separately, and then to combine the two resulting bytes into a full word again. The AND instruction is useful for separating words into bytes and the OR instruction for combining bytes into

Program	Accumulator	Location 21	Location 22	Location 23
LOAD ACC, 20	0011 1010 1110 0101	–	–	–
AND, 30	0011 1010 0000 0000	–	–	–
STORE ACC, 21	0011 1010 0000 0000	0011 1010 0000 0000	–	–
LOAD ACC, 20	0011 1010 1110 0101	0011 1010 0000 0000	–	–
AND, 31	0000 0000 1110 0101	0011 1010 0000 0000	–	–
STORE ACC, 22	0000 0000 1110 0101	0011 1010 0000 0000	0000 0000 1110 0101	–
LOAD ACC, 21	0011 1010 0000 0000	0011 1010 0000 0000	0000 0000 1110 0101	–
OR, 22	0011 1010 1110 0101	0011 1010 0000 0000	0000 0000 1110 0101	–
STORE ACC, 23	0011 1010 1110 0101	0011 1010 0000 0000	0000 0000 1110 0101	0011 1010 1110 0101

Location 20	0011 1010 1110 0101
Location 30	1111 1111 0000 0000
Location 31	0000 0000 1111 1111

FIGURE 2-3. **Details of the execution of a program to separate a word into two bytes and combine two bytes into a word.**

words. A program which illustrates this procedure is

```
1    LOAD ACC, 20
2    AND, 30
3    STORE ACC, 21
4    LOAD ACC, 20
5    AND, 31
6    STORE ACC, 22
7    LOAD ACC, 21
8    OR, 22
9    STORE ACC, 23
.      .
.      .
.      .
20   0011 1010 1110 0101
.      .
.      .
.      .
30   1111 1111 0000 0000
31   0000 0000 1111 1111
```

The contents of locations 20, 30, and 31 are shown in binary, for convenience. Figure 2-3 illustrates the step-by-step execution of the program which separates the word stored in location 20 into two bytes and then combines the two bytes back into a full word. Locations 21 and 22 are used to store the two bytes, with ZERO's replacing the unused byte in each case. Finally, location 23 is used to store the word obtained from the two bytes, which, in this case, is the same word with which we started in location 20, since no intermediate manipulation occurred.

The next instructions to be examined are the load and store instructions. These are responsible for setting the accumulator and index register to their initial values and storing data from the two registers in the memory.

2.6 THE LOAD AND STORE INSTRUCTIONS

The load and store instructions are used to transfer data between the memory and the accumulator and index register. Bits 4 and 5 of the command bits are used to distinguish between the four types of load and store instructions, as follows:

Bit 4	Bit 5	Type of operation
0	0	LOAD ACC
0	1	STORE ACC
1	0	LOAD INDEX
1	1	STORE INDEX

Thus,

011 000 00 0001 0011

is equivalent to LOAD ACC, 19, while

011 110 00 0001 0011

is STORE INDEX, 19. Bits 6, 7, and 8 have the same interpretation as for the arithmetic and logic instructions. Therefore,

011 101 00 0001 0011

is the instruction LOAD INDEX, (19), whereas

011 010 10 0001 0011

is STORE ACC, 19+INDEX. In the former example, the index register is set to 19. In the latter example, the contents of the accumulator is stored in the memory location whose address is obtained by adding the contents of the index register to the number 19.

We next describe the **test** instructions. In connection with these we will introduce the concept of **relative addressing.**

2.7 THE TEST INSTRUCTIONS

The two test instructions are IF ACC and IF INDEX. Bits 4, 5, and 6 together determine the type of test. The interpretation of these bits is summarized below:

Bit 4	Bit 5	Bit 6	Type of test
0	0	0	IF ACC=O
0	0	1	IF ACC=+
0	1	0	IF ACC=–
0	1	1	NO TEST
1	0	0	IF INDEX=0
1	0	1	IF INDEX=+
1	1	0	IF INDEX=–
1	1	1	SAVE

As an example,

100 001 00 0001 0011

is the instruction IF ACC=+, TRANSFER TO 19, whereas

100 100 00 0001 0011

is equivalent to IF INDEX=0, TRANSFER TO 19. If bits 4, 5, and 6 are 011, the test is dispensed with and the computer proceeds to execute the instruction in the memory location given by the address. That is,

100 011 00 0001 0011

is equivalent to the instruction TRANSFER TO 19.

As with the previous types of instructions, if bit 8 is a ONE, then indirect addressing is used. Thus, the instruction

100 011 01 0001 0011

is equivalent to TRANSFER TO* 19. The instruction whose address is stored in memory location 19 is then executed immediately. As we shall see, indirect addressing for the test instructions is useful on both large and small machines and is therefore implemented in some manner on most computers.

If bits 4, 5, and 6 are 111, the test is dispensed with, and the instruction becomes SAVE AND TRANSFER TO n. In this case, an additional step takes place during the execution of the instruction: The address of the instruction following the SAVE AND TRANSFER TO n instruction is saved by being stored in memory location n, and the instruction in location n + 1 is executed next. For example, during the execution of the program

```
.       .
.       .
.       .
m       SAVE AND TRANSFER TO n
m + 1   ----
.       .
.       .
.       .
n       ----
n + 1   ADD, k
.       .
.       .
.       .
```

the number m + 1 is stored in location n and the instruction ADD, k is executed next. The instruction TRANSFER TO* n would then cause the instruction stored in location m + 1 to be executed. By using the TRANSFER TO* n instruction, we can resume the execution of the original sequence of instructions at any time after the SAVE AND TRANSFER instruction. The SAVE AND TRANSFER instruction is therefore useful when we wish to insert a self-contained set of instructions called a **subroutine** in more than one place in the main program. Regardless of where the SAVE AND TRANSFER instruction is located, we are able to return to the original program from the subroutine by

n	– – –
n + 1	STORE ACC, n+10
n + 2	MULTIPLY, n+7
n + 3	ADD, n+8
n + 4	MULTIPLY, n+10
n + 5	ADD, n+9
n + 6	TRANSFER TO * n
n + 7	a
n + 8	b
n + 9	c
n + 10	– – –

FIGURE 2-4. Subroutine which computes the function $ax^2 + bx + c$.

using the TRANSFER instruction with an indirect address. An example of a subroutine which computes the function $ax^2 + bx + c$ is given in Figure 2-4. In the example, it is assumed that the value of x to be used for the computation is contained in the accumulator when the instruction SAVE AND TRANSFER TO n is used to transfer control to the subroutine. Before proceeding with the computation of the function, the value of x, which is contained in the accumulator, is stored in location n + 10 for later use. Note that the STORE ACC instruction does not change the contents of the accumulator. The function is then computed by the subroutine from the formula

$$ax^2 + bx + c = (ax+b)x + c \tag{2-1}$$

and the result is left in the accumulator. Finally, the instruction TRANSFER TO* n causes the computer to execute the next instruction of the original program.

For all tests, if bit 7 is a ONE, then the associated binary number is used as a **relative address.** For example, in the instruction

m TRANSFER TO *+k

the associated binary number k is added to the current address m to determine the actual address to be used. The asterisk, in this case, is interpreted as the current address m so that *+k becomes m + k. An example of a program using relative addressing is given below. In this program, the 80 numbers stored in locations 101–180 are added together and the sum is stored in location 100.

```
908    LOAD ACC, (0)
909    LOAD INDEX, (–80)
910    ADD, 181+INDEX
911    INCREMENT INDEX
912    IF INDEX=–, TRANSFER TO * –2
913    STORE ACC, 100
```

In the example, direct addressing cannot be used for the test instruction, since the address 910 cannot be represented by an eight-bit number. Therefore, relative addressing provides a simple way to specify the location to which control is to be transferred by the test instruction. Note that for relative addressing a plus or minus sign follows the asterisk to distinguish it from indirect addressing.

In some cases, either relative addressing or indirect addressing can be used with the same end result. However, relative addressing, whenever it can be used, is more efficient, since it does not tie up an additional memory location. In both the following examples,

```
912   TRANSFER TO *-2
```

and

```
  2   910
  .    .
  .    .
  .    .
912   TRANSFER TO*2
```

the instruction in memory location 910 is executed next by the computer. But the latter example ties up location 2 in the memory and further requires that the main control wait to receive the contents of location 2 before it continues with the execution of the program. Thus, it is advantageous to use relative addressing whenever possible. In a large computer with a long word length, relative addressing has no advantage over direct addressing. As we have stated, however, indirect addressing is useful for returning from a subroutine and is therefore available in some form in all size machines for use with the TRANSFER instruction.

In our description of the test instructions, we used a **symbol**, such as n, in place of the actual address. The practice of using symbols in place of addresses is common, and we do so often throughout this book. The computer assigns an address to each symbol when it translates the instructions into binary machine language. We describe the translation process and the use of **symbolic addresses** in Chapter 11.

Thus far, the only nonarithmetic instructions which we described and which are executed by the arithmetic unit are the logic instructions. The arithmetic unit can also execute other nonarithmetic operations as specified by the shift instructions.

2.8 THE SHIFT INSTRUCTIONS

The shift instructions cause each bit in the accumulator to be moved, or shifted. Four types of shift instructions are possible. These are specified by bits 4 and 5 as shown below:

Bit 4	Bit 5	Type of shift
0	0	LOGICAL
0	1	ARITHMETIC
1	0	CIRCULAR
1	1	NORMALIZE

For the shift instructions, bit 6 specifies the direction that the bits are shifted: If it is a ZERO, they are shifted to the left; if it is a ONE, they are shifted to the right. The number of positions that the bits are shifted is specified by the associated binary number of the instruction. The instruction

101 000 00 0000 0011

is, therefore, the logical shift instruction, SHIFT LEFT, 3. If the accumulator originally contains the word

0100 1100 0111 0001

the execution of the SHIFT LEFT, 3 instruction changes the accumulator contents to

0110 0011 1000 1000

The three left-hand bits are shifted out of the accumulator and lost in the process, and ZERO's are automatically shifted into the right-hand bit positions. In the above example, the execution of the instruction SHIFT RIGHT, 3 causes the accumulator contents to become

0000 1001 1000 1110

In this case, the three right-hand bits are shifted out of the accumulator and lost, and ZERO's are shifted into the left-hand bit positions.

The arithmetic shift is distinguished by adding the letter A to the instruction. Thus

101 011 00 0000 0011

is equivalent to SHIFT RIGHT A, 3. In a similar manner, the letter C is used to identify, a circular shift. These instructions are described below. The normalizing shift, which is written simply as NORMALIZE, is described in Chapter 4.

The left arithmetic shift is identical to the left logical shift. However, the right arithmetic shift differs because ZERO's are not always shifted in from the left. If the left-hand bit of the accumulator is a ONE, then ONE's are shifted in from the left. Thus, if the accumulator contains

1000 1100 1001 0001

then SHIFT RIGHT A, 5 changes the accumulator contents to

1111 1100 0110 0100

Compare this result to

0000 0100 0110 0100

which would be obtained if the instruction SHIFT RIGHT, 5 were executed instead. If the extreme left-hand bit of the accumulator is a ZERO, then SHIFT RIGHT A, n and SHIFT RIGHT, n yield the same result. The arithmetic shift derives its name from the fact that SHIFT RIGHT A, n has the effect of dividing the number by 2^n, whereas SHIFT LEFT A, n causes the number to be multiplied by 2^n. This result holds true for both positive and negative binary numbers as long as the twos complement representation is used for negative numbers.

The circular shift causes the accumulator to be treated as if the left and right-hand bits are adjacent and the accumulator forms a circle. In this case, no bits are lost, as all of the bits are always shifted into a new position. For example, if the accumulator contains the word

1100 0000 1111 0011

then SHIFT RIGHT C, 3 causes the accumulator contents to become

0111 1000 0001 1110

If the instruction SHIFT LEFT C, 3 were executed in the above example, the result would be

0000 0111 1001 1110

Two instruction groups remain to be described: the **input–output** and **miscellaneous** instructions. We briefly introduce these in Section 2.9.

2.9 THE INPUT–OUTPUT AND MISCELLANEOUS INSTRUCTIONS

All **input** and **output** operations which are executed by the computer are initiated by a START I/O instruction. If bit 4 of this instruction is a ZERO, then information is to be read into the computer. If it is a ONE, then the computer is to write information onto an output medium. If bit 5 is a ZERO, then the data is transferred via the accumulator, whereas if it is a ONE, the transfer is directly into or out of the memory. If the accumulator is used, then the associated binary number specifies the I/O device. If a memory transfer is indicated, then the associated binary number specifies the address of the first location of a complete block of consecutive locations in the memory. The first two locations of this block then contain numbers which specify the I/O device and the length

Instruction		Bit number					
		1–3	4	5	6	7	8
ARITHMETIC	ADD SUBTRACT MULTIPLY DIVIDE	0 0 1	0 0 1 1	0 1 0 1	1 = LITERAL	1 = INDEXING	1 = INDIRECT ADDRESS
LOGIC	COMPLEMENT AND OR EXCLUSIVE OR	0 1 0	0 0 1 1	0 1 0 1			
LOAD AND STORE	LOAD ACC STORE ACC LOAD INDEX STORE INDEX	0 1 1	0 0 1 1	0 1 0 1			

TEST	IF ACC=0 IF ACC=+ IF ACC=– NO TEST IF INDEX=0 IF INDEX=+ IF INDEX=– SAVE	1 0 0	0 0 0 0 1 1 1 1	0 0 1 1 0 0 1 1	0 1 0 1 0 1 0 1	1 = RELATIVE ADDRESS	
SHIFT	LOGICAL ARITHMETIC CIRCULAR NORMALIZE	1 0 1	0 0 1 1	0 1 0 1	0 = LEFT 1 = RIGHT	–	–
INPUT–OUTPUT	START I/O	1 1 0	0 = READ 1 = WRITE	0 = ACC 1 = MEMORY	–	–	1 = INDIRECT ADDRESS
MISCELLANEOUS	INCREMENT INDEX	1 1 1	0	0	0	–	–

FIGURE 2-5. Interpretation of the command bits as an instruction.

of the block; the remainder of the block either contains the data to be transferred during a WRITE operation or is used to store data transferred to the memory during a READ operation. The details of block transfers are described in Chapter 6. For memory transfers, if bit 8 of the instruction is a ONE, the associated binary number is interpreted as an indirect address. The block address is then stored in the location given by the indirect address.

The instructions OUTPUT ACC, TYPE and INPUT ACC, TYPE, which were introduced in Chapter 1, are specific examples of START I/O instructions. In both cases, bit 5 of the START I/O instruction is a ZERO, and the associated binary number specifies the typewriter. However, if bit 4 is a ONE, the instruction is OUTPUT ACC, TYPE, whereas, if it is a ZERO, the instruction becomes INPUT ACC, TYPE. Phrases such as OUTPUT ACC, TYPE are used to simplify a program. This instruction could also be written as START OUTPUT, ACC, TYPE.

The **miscellaneous** group contains a set of instructions which are specified by bits 4, 5, and 6. The only instruction of this group which we have used thus far is the INCREMENT INDEX instruction for which bits 4, 5, and 6 are all ZERO. This instruction causes the index register to be incremented, as described in Chapter 1, where it was assumed that the index register is always incremented by one. This will be true if the associated binary number of the instruction is equal to one. However, if any other number is specified, then the index register is incremented by this number. Thus, the instruction

111 000 00 0000 0011

is equivalent to INCREMENT INDEX, 3. If the associated binary number represents a twos complement negative number, then the contents of the index register are decreased. INCREMENT INDEX written alone, however, implies that the index register is to be incremented by one.

This completes the description of the machine language instruction format which we introduced at the beginning of the chapter. A summary of the interpretation of the command bits of the computer word as an instruction is contained in Figure 2-5.

Throughout this chapter, we encountered sequences of ZERO's and ONE's which represented instructions or numbers. To simplify dealing with these long sequences of bits, we divided each sequence into groups of bits. We can further simplify the interpretation of a long sequence of bits by assigning a symbol to each group of bits. The **hexadecimal number system** described in Section 2.10 provides a simple method for assigning a symbol to each group of four bits.

2.10 HEXADECIMAL NUMBERS

If an error occurs during the execution of a program, the computer can be made to execute a subroutine to print out the contents of the memory as an aid to the programmer in locating the error. If the printout were in binary, not only would

TABLE 2-1. Assignment of Hexadecimal Codes

Binary sequence	Decimal equivalent	Hexadecimal equivalent
0000	0	0
0001	1	1
0010	2	2
0011	3	3
0100	4	4
0101	5	5
0110	6	6
0111	7	7
1000	8	8
1001	9	9
1010	10	A
1011	11	B
1100	12	C
1101	13	D
1110	14	E
1111	15	F

a great deal of paper be required to print it, but it would be difficult to interpret. Use of a hexadecimal symbol to represent each group of four bits condenses the printout by a factor of four and also improves legibility.

If a sequence of four bits is converted into a positive decimal number, it assumes a value from 0 to 15. The hexadecimal number system assigns the symbols 0–9 to the sequences whose decimal equivalents are 0–9 and the symbols A–F to the sequences whose values are 10–15, respectively. This assignment is summarized in Table 2-1. Let us illustrate the use of the hexadecimal number system with an example:

The equivalent hexadecimal representation for the sixteen-bit binary number 0100 1101 0101 1110 is 4D5E. To convert this number from hexadecimal into decimal, we note that, just as for the decimal and binary number systems, each digit must be multiplied by a weighting factor. In the hexadecimal case, the first digit to the left of the "hexadecimal point" is weighted by 16^0, the second digit by 16^1, then 16^2, and the nth digit is weighted by 16^{n-1}. Thus, 4D5E is equal to the decimal number

$$
\begin{aligned}
4 \times 16^3 + 13 \times 16^2 + 5 \times 16^1 + 14 \times 16^0 &= 4 \times 4096 + 13 \times 256 + 5 \times 16 + 14 \\
&= 19{,}806
\end{aligned}
$$

The reader can verify this result by converting the original binary number directly into decimal in the manner described in Section 2.1.

A binary code which represents an instruction can be converted into hexadecimal in the same manner. For example, the binary code for the instruction ADD, 19+INDEX is

001 000 10 0001 0011

and the equivalent hexadecimal representation is given by 2213. Although we have separated the first eight bits of the instruction into three groups, only two hexadecimal digits are used to represent these eight bits. With a little experience, it is possible to interpret the first two hexadecimal digits directly as an instruction without the need to first convert them into binary. The two hexadecimal digits which represent the associated binary number can be converted into decimal in the manner described above if they represent a positive number. In the example, 13 is therefore equivalent to

$$1 \times 16^1 + 3 \times 16^0 = 19$$

Negative hexadecimal numbers can be interpreted in a similar manner. However, it is first necessary to separate the left-hand bit or sign bit of the equivalent binary number from the rest of the number and weight it by a suitable negative factor. For example, the twos complement binary number 1100 1101 0101 1110 is equivalent to the hexadecimal number CD5E. To convert this number into decimal, the sign bit is separated out, leaving 100 1101 0101 1110, which is 4D5E. The negative factor which must be used is –32,768 so that the number becomes

$$-32{,}768 + 19{,}806 = -12{,}962$$

since the hexadecimal number 4D5E is equal to the decimal number 19,806.

An alternate method for interpreting hexadecimal numbers is to use a set of tables. Such tables are usually contained in the manual supplied by the computer manufacturer. Table 2-2 provides an example of a table which can be used to convert a two-digit hexadecimal number into its decimal equivalent. We have assumed that the equivalent binary numbers use the twos complement representation for negative numbers.

In Chapters 1 and 2 we assumed that, when the arithmetic instructions ADD, SUBTRACT, MULTIPLY, and DIVIDE are specified, the arithmetic unit manipulates the operands to yield correct results. We have been totally unconcerned with how these operands are treated. In Chapter 3 we discuss the arithmetic operations in order to learn how the arithmetic unit manipulates numbers.

EXERCISES

2.1 Convert the eight-bit ninary numbers 0101 0110, 0011 1111, and 0100 0101 into their decimal counterparts.

TABLE 2-2. Hexadecimal-to-Decimal Conversion Table*

	Second digit															
First digit	0	1	2	3	4	5	6	7	8	9	A	B	C	D	E	F
0	0	1	2	3	4	5	6	7	8	9	10	11	12	13	14	15
1	16	17	18	19	20	21	22	23	24	25	26	27	28	29	30	31
2	32	33	34	35	36	37	38	39	40	41	42	43	44	45	46	47
3	48	49	50	51	52	53	54	55	56	57	58	59	60	61	62	63
4	64	65	66	67	68	69	70	71	72	73	74	75	76	77	78	79
5	80	81	82	83	84	85	86	87	88	89	90	91	92	93	94	95
6	96	97	98	99	100	101	102	103	104	105	106	107	108	109	110	111
7	112	113	114	115	116	117	118	119	120	121	122	123	124	125	126	127
8	−128	−127	−126	−125	−124	−123	−122	−121	−120	−119	−118	−117	−116	−115	−114	−113
9	−112	−111	−110	−109	−108	−107	−106	−105	−104	−103	−102	−101	−100	−99	−98	−97
A	−96	−95	−94	−93	−92	−91	−90	−89	−88	−87	−86	−85	−84	−83	−82	−81
B	−80	−79	−78	−77	−76	−75	−74	−73	−72	−71	−70	−69	−68	−67	−66	−65
C	−64	−63	−62	−61	−60	−59	−58	−57	−56	−55	−54	−53	−52	−51	−50	−49
D	−48	−47	−46	−45	−44	−43	−42	−41	−40	−39	−38	−37	−36	−35	−34	−33
E	−32	−31	−30	−29	−28	−27	−26	−25	−24	−23	−22	−21	−20	−19	−18	−17
F	−16	−15	−14	−13	−12	−11	−10	−9	−8	−7	−6	−5	−4	−3	−2	−1

* It is assumed that the equivalent eight-bit binary numbers use the twos complement representation for negative numbers.

2.2 Convert the eight-bit binary numbers 1101 0110, 1111 0000, and 1000 0010 into decimal numbers assuming that they are twos complement numbers.

2.3 Repeat Exercise 2.2 assuming that the numbers are positive.

2.4 What is the difference between the instructions ADD, 100; ADD*, 100; ADD, (100); and ADD, 100+INDEX?

2.5 Assume that the accumulator and memory location 50 contain the sixteen-bit numbers 0101 1010 0011 1100 and 0100 1110 1100 1110, respectively. What does the accumulator contain after the execution of the COMPLEMENT instruction? After the execution of the instruction AND, 50 using the original data in the accumulator? After the execution of the program

```
OR, 50
COMPLEMENT
```

on the original data?

2.6 Write a loop which sets the accumulator to −20 and increments it repeatedly by 2 until it is no longer negative. Store each of the computed numbers in the memory in locations 101–110.

[Hint: Use the index register to determine which storage location to use for each number computed. Test the accumulator to determine when to terminate the loop.]

2.7 It is occasionally useful to know how many ONE bits are contained in a number stored in the accumulator. Write a loop to count the number of ONE bits in a sixteen-bit accumulator.

[Hint: Use a test instruction to determine if the extreme left-hand bit is a ONE. Then use a shift instruction to move each successive bit into position to be tested. Use the index register to keep track of the number of ONE bits found and test the accumulator to terminate the loop.]

2.8 Convert the binary numbers given in Exercises 2.1, 2.2, and 2.5 into their hexadecimal counterparts.

2.9 Convert the positive hexadecimal numbers 3AD7, 705F, and 16F2 into decimal numbers.

2.10 What computer instructions are represented by the hexadecimal codes 5208, 7C10, and B803?

2.11 What arithmetic shift instruction causes a binary number to be doubled? To be halved? Verify your answer by actually shifting the eight-bit number 0011 0100 and converting the original number and the shifted numbers into decimal. Repeat using the negative number 1111 0100.

3

ARITHMETIC

An arithmetic operation is a universal operation; that is, it is independent of the number system in which its operands are represented. The sum of 50 and 8 is 58, regardless of whether the numbers are represented in the binary, decimal, or any other number system. We therefore use the more familiar decimal system to illustrate the rules used in performing arithmetic. Once the concepts involved have been established, they are easily extended to the binary number system and to the digital computer operating either as a binary machine or as a binary-coded-decimal machine.

3.1 DECIMAL ADDITION

The operations of addition, subtraction, multiplication, and division in the decimal number system are so familiar to us that we tend to overlook the significance of the details of these operations. If we wish to add two numbers, 172 and 455 for example, we write the numbers one above the other and apply the rules of addition shown in Table 3-1, as follows:

(a)	2 plus 5 equals 7	1
(b)	7 plus 5 equals 2, carry 1*	455
(c)	1 plus 4 plus carry 1 equals 6	<u>172</u>
		627

* In all examples, the carry digits are shown above the columns into which the carries are induced.

TABLE 3-1. **Rules of Decimal Addition**

+	0	1	2	3	4	5	6	7	8	9
0	0	1	2	3	4	5	6	7	8	9
1	1	2	3	4	5	6	7	8	9	0*
2	2	3	4	5	6	7	8	9	0*	1*
3	3	4	5	6	7	8	9	0*	1*	2*
4	4	5	6	7	8	9	0*	1*	2*	3*
5	5	6	7	8	9	0*	1*	2*	3*	4*
6	6	7	8	9	0*	1*	2*	3*	4*	5*
7	7	8	9	0*	1*	2*	3*	4*	5*	6*
8	8	9	0*	1*	2*	3*	4*	5*	6*	7*
9	9	0*	1*	2*	3*	4*	5*	6*	7*	8*

* The asterisks indicate a carry digit.

Thus, we arrive at the result 627. In adding 7 and 5 in step (b), the symbol 9, which is the largest symbol that can be written in the decimal number system has been exceeded; this induces a carry into the next column. In step (c), the table is used twice: first to add 1 and 4, totaling 5, then 5 and 1, totaling 6.

Although each decimal digit represents a different factor of ten, it is significant that the addition table applies to each digit individually, regardless of its actual value. The interaction between digits is taken care of by the carry digits. Thus, it is possible to write an **algorithm**, or set of repetitive rules, governing the addition of two numbers in the decimal system, as follows:

1. Add the digits on the right according to the addition rules, thus forming the first sum digit.
2. Add the next digits and the carry digit (if one was induced in the last step), forming the next sum digit.
3. If additional digits remain to be added, repeat step 2; otherwise, go on to step 4.
4. If the last addition induced a carry digit, set the next sum digit to one; if no carry digit was induced, set the next sum digit to zero.

In step 4, if the carry digit is zero, the leading sum digit of zero is usually omitted; that is 0627 is writen as 627.

Thus far, only whole numbers, or integers, have been considered; the decimal point, although omitted, was always assumed to lie on the right. In order to add numbers with nonzero fractional parts, it is first necessary to ensure that the decimal points are lined up. Zeros are then inserted for blank digits, and finally the addition algorithm is applied directly. An example is given below.

To add 8.375 and 146.84

(a)	Line up decimal points	8.375 146.84
(b)	Insert zeros into blanks	008.375 146.840
(c)	Apply addition algorithm	11 1 008.375 146.840 155.215

Let us now consider the general interpretation of the digits of a decimal number. Each digit can be represented by a symbol of the form d_n, where n indicates the position of the digit relative to the decimal point. Let us adopt the usual convention that d_0 lies to the immediate left of the decimal point, digits with positive subscripts lie to the left of d_0, and digits with negative subscripts lie to the right of d_0. Then the weighting factor for a digit d_n is 10^n so that the interpretation of the sequence of digits

$$\cdots d_2\ d_1\ d_0 \cdot d_{-1}\ d_{-2} \ldots$$

is given by

$$\cdots + d_2 \times 10^2 + d_1 \times 10^1 + d_0 \times 10^0 + d_{-1} \times 10^{-1} + d_{-2} \times 10^{-2} + \cdots$$

and we see that the number 8.375 is equivalent to

$$8 \times 10^0 + 3 \times 10^{-1} + 7 \times 10^{-2} + 5 \times 10^{-3} = 8 + \frac{3}{10} + \frac{7}{100} + \frac{5}{1000}$$

Only the addition of positive numbers was considered above. However, if negative numbers are represented in the **tens complement** format, the addition algorithm applies equally well to the addition of any two numbers, regardless of sign. The representation of negative numbers in tens complement and the addition of tens complement numbers are the subjects of Sections 3.2 and 3.3.

3.2 NEGATIVE NUMBERS

The most familiar method of representing a negative number is in the **sign-magnitude** system. In this system, positive numbers are preceded by a plus sign, which is often omitted, while negative numbers are preceded by a minus sign. If two numbers being added are both positive or both negative, the addition algorithm can be applied directly. However, if one is positive while the other is negative, a more complicated algorithm is required. As a result, very few computers have arithmetic units which add sign-magnitude numbers directly.

If instead of sign-magnitude the tens complement representation is used for negative numbers, the addition algorithm is directly applicable. To simplify the description of the tens complement representation, let us restrict our number system so that all numbers are of magnitude less than 50.000* and extend no more than three digits to the right of the decimal point. The numbers between 50.000 and 99.999, which are not legitimate positive numbers in our system, are then used to represent the negative numbers between –50.000 and zero without ambiguity. We can convert every negative number in this range into a unique number between 50.000 and 99.999 by adding 100.000 to the number. Thus, –15.000 becomes 85.000.

In some computers, numbers are stored in the memory in the sign-magnitude representation. In these computers, each negative number must first be converted into tens complement before being used as an operand for an ADD instruction. Therefore, before proceeding to describe the addition of tens complement numbers, let us consider the problem of converting a negative number from sign-magnitude to tens complement and back again in the computer. Direct addition of 100.000 is not possible, since the number 100.000 does not exist in our number system. Fortunately, however, a simple rule exists for converting a negative number into its tens complement counterpart. The tens complement y of any negative number x is given by

$$y = x + 100.000 = [x + 99.999] + 00.001 \tag{3-1}$$

The number [x + 99.999] can be formed by applying a simple substitution for each digit of x according to the rules given in Table 3-2. As an example, –39.621 becomes 60.378. To form the tens complement, it remains only to add 00.001 to this number. This produces the result 60.379, which is the tens complement of –39.621.

To convert a negative number into sign-magnitude from its tens complement representation, it is necessary to subtract 100.000 from the number. This is the inverse of the operation given in (3-1) and can be written as

$$x = y - 100.000 = -(-y + 100.000) = -([-y + 99.999] + 00.001) \tag{3-2}$$

The expression [–y + 99.999] can be formed in exactly the same manner as before using the substitution rule. The addition of 00.001 completes the task except that a minus sign must be inserted on the left in accordance with (3-2). As an example, let us convert the tens complement number 60.379, which was

* It is a simple matter to scale all numbers by a suitable factor to ensure that they never exceed 49.999 in magnitude. Methods which allow this restriction to be relaxed are described in Chapter 4.

TABLE 3-2. Substitution Rule

– →	+
0 →	9
1 →	8
2 →	7
3 →	6
4 →	5
5 →	4
6 →	3
7 →	2
8 →	1
9 →	0

obtained in the last example, into a sign-magnitude number. Applying the substitution rule, 60.379 becomes 39.620; adding 00.001 yields 39.621; and inserting the minus sign, the result –39.621 is obtained. This is the correct result, since it is the number with which we started.

These algorithms allow the computer to convert automatically negative numbers stored in sign-magnitude into tens complement before proceding to add them. In a similar manner, a negative tens complement sum can easily be converted into sign-magnitude before being stored back into the memory. Note that in a machine which stores negative numbers in the tens complement representation, these conversions are omitted.

3.3 ADDITION OF TENS COMPLEMENT NUMBERS

What we must now establish is that the algorithm previously set forth for the addition of two positive numbers applies equally well to the addition of any two numbers if the tens complement representation is used for negative numbers. One restriction is made at the outset: The result of the addition must be a number which is within the range of the number system; that is, its magnitude must be less than 50.000. The difficulties which arise when this restriction is removed are dealt with in Chapter 4 under the heading of **overflow** (Section 4.5).

Three cases which involve the addition of negative numbers can occur:

(a) Only one number is negative and the result is positive.
(b) Only one number is negative and the result is negative.
(c) Both numbers are negative.

In cases (a) and (c), a rather odd result is obtained. The sum is in the range

100.000–199.999 and larger than the desired result by exactly 100.000. Since we have stipulated that the result must always be in range, and since the excess 100.000 is an idiosyncrasy which arises from the use of the tens complement representation, we can agree to delete the carry into digit position d_2; this is equivalent to eliminating the extraneous 100.000 which occurs in these two cases. The three cases involving the addition of negative numbers are illustrated in Figure 3-1. The first column shows the numbers in tens complement, the second in sign-magnitude, and the third in a hybrid format. In the hybrid examples, each negative number is written in the form (100.000 + x) which is

Delete (carry)

1 1 11		
46.832	46.832	46.832
60.379	-39.621	100.000 - 39.621
107.211	07.211	100.000 + 07.211

(a) Only one number is negative — the result is positive

11		
60.379	-39.621	100.000 - 39.621
21.462	21.462	21.462
81.841	-18.159	100.000 - 18.159

(b) Only one number is negative — the result is negative

Delete (carry)

1 1 11		
60.379	-39.621	100.000 - 39.621
90.846	- 9.154	100.000 - 09.154
151.225	-48.775	200.000 - 48.775

(c) Both numbers are negative

FIGURE 3-1. Examples of the addition of negative numbers. The first column shows tens complement, the second sign-magnitude, and the third a hybrid format showing the source of the deleted carry digit.

numerically equivalent to the tens complement of x. By examining the hybrid examples, we see that the presence of the extraneous 100.000, which occurs in cases (a) and (c), is a direct consequence of using the tens complement representation for negative numbers.

Thus, the addition algorithm can be used for adding any two numbers together if the tens complement representation is used for negative numbers, and if the carry into digit position d_2 is deleted. Now that we have shown that the addition algorithm applies regardless of whether positive or negative numbers are added, it is a comparatively simple task to apply the same algorithm to subtraction. This is discussed in Section 3.4.

3.4 DECIMAL SUBTRACTION

A simple relationship exists between addition and subtraction which allows the addition algorithm to be used for subtraction. This relationship is given by

$$a - b = a + (-b) \tag{3-3}$$

where $-b$ is the **arithmetic complement*** of b. The equation states that subtracting b from a is equivalent to adding the complement of b to a. Equation (3-3) is an algebraic equation and therefore holds true regardless of whether the numbers involved are positive or negative.

To complement a sign-magnitude number, it is merely necessary to change its sign. To complement a decimal number in the tens complement representation, however, the following rule is used: Apply the substitution rule of Table 3-2 and then add 00.001 to the result. The reader can verify for himself that every positive number from zero to 49.999 is thereby converted into its equivalent negative number between 50.000 and 99.999, and conversely.

Let us illustrate subtraction with two examples: To subtract the number 06.254 from 26.254, we add the complement of 06.254, which is 93.746, to 26.254. We then obtain 20.000, which is the correct result. To subtract the negative number 90.846 from 26.254, we add the complement of 90.846, which is 09.154, to 26.254, obtaining the result 35.408.

Although other subtraction algorithms do exist, the sheer simplicity of the algorithm just described has been sufficient motivation for its almost universal adoption by computer designers.

Multiplication and division are considerably more complex operations than addition and subtraction. Nevertheless, they can be reduced to fairly simple algorithms in which addition and subtraction are used. Sections 3.5 and 3.6 describe the multiplication and division algorithms in detail.

* The arithmetic complement is not the same as the logic complement introduced in Chapter 2. However, the term "complement," when used, should cause no confusion.

3.5 DECIMAL MULTIPLICATION

The algorithm for multiplying two positive numbers together can be deduced from a simple example. If we multiply 4.51 (the multiplicand) by 3.62 (the multiplier), then the product, 16.3262, is formed, as shown below:

4.51	
3.62	
902	451 x 2
2 706	451 x 60
13 53	451 x 300
16.3262	

451 is multiplied by 2, 6, and 3, successively, and the positional significance of the 6, as 60, and the 3, as 300, is taken into account by shifting the three partial products relative to one another. The order in which the multiplier digits are used and the direction of shifting are immaterial, as long as the relative position of the partial products is maintained. This can be seen by comparing the above example with the one below:

4.51	
3.62	
13 53	451 x 300
2 706	451 x 60
902	451 x 2
16.3262	

The position of the decimal point is determined by the total number of digits to the right of the decimal point in both the multiplier and the multiplicand, in this case four.

If we attempt to formulate a multiplication algorithm based on this procedure, we immediately encounter the problem of how to compute partial products such as 451 x 2. Of the two ways that partial products can be formed, the method which uses the multiplication tables (2 x 3 = 6, 2 x 4 = 8, etc.) is difficult to implement on a computer and is not pursued further. The method commonly used in computers causes the multiplicand to be added to the sum of all previous partial products as many times as required by each multiplier digit. Thus, 451 x 2 is formed by adding 451 twice, and so on. The convention usually adopted is that shown in the second example, wherein the most significant digit* of the multiplier is used first. However, instead of shifting each successive partial product to the right, the partial product **sum** is shifted to the left. The same product is obtained in either case. With these points in mind, we can now formulate the multiplication algorithm for positive numbers, as follows:

* The most significant digit of a number is the left-hand digit of that number.

1. Add the multiplicand d times, where d is the most significant digit of the multiplier, to form the first partial product.
2. Shift the partial product sum to the left by one digit position, and add the multiplicand to this sum d times, where d is the next significant digit of the multiplier.
3. If additional digits remain in the multiplier, repeat step 2; otherwise, go on to step 4.
4. Place the decimal point n places from the right of the product, where n is the total number of digits to the right of the decimal points in both the multiplier and the multiplicand.

451	
451	
902	Add 451, three times
451	
1353	
13530	Shift partial product sum left
451	
13981	
451	
14432	
451	
14883	Add 451, six times
451	
15334	
451	
15785	
451	
16236	
162360	Shift partial product sum left
451	
162811	Add 451, twice
451	
163262	
16.3262	Insert decimal point four places from right

FIGURE 3-2. Example of decimal multiplication.

The steps which are carried out when we compute the product 4.51 x 3.62 using the algorithm are shown in Figure 3-2.

To determine the algorithm for multiplying a positive number by a negative number, observe that

$$a \cdot (-b) = -(a \cdot b) \qquad (3\text{-}4)$$

where both a and b are positive. Thus, if the numbers are in sign-magnitude representation, the magnitude of the product can be determined by multiplying the magnitudes of the two numbers together using the multiplication algorithm for positive numbers. Then, following (3-4), the product is assigned a minus sign. The algorithm for multiplying two negative numbers together follows from

$$(-a) \cdot (-b) = a \cdot b \qquad (3\text{-}5)$$

In this case, the product is formed by multiplying the magnitudes of the two numbers together and leaving the product positive.

Because of the relative simplicity of this multiplication scheme as compared to one utilizing negative numbers in tens complement notation, the latter method is not presented. Therefore, to multiply any two numbers together, convert the negative numbers to sign-magnitude, if necessary, multiply the magnitudes together, and evaluate the sign of the product from the following rule:

> If either, but not both, of the two numbers is negative, the product is negative; otherwise it is positive.

3.6 DECIMAL DIVISION

For division, as for multiplication, it is far simpler to manipulate the magnitudes of the numbers and account for the signs separately.* Therefore, it will be assumed that all numbers are in the sign-magnitude format, suitable conversions having been performed, if necessary. An example illustrating the division of the magnitudes of two numbers is shown below; the division algorithm can be deduced from it. The decimal points are omitted for simplicity.

```
         312
457 | 142601
      1371        457 x 3
      ----
        5501
         457      457 x 1
        ----
         931
         914      457 x 2
         ---
          17
```

* In summary, the arithmetic unit manipulates sign-magnitude numbers for multiplication and division, and tens complement numbers for addition and subtraction. A similar convention is used for binary arithmetic, as is pointed out later.

In the example, 457 is the divisor, 142601 is the dividend, 312 is the quotient, and 17 is the final remainder. The division is carried out by performing a sequence of subtractions. The numbers which are subtracted, 457 x 3, 457 x 1, and 457 x 2, must be properly lined up and the numbers 3, 1, and 2 become the quotient digits. Each quotient digit is the largest digit which, when multiplied by the multiplier, 457, and subtracted, leads to a nonnegative remainder. For example, since 1426 – (457 x 3) = 55, but 1426 – (457 x 4) = –402, the first quotient digit is 3. This leads to a trial and error procedure which is unsuitable for direct implementation on a computer. A slight modification yields a more direct procedure.

In the modified algorithm, if the divisor is repeatedly subtracted by adding its complement to the dividend until the remainder actually becomes a negative number, and then the divisor is added once, the remainder is always positive or zero. Moreover, if the number of subtractions is counted and decreased by one to compensate for the final addition, the correct quotient digit is obtained. This procedure is illustrated below using the same example.

	142601	
	9543	1
	096901	
	9543	2
	051201	
	9543	3
	005501	
	9543	4
Negative remainder	959801	
	0457	3
	005501	
Shift remainder	055010	
	9543	31
	009310	
	9543	32
Negative remainder	963610	
	0457	31
	009310	
Shift remainder	093100	
	9543	311
	047400	
	9543	312
	001700	
	9543	313
Negative remainder	956000	
	0457	**312 Final quotient**
Final remainder	001700	

In the example, the subtractions are accomplished by adding the tens complement of 0457, which is 9543, at each step except the last of each sequence. Moreover, the remainder, rather than the divisor, is shifted after each quotient digit is formed. The step-by-step formation of the quotient digits is shown in the second column.

Regardless of where the decimal points lie in the dividend and the divisor, the division is carried out exactly as described above. Then the number of digits to the right of the decimal point in the quotient is m − n, where m digits lie to the right of the decimal point in the dividend and n digits lie to the right of the decimal point in the divisor. The number of digits to the right of the decimal point in the remainder is m + s, where s is the number of shifts performed. Thus, for example, if we divide 14.2601 by 4.57, the quotient is 3.12 and the remainder is .001700.

We are now in a position to formulate the division algorithm for two positive numbers:

1. Repeatedly subtract the divisor from the most significant part of the dividend until the remainder becomes a negative number, and then add the divisor once to form a positive remainder. During this step, count the number of subtractions, and deduct one to form the first quotient digit.
2. Shift the remainder to the left by one digit position and repeatedly subtract the divisor from the remainder following the same rule as in step 1. Count the number of subtractions and deduct one to form the next quotient digit.
3. If the number of shifts performed equals the difference between the number of digits in the dividend and the divisor, go to step 4; otherwise, repeat step 2.
4. Place the decimal point of the quotient m − n places from the right, m and n being the number of fractional digits in the dividend and divisor, respectively.
5. Place the decimal point of the remainder m + s places from the right, where m is defined above and s is the number of shifts performed in step 2.

Since the quotient of two negative numbers is a positive number, dividing the magnitude of the dividend by the magnitude of the divisor yields the correct quotient. However, since the sign of the remainder should be the same as the sign of the dividend, it should be changed to a minus sign. If only one of the two numbers is a negative number, the quotient of the two magnitudes is correct in magnitude, but its sign should be changed to a minus sign. Again, the sign of the remainder should be the same as the sign of the dividend and should be changed, if necessary.

Thus, for numbers which are in sign-magnitude, having been converted from tens complement, if necessary, the division algorithm stated above can be used to determine the magnitudes of the quotient and remainder. The signs of the quotient and remainder are then determined as follows:

> If either, but not both, of the two numbers is negative, the quotient is negative; otherwise, it is positive. The sign of the remainder is always the same as the sign of the dividend.

As we have seen, both the multiplication and division algorithms are composed of specific sequences of additions, subtractions, shifts, and tests. It should not be inferred, however, that the programmer must write out each of these steps in detail in order to be able to multiply and divide numbers. Many small computers and virtually all of the larger ones have provisions for automatically executing the correct sequence of additions, subtractions, shifts, and tests whenever a MULTIPLY or DIVIDE instruction is specified.

Thus far in this chapter, we have developed the algorithms for addition, subtraction, multiplication, and division in the decimal number system. In Sections 3.7 and 3.8 we show that, with only minor modifications, these algorithms apply equally well for performing arithmetic operations using binary numbers.

3.7 BINARY ADDITION AND SUBTRACTION

The general interpretation of the bits of a binary number is similar to that used for the digits of a decimal number; that is, if the symbol b_n is used to represent the nth bit and if bit b_0 lies to the immediate left of the binary point, then the weighting factor for b_n is 2^n. Therefore, the sequence of bits

$$\cdots b_2\ b_1\ b_0 \cdot b_{-1}\ b_{-2} \cdots$$

is interpreted as

$$\cdots + b_2 \times 2^2 + b_1 \times 2^1 + b_0 \times 2^0 + b_{-1} \times 2^{-1} + b_{-2} \times 2^{-2} + \cdots$$

Because the interpretation of the bits of a binary number is similar to the interpretation of the digits of a decimal number, the binary addition algorithm is similar to the decimal addition algorithm. We state the binary algorithm below in a form which is applicable to both positive and negative numbers, assuming that the sum is always within range. The binary addition rules which are used are shown in Table 3-3. The algorithm is:

1. Add the least significant bits according to the addition rules, thus forming the least significant sum bit.

2. Add the next bits and the carry bit, if one was induced in the last step, forming the next sum bit.
3. If additional bits remain to be added, repeat step 2; otherwise, go on to step 4.
4. If the last addition induced a carry bit, delete it.

TABLE 3-3. Rules of Binary Addition

+	0	1
0	0	1
1	1	0*

* The asterisk denotes that a carry bit is produced.

Step 4 is needed when adding negative numbers, as we shall see. An example illustrating the addition of two positive binary numbers is shown below along with its decimal equivalent for comparison.

111 111	
0011 0101	+53
0000 1111	+15
0100 0100	+68

Before introducing subtraction, we must first consider the representation of negative binary numbers.

For negative binary numbers, the twos complement representation is used in the same way that the tens complement representation is used for negative decimal numbers. If, for simplicity in discussing negative binary numbers, we restrict our number system to integers whose magnitude is less than 128, then each number consists of eight bits. Then, to convert a negative number from sign-magnitude to its twos complement representation, 256 must be added to the number.* As before, direct addition is not possible, and a procedure for converting a negative number x into its twos complement counterpart y can be deduced from

$$y = x + 256 = [x + 255] + 1 \qquad (3\text{-}6)$$

$$= [x + 1111\ 1111] + 0000\ 0001$$

* The conversion factor used is twice the largest magnitude representable in the number system. Thus, in the decimal case considered earlier, it was 100. (2 x 50.), while here it is 256. (2 x 128.).

The number [x + 1111 1111] can be formed from x by applying the substitution rule

$$\begin{aligned} - &\longrightarrow + \\ 0 &\longrightarrow 1 \\ 1 &\longrightarrow 0 \end{aligned}$$

As an example, –0011 0000 (–48) becomes 1100 1111 (207). Adding 0000 0001, we obtain 1101 0000 (208), which is the correct result. To convert a twos complement number into sign magnitude, 256 is subtracted from the number. Examining the equation

$$\begin{aligned} x = y - 256 &= -\,[-y + 256] \\ &= -\,([-y + 255] + 1) \\ &= -\,([-y + 1111\ 1111] + 0000\ 0001) \end{aligned} \tag{3-7}$$

we find that the conversion of a twos complement number into sign-magnitude requires the application of the binary substitution rule followed by the addition of 0000 0001 and a change of sign. Thus, 1101 0000 (208) becomes 0010 1111 (47). Adding 0000 0001 yields 0011 0000 (48); and, after changing the sign, the result –0011 0000 (–48), the number with which we started, is obtained.

In Chapter 2 we introduced a method for the interpretation of negative binary numbers which entails using -2^N as the weighting factor for the most significant bit b_N. Regardless of which method we use to convert a negative binary number into decimal, the same result is obtained. For example, using the method of Chapter 2, 1101 0000 becomes

$$\begin{aligned} -2^7 + 2^6 + 2^4 &= -128 + 64 + 16 \\ &= -48 \end{aligned}$$

which is the same as the result obtained above.*

We have now established the rules for converting numbers into and out of the twos complement representation. If we assume that all negative numbers are in the twos complement representation, having been converted from sign-magnitude if necessary, then any two binary numbers can be added together using the binary addition algorithm, as shown in the example below:

Delete ⟶ 1	1	
	1101 0000	-48
	0110 0011	+99
	0011 0011	+51

* The methods presented for interpreting binary numbers constitute a procedure for converting binary numbers into decimal. It is also useful to be able to convert decimal numbers into binary. A procedure for this purpose is described in Exercises 3.10 and 3.11.

Step 4 of the algorithm deletes the extraneous carry bit which arises from using the twos complement representation.

Let us now consider the subtraction of binary numbers. The subtraction of b from a is accomplished by adding the complement of b to a. This rule is precisely the same as that used for the subtraction of decimal numbers. To find the complement of a binary number in the twos complement representation, the binary substitution rule is applied and 0000 0001 is added to the result. All positive numbers in the range 0000 0000 to 0111 1111 are thereby converted into negative numbers between 1000 0000 and 1111 1111, and conversely, and the magnitudes of the original number and its complement are equal. An example of subtraction by complementation and addition is shown below:

$$\begin{array}{r} \\ 0110\,0011 \\ -\,0001\,1000 \\ \hline \end{array} \xrightarrow{\text{Complement}} \begin{array}{r} 1\quad 11\qquad\quad \\ 0110\,0011 \\ +\,1110\,1000 \\ \hline 0100\,1011 \end{array} \qquad \begin{array}{r} \\ +99 \\ -24 \\ \hline +75 \end{array}$$

We have seen that the algorithms for binary addition and subtraction are similar to their decimal counterparts. In Section 3.8 we develop the algorithms for binary multiplication and division, and in so doing see that they too are similar to their decimal counterparts.

3.8 BINARY MULTIPLICATION AND DIVISION

The algorithm for binary multiplication of two numbers is actually a simplified version of the decimal multiplication algorithm. It is simplified because at each step either a single addition or no addition is performed, depending upon whether the corresponding multiplier bit is a ONE or a ZERO, respectively. Numbers to be multiplied are first converted into sign-magnitude, if necessary; the two magnitudes are then multiplied together; and the rules stated earlier for determining the sign of the product in the decimal case are applied. The complete algorithm for multiplying any two binary numbers together is given below:

1. Convert twos complement negative multipliers and multiplicands into sign-magnitude and ignore the sign bits which are always ZERO.
2. If the left-hand bit of the multiplier is a ONE, use the multiplicand as the first partial product sum; if it is a ZERO, use zero as the first partial product sum.
3. Shift the partial product sum to the left by one bit position, and add the multiplicand to the sum if the next significant bit of the multiplier is a ONE; if it is a ZERO, go on to step 4.
4. If additional bits remain in the multiplier, repeat step 3; otherwise go on to step 5.

5. Place the binary point n places from the right of the product, where n is the total number of bits to the right of the binary points in both the multiplier and the multiplicand.
6. Check the signs of the multiplier and the multiplicand. If either, but not both, of the two numbers is negative, convert the product to a negative number in the desired format; otherwise, leave it positive.

As illustrated by the multiplication example shown in Figure 3-3, the product obtained when two seven-bit positive numbers are multiplied together is a fourteen-bit positive number. The sign bits are not shown in the example, since they are always ZERO. That the product is a double-length number follows from the nature of the multiplication operation. In the example, the number 1110 1000 (−24) is multiplied by the number 0011 0011 (51). The negative multiplicand is first converted into the sign-magnitude number −0001 1000, and the two unsigned magnitudes 001 1000 and 011 0011 are then multiplied

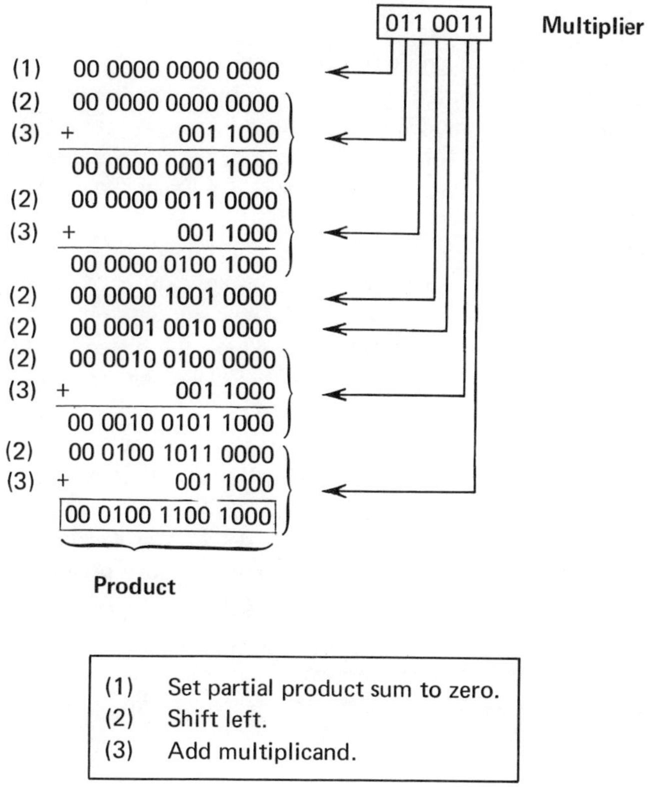

FIGURE 3-3. Example of binary multiplication of 001 1000 by 011 0011.

together using the algorithm. The binary point is placed at the extreme right so that the resulting product, 00 0100 1100 1000., is equivalent to

$$2^{10} + 2^7 + 2^6 + 2^3 = 1024 + 128 + 64 + 8 = 1224$$

which is the product of 51 and 24. Finally, since the multiplicand is a negative number, the sign of the product is changed, yielding –00 0100 1100 1000. or –1224. If desired, a sign bit can be added to the product which can then be converted into a fifteen-bit twos complement number using the same rule previously stated for eight-bit numbers. Thus, - 00 0100 1100 1000 becomes 111 1011 0011 1000.

Because division is the inverse of multiplication, a fourteen-bit dividend divided by a seven-bit divisor yields a seven-bit quotient, exclusive of the sign bits. The remainder is also a seven-bit number. As with multiplication, the binary division algorithm is a simplified version of the decimal division algorithm with all numbers converted into sign-magnitude initially, if required. We first state the division algorithm and then provide an example to illustrate it.

1. Convert twos complement negative divisors and negative dividends into sign-magnitude and ignore the ZERO sign bits.
2. Subtract the divisor from the dividend by adding the twos complement of the divisor to the dividend. If the remainder is a positive number, set the first quotient bit to ONE and proceed to the next step; if the remainder is negative, add the divisor to the remainder and set the first quotient bit to ZERO.
3. Shift the remainder to the left by one bit position and subtract the divisor from the remainder. Follow the same rule as in step 2 to determine the new remainder and the next quotient bit.
4. If the number of shifts performed equals the difference between the number of bits in the dividend and the divisor, go to step 5; otherwise, repeat step 3.
5. Place the binary point of the quotient $m - n$ places from the right, m and n being the number of fractional bits in the dividend and divisor, respectively.
6. Place the binary point of the remainder $m + s$ places from the right, where m is defined above and s is the number of shifts performed in step 3.
7. Check the signs of the divisor and the dividend. If either, but not both, of the two numbers is negative, convert the quotient to a negative number in the desired format; otherwise, leave it positive. If the dividend is negative, convert the remainder to a negative number; otherwise leave it positive.

To provide a simple example of binary division, let us divide 111 1011 0011 0100 (–1228) by 1110 1000 (–24). Converting both the dividend and the divisor into sign-magnitude, we obtain –00 0100 1100 1100 and –001 1000. We then proceed as shown in Figure 3-4, using the binary addition and subtraction

	Sign bits	Quotient
Dividend →	000 0100 1100 1100	
(1)	111 0100 0	
(2)	111 1000 1100 1100	0
(3)	000 1100 0	
	000 0100 1100 1100	
(4)	000 1001 1001 1000	
(1)	111 0100 0	
(2)	111 1101 1001 1000	00
(3)	000 1100 0	
	000 1001 1001 1000	
(4)	001 0011 0011 0000	
(1)	111 0100 0	
(5)	000 0111 0011 0000	001
(4)	000 1110 0110 0000	
(1)	111 0100 0	
(5)	000 0010 0110 0000	0011
(4)	000 0100 1100 0000	
(1)	111 0100 0	
(2)	111 1000 1100 0000	0011 0
(3)	000 1100 0	
	000 0100 1100 0000	
(4)	000 1001 1000 0000	
(1)	111 0100 0	
(2)	111 1101 1000 0000	0011 00
(3)	000 1100 0	
	000 1001 1000 0000	
(4)	001 0011 0000 0000	
(1)	111 0100 0	
(5)	000 0111 0000 0000	0011 001
(4)	000 1110 0000 0000	
(1)	111 0100 0	
(5)	0 [00 0010 0] 000 0000	0 [011 0011]
	Final remainder	

(1) Subtract divisor (by adding twos complement of divisor).
(2) Negative remainder.
(3) Add divisor.
(4) Shift left.
(5) Positive remainder.

FIGURE 3-4. Example of binary division of 00 0100 1100 1100 by 001 1000.

rules previously set forth.* The binary point of the quotient is at the extreme right because both the dividend and divisor are integers. The binary point in the final remainder is seven places from the right, leaving an exact seven-bit integral remainder. The least significant half of the remainder always consists of ZERO's, so that only the most significant seven bits need be retained, as shown in the figure. The quotient is positive, since both the divisor and the dividend are negative numbers; but the remainder should be a negative number, and so 000 0100 becomes 1111 1100 (−4) in twos complement. Thus, dividing 111 1011 0011 0100 (−1228) by 1110 1000 (−24), we obtain the quotient 0011 0011 (51) and a remainder 1111 1100 (−4). The reader can verify for himself that this is the correct result.

In the example, the quotient is eight bits rather than seven bits long. The most significant bit, which is the first one formed, will always be ZERO unless the quotient is out of the range of the number system and cannot be represented as a valid number. We return to the significance of this bit when we discuss overflow in Section 4.5.

In the preceding sections, both the decimal and the binary algorithms for performing arithmetic were established. The arithmetic unit of a binary computer implements the binary algorithms in a straightforward manner. The decimal algorithms, on the other hand, cannot be implemented as easily and require a machine which encodes each decimal digit as a binary number. We now consider the decimal computer and show that with a suitable encoding the decimal algorithms can be implemented directly.

3.9 THE DECIMAL COMPUTER

The rules for performing binary arithmetic can be implemented directly, since electronic digital computers are composed of two-state devices which represent ONE's and ZERO's quite naturally. However, the same is not true of decimal arithmetic, since ten-state devices are nonexistent. Therefore, a binary format must be devised for representing decimal numbers. It is possible to convert all numbers into ordinary binary, perform the required arithmetic manipulation, and then convert back again for presentation to the computer user. The conversions, however, are very time-consuming. For some tasks, especially in the scientific fields where a great deal of arithmetic manipulation is required, the conversions are justifiable because binary computers are extremely efficient. However, for many tasks, especially in the business and accounting fields, it is desirable to avoid the decimal-to-binary and binary-to-decimal conversions, if

* In Figure 3-4, the sign bits are shown since they are needed for correctly representing negative partial remainders and for the subtraction steps. They do not affect the final results and are therefore not considered in the discussion.

possible. Thus, the **binary-coded-decimal**, or **BCD**, computer has found wide acceptance in the business world.

TABLE 3-4 Binary-Coded-Decimal Code

Decimal digit	BCD equivalent
0	0000
1	0001
2	0010
3	0011
4	0100
5	0101
6	0110
7	0111
8	1000
9	1001

In the BCD machine, each decimal digit is represented by a four-bit code, as shown in Table 3-4. The code assignment is made simply: The binary numbers 0000 through 1001 represent their decimal equivalents from 0 through 9, while the remaining six codes, 1010 through 1111, represent signs or special markers. For now, let us assume that, of the latter six codes, only 1010 and 1111 are used and represent the plus and minus signs, respectively. Two examples of BCD numbers* are shown in Figure 3-5. In this and in the following figures, the decimal point is not shown. To be consistent with previous definitions, the reader should assume that the point lies between the second and third digit in every example.

In the decimal computer, the addition rules of Table 3-1 are implemented in the following manner:

> Add the BCD equivalents of each digit, and the carry bit if one exists, as if they were binary numbers. This yields a result which lies between 0 0000

Decimal	**BCD**
+ 15027	1010 0001 0101 0000 0010 0111
−32576	1111 0011 0010 0101 0111 0110

FIGURE 3-5. Examples of BCD numbers.

* In some computers, the term "packed-decimal" is used in place of BCD to designate numbers coded in this manner. However, BCD is more general, and we shall use it throughout this book.

11	1			11	1
15027	0001	0101	0000	0010	0111
32576	0011	0010	0101	0111	0110
	0 0100	0 0111	0 0101	0 1001	0 1101
	0 0000	0 0000	0 0001	0 0001	0 0000
	0 0100	0 0111	0 0110	0 1010	0 1101
	—	—	—	0 0110	0 0110
	(0)0100	(0)0111	(0)0110	(1)0000	(1)0011
47603	0100	0111	0110	0000	0011

FIGURE 3-6. BCD addition.

and 1 0011 (0 and 19). If the result is 0 0000 through 0 1001 (0 through 9), it can be used directly. Note that the most significant bit, which is the carry bit, is a ZERO in this case. If the result of the addition is 0 1010 through 1 0011 (10 through 19), then the correction factor* 0 0110 is added to it, resulting in a number between 1 0000 and 1 1001. The least significant four bits are now the correct BCD sum digit, while the most significant bit, the carry bit, is a ONE.

Figure 3-6 illustrates the addition of two positive BCD numbers and includes the manipulation of the carry digit as stipulated by the addition algorithm of Section 3.1.

If negative BCD numbers are first converted into tens complement, when necessary, then the addition algorithm applies universally. To convert a negative number into tens complement we use the rules stated earlier in connection with (3-1). This requires that we be able to implement the substitution rule of Table 3-2 for each BCD digit. The substitution rule is implemented in BCD in the following manner:

> Interchange ONE'S and ZERO'S for each BCD digit, thereby forming the logic complement of the BCD number. Add 1010 to each BCD digit and delete the carry bits.

This procedure is illustrated in detail in Figure 3-7. Note that the choice of 1010 to represent a plus sign and 1111 for a minus sign causes the sign to be changed automatically when applying the substitution rule. To complete the conversion,

* The correction factor 0110 is used to ensure that the codes 1010 through 1111, which do not represent decimal digits, are prevented from occurring during the addition of two BCD digits.

− 32576	1111	0011	0010	0101	0111	0110
Logic complement	0000	1100	1101	1010	1000	1001
Add 1010	1010	1010	1010	1010	1010	1010
	1010	①0110	①0111	①0100	①0010	①0011
Delete						
(+)67423	(1010)	0110	0111	0100	0010	0011

FIGURE 3-7. The BCD substitution rule.

From Figure 3-7		0110	0111	0100	0010	0011
		0000	0000	0000	0000	0001
67424		0110	0111	0100	0010	0100
Converting back		1001	1000	1011	1101	1011
		1010	1010	1010	1010	1010
		0011	0010	0101	0111	0101
		0000	0000	0000	0000	0001
− 32576	1111	0011	0010	0101	0111	0110

FIGURE 3-8. Conversion of a BCD number into tens complement and back.

it is merely necessary to add the decimal number 00001 to this number, ignoring the sign digit. Figures 3-7 and 3-8 together illustrate the conversion of a negative BCD number into tens complement and back again into sign-magnitude. In Figure 3-7, the BCD substitution rule is applied to the number −32576, and 67423 is the result. In Figure 3-8, decimal 00001 is added to 67423, and the result 67424 is obtained. Applying the same steps to 67424, we obtain −32576, which is the number we started with. Addition of negative numbers and subtraction now follow directly, as illustrated in Figure 3-9.

Finally, to implement multiplication and division, the computer must be able to shift the digits as required by the algorithms. In the BCD machine, a shift of four bits is the same as a shift of a single decimal digit. Thus, all the decimal arithmetic algorithms, including multiplication and division, can be implemented on the BCD computer using the rules previously set forth.

In this chapter, we have concentrated on the algorithms used by computers for performing arithmetic in both binary and decimal. Next, we consider several methods for extending the range of the numbers which can be manipulated by the machine so that we are no longer limited by the computer word length.

15027	0001	0101	0000	0010	0111
+67424	0110	0111	0100	0010	0100
	0 0111	0 1100	0 0100	0 0100	0 1011
	0 0001	0 0000	0 0000	0 0001	0 0000
	0 1000	0 1100	0 0100	0 0101	0 1011
	–	0 0110	–	–	0 0110
	⓪1000	①0010	⓪0100	⓪0101	①0001
82451	1000	0010	0100	0101	0001

(a) Addition example: (+ 15027) + (–32576) = (– 17549)

15027	0001	0101	0000	0010	0111
–67424 * →	0011	0010	0101	0111	0110
	0 0100	0 0111	0 0101	0 1001	0 1101
	0 0000	0 0000	0 0001	0 0001	0 0000
	0 0100	0 0111	0 0110	0 1010	0 1101
	–	–	–	0 0110	0 0110
	⓪0100	⓪0111	⓪0110	①0000	①0011
47603	0100	0111	0110	0000	0011

(*) Tens complement of 67424 is 32576 (from Figure 3-8).

(b) Subtraction example: (+ 15027) – (–32576) = (+ 47603)

FIGURE 3-9. Examples of addition and subtraction of tens complement BCD numbers.

EXERCISES

3.1 What advantage does the tens complement representation for negative decimal numbers have over the sign-magnitude representation?

3.2 Convert the numbers –15.257 and –33.126 into tens complement numbers using the rules presented in the text.

3.3 Form the sums

$$22.962 + (-15.257)$$
$$16.857 + (-33.126)$$

using the tens complement numbers obtained in Exercise 3.2. Check your results by subtracting in the sign-magnitude system and comparing the results. Note that in the second case it is necessary to convert the tens complement result back into sign-magnitude before comparing the two answers.

3.4 Convert the binary numbers –0011 0101 and –0100 0000 into twos complement binary numbers.

3.5 Add the binary number 0101 0000 to each of the twos complement numbers computed in Exercise 3.4. Verify the results by converting all binary numbers to decimal and reworking the calculations in decimal.

3.6 Multiply the binary numbers 00011 and 00100 together and check the result in decimal.

3.7 Divide the binary number 0010 0000 by 0011. Check the result by performing a binary multiplication and also by reworking in decimal When checking by multiplication, do not forget to add the remainder back in.

3.8 Convert the decimal numbers 1059 and 2468 into the binary-coded-decimal representation.

3.9 Add together, in BCD, the two numbers given in Exercise 3.8. Check your result by converting the sum into decimal and adding the numbers together.

3.10 To convert a decimal integer x whose value lies between 0 and 255 into an eight-bit binary number, the following algorithmic procedure is used:

1. Is $x \geqslant 128$? If so, set the most significant bit to ONE and subtract 128 from x. Otherwise, set the most significant bit to ZERO and omit the subtraction step.
2. Repeat step 1 using one-half of the previous test constant to determine the next significant bit.
3. Repeat until eight bits have been obtained.

Convert the decimal numbers 235, 189, 137, 127, 89, 25, and 6 into eight-bit binary numbers. Check your answers by converting them back into decimal.

3.11 To convert a negative decimal number into twos complement binary, convert its magnitude into binary using the algorithm of Exercise 3.10 and then complement the result. Convert the decimal numbers –120, –84, –61, –37, and –5 into eight-bit twos complement numbers. Check your answers by converting them back into decimal.

4

NUMBERS

In Chapter 3, we restricted the range of the numbers which the computer could manipulate. This allowed us to simplify the description of computer arithmetic. Although it is possible to scale all numbers to fall within the range of the computer, this puts unnecessary restrictions on the programmer who is using the machine. In this chapter we consider number formats to show how the useful range of the computer can be extended. Several related topics, such as overflow, are also considered.

4.1 THE FIXED-POINT FORMAT

Thus far, both the binary point and the decimal point, which we shall simply call the **point**, entered into the discussion only where necessary to avoid confusion. For example, we stated that in addition and subtraction the points must first be lined up. We also provided rules for determining the locations of the points in the product, quotient, and remainder in multiplication and division. Perhaps we gave the impression that in the computer the point would always automatically appear where it belongs. This is not so. In fact, in most machines, the point is not physically represented as part of the number. Depending on the type of number format used, either the programmer or the computer keeps track of where the point lies. If it lies in a fixed position in the number, as in the **fixed-point** format, the programmer has the responsibility of specifying its position and keeping track of it. If the point can "float" around and thereby

150 x 075 = 011250	Computer result
150. x 075. = 011250.	Integers
.150 x .075 = .011250	Fractions

FIGURE 4-1. Decimal multiplication and the decimal point.

assume any position in the number, as in the **floating-point** format, the computer then keeps track of its position, as described in Section 4.2.

In a fixed-point machine, regardless of where the point is assumed to lie in any given number, the arithmetic algorithms remain the same; that is, the computer treats all numbers as strings of digits for the purpose of performing arithmetic. We have illustrated this in Figure 4-1 for decimal multiplication. In the example, the product is interpreted as either an integer or a fraction, depending on where the point is assumed to lie in the multiplier and multiplicand. The programmer has the option of placing the point anywhere in the number, and it is his responsibility to keep track of where he has placed it. For example, he might choose to have the point lie in the middle of the number, rather than on the left or right, or even in different places in different numbers. In the latter situation, keeping track of the point is not a trivial matter.

The necessity of keeping track of the point is a major drawback of the fixed-point format. Thus, when using a fixed-point machine, most programmers use either integer arithmetic or fractional arithmetic with the point to the right or left of the number, respectively. This, of course, greatly simplifies the programs but does restrict the range of numbers which can be represented. For example, it is impossible to represent the decimal number 54260000. in a four-digit fixed-point machine. However, if the number is scaled by 10,000, then it becomes 5426., which can be represented by a four-digit number. In a fixed-point machine, the programmer must do his own scaling; in a floating-point machine, the number is scaled automatically, as we shall see.

4.2 THE FLOATING-POINT FORMAT

Scaling the number 54260000. by 10,000 is only one way of reducing it to a four-digit number. Another method is to scale all numbers so that the point lies on the left. Thus, in our example,

$$54260000. = .5426 \times 10^{8}$$

The digits 5426 along with the **exponent** 8 constitute a **floating-point** number which gives us sufficient information to determine what the original number is. The digits 5426 are always interpreted as a **fraction**,* since we have scaled the

* The fractional and exponent parts of a floating-point number have been called by a variety of other names whose usage is not standardized. Therefore, we have chosen to use the terms "fraction" and "exponent," which should cause no confusion.

number accordingly. Thus, although it requires eight digits to represent the number 54260000. in fixed-point, it requires only the 5 digits 5426,8 to represent it in floating-point. The exponent, which tells us where the point lies, is stored along with the fraction in the computer.

Let us now compare the range of numbers which can be represented by five-digit numbers in the fixed-point and floating-point formats. For simplicity, only positive fractions and exponents are considered. In fixed-point, we can represent either fractions from .00000 to .99999 or integers from 00000. to 99999. in a simple manner by a five-digit number. In floating-point, any number from $.0000 \times 10^0$ to $.9999 \times 10^9$, that is, from .0000 to 999900000., can be represented by the five digits. Although the accuracy is slightly greater in the fixed-point format because more significant digits are available, the range is far greater in the floating-point format. Moreover, as we have stated, the programmer does not have to be concerned with where the point lies.

The general floating-point number representation is given by f,e, which is interpreted as the number

$$f \times b^e$$

where f is the fraction, e is the exponent, and b is the base of the number system. For decimal machines, b = 10, and f,e is stored as a sequence of decimal digits. For example, 54260000. is stored as the sequence 5426,8. Note that in many computers, the exponent and fraction are stored in reverse order. That is, 54260000. is stored as 8,5426. Conceptually, there is no difference between the two conventions, and we shall assume that the exponent is always stored on the right. For binary machines, b = 2, and f,e is stored as a sequence of bits. An example of a sixteen-bit binary floating-point number, wherein the fraction is twelve bits long and is represented by the leftmost bits of the computer word, while the exponent is represented by the remaining four bits, is given by

0010 0001 0000 0110

This is equivalent to the decimal number 16.5.* Although other bases, such as 4 and 16, are in use, we shall restrict ourselves to the binary and decimal cases.

Both the fraction and the exponent can be negative numbers. If the fraction is negative, then the number itself is negative. For example, –5426,+8 is –54260000., assuming the sign-magnitude representation is used for negative numbers. If the exponent is negative, the value of the number is changed significantly. For example, the floating-point number +5426, –8 is equal to +.000000005426. Negative fractions and exponents can also be represented by tens complement or twos complement numbers which are then interpreted

* To verify this, note that the extreme left-hand bit of the fraction is the **sign** bit, the remaining bits are weighted $\frac{1}{2}, \frac{1}{4}, \frac{1}{8}, \ldots$, and the exponent is treated as an integer. Thus, 0010 0001 0000 0110 is

$$[\tfrac{1}{4} + \tfrac{1}{128}] \times 2^6 = 16.5$$

according to the rules given in Chapter 3. An example of a floating-point binary number which uses the twos complement representation for the fraction and exponent is 1110 0000 0000 1101. This number is equivalent to the decimal number −.03125.* Although other number representations are often used for the exponent, we will not present the details here.†

Thus far in our discussion of floating-point, we have described the floating-point format and have given examples of binary and decimal numbers. We now show how arithmetic is performed using floating-point numbers.

4.3 FLOATING-POINT ARITHMETIC

The first step in carrying out floating-point addition is to line up the points. The fixed-point computer assumes that they are lined up, since it is the programmer's responsibility to do so. In floating-point, the points are correctly lined up whenever the exponents are equal. Thus, to line up the points, it is necessary to adjust one of the exponents until it is equal to the other. This adjustment can be made without changing the value of the number by shifting the fraction one digit position to the right each time the exponent is **incremented.** The following example serves to illustrate this procedure:

$$.3218 \times 10^6 = .0321(8) \times 10^7 = .0032(18) \times 10^8$$

Thus, the floating-point numbers 3218,6 and 0032,8 are equal except for the digits lost in the shifting process. The loss of digits occurs because a fixed number of digits is used to represent a floating-point number in the computer. Therefore, to add together the numbers 5426,8 and 3218,6 the latter is first converted into 0032,8 and the fractions are then added together. The sum, in this case, is 5458,8. The four-digit accuracy of the sum is consistent with the four-digit accuracy of the original numbers. Thus, the shifting process used to make the exponents equal does not affect the accuracy of the sum. Note that, in the process of making the two exponents equal, the smaller of the two was incremented. This is done so that the least significant rather than the most significant digits are lost in the shifting process.

Subtraction is accomplished by complementing the fraction part of the number to be subtracted and then performing a floating-point addition as described above. For both addition and subtraction, whenever negative numbers in sign-magnitude representation are encountered, the fraction parts are first

* The sign bit of the fraction is weighted −1 and the sign bit of the exponent, −8. Thus, 1110 0000 0000 1101 is

$$[-1 + \tfrac{1}{2} + \tfrac{1}{4}] \times 2^{-8+4+1} = -\tfrac{1}{4} \times 2^{-3} = -.03125$$

† The **excess 64** representation which is often used for the exponent is described in Exercise 4.6.

converted into either twos complement or tens complement numbers in accordance with the rules stated in Chapter 3.

The rules for floating-point multiplication can be derived by examining how the product p of the two numbers $f_1 \times b^{e_1}$ and $f_2 \times b^{e_2}$ is formed:

$$\begin{aligned} p &= [f_1 \times b^{e_1}] \times [f_2 \times b^{e_2}] \\ &= [f_1 \times f_2] \times b^{(e_1+e_2)} \end{aligned} \tag{4-1}$$

To obtain this result, the usual laws of arithmetic have been applied. This equation states that the product of two floating-point numbers is composed of the product of the fractional parts and the sum of the exponents. Thus, (1250,4) x (4000,–2) = (50000000,2). In ordinary decimal, 1250. x .004000 = 50.000000. Note that, just as in fixed-point multiplication, the product contains twice the number of digits of the multiplier and multiplicand. The rules of fixed-point multiplication and addition thus apply to the fractions and exponents, respectively.

In a similar manner, the quotient of two general floating-point numbers is given by

$$q = \left[\frac{f_1}{f_2}\right] \times b^{(e_1-e_2)} \tag{4-2}$$

We will assume that $f_1 < f_2$* to ensure that $[f_1/f_2]$ will itself be a fraction. Then the quotient of two floating-point numbers is composed of the quotient of the fractional parts and the difference between the exponents. The fractional part of the remainder is the remainder obtained when f_1 is divided by f_2 and the exponent part of the remainder is $[e_1 - e_2 - s]$ where s is the number of shifts performed. In both multiplication and division, whenever negative numbers whose fraction parts are in twos complement or tens complement representation are encountered, they are first converted into sign-magnitude numbers in accordance with the rules stated in Chapter 3. Since the exponents are to be added or subtracted, they are manipulated in the complement representation.

In a floating-point computer, the exponents are manipulated automatically by the arithmetic unit. Thus, for example, the shifting steps, which are used to line up the points for addition and subtraction, are executed without any intervention on the part of the programmer. It is possible, however, to perform floating-point arithmetic on a fixed-point machine. In this case, step-by-step instructions for manipulating the exponents must be provided by the programmer. The algorithms used for floating-point arithmetic remain the same whether

* It is a simple matter to test for this condition and ensure that it is true by shifting the fraction of the dividend and adjusting its exponent. The details are presented in the sections on overflow and normalization (Sections 4.5–4.7).

they are programmed in a step-by-step manner for a fixed-point machine or implemented automatically in a floating-point machine.

Most floating-point computers can also perform fixed-point arithmetic directly. For this reason, two sets of arithmetic instructions are provided. The instructions ADD, SUBTRACT, MULTIPLY, and DIVIDE refer to the fixed-point operations, whereas FLOATING ADD, FLOATING SUBTRACT, FLOATING MULTIPLY, and FLOATING DIVIDE refer to the corresponding floating-point operations.

As we have seen, the floating-point format allows a wider range of numbers to be represented by a given number of digits than the fixed-point format. However, numbers requiring high absolute accuracy cannot be handled in either format unless a large number of digits is available to represent the number in the computer. Most large computers have long word lengths which enable them to perform high-precision arithmetic directly. In the smaller computers, **multiple-precision arithmetic** is commonly used for high-precision computations. Multiple-precision arithmetic can also be used on a large computer when higher precision is needed than can be obtained with the existing word length. In Section 4.4, we discuss **double-precision arithmetic**, which allows a computer to operate with the same accuracy as a machine with twice the word length.

4.4 DOUBLE-PRECISION ARITHMETIC

Cost is often a prime consideration when a computer is purchased. Thus, a small computer with a word length which is less than twenty-four bits long is often acquired whenever the amount of high-precision computing to be done is small or the length of time required to complete a problem requiring high precision is relatively unimportant. Let us examine a sample problem to see why double-precision arithmetic is required and how it can be implemented on a typical small machine.

In the right-angled triangle shown in Figure 4-2, the lengths of sides c and a are known, and we wish to find the length of side b. The relation between the sides of a right-angled triangle is given by the Pythagorean theorem, which can be stated as

$$c^2 = a^2 + b^2 \tag{4-3}$$

Solving for b, we obtain

$$b = \sqrt{c^2 - a^2} \tag{4-4}$$

Let us assume that our computer performs four-digit fixed-point arithmetic* and that the values of c and a are .1336 and .1289, respectively. Squaring .1336 and .1289, we obtain .01784896 and .01661521, since we automatically obtain a double-precision product when performing multiplication. However, if we then

* This is very nearly equivalent to fourteen-bit binary arithmetic.

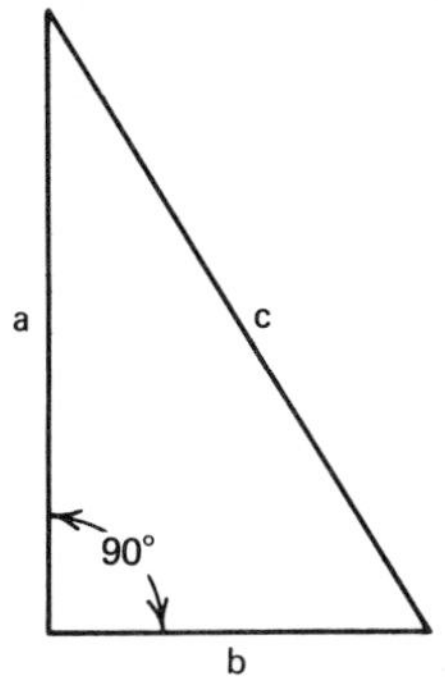

FIGURE 4-2. Example problem illustrating double-precision arithmetic.

perform the usual type of subtraction, which allows us to manipulate only the four most significant digits, we obtain the single-precision result .0012. Compare this result to the double-precision difference .00123375. If we then calculate the square roots to four-digit accuracy, we obtain .0346 and .0351, respectively, in the two cases. The two results differ by almost 1½%! This is an intolerable error in most cases. If, for example, the right-angled triangle represents a parcel of land whose dimensions are given in fractions of a mile, then the error in side b would be over 2½ feet. For comparison, the original values given for sides a and c are accurate to within approximately ½ foot. Let us now examine some techniques for storing and manipulating double-precision numbers.

A double-precision fixed-point number is most easily stored in two consecutive memory locations. One format commonly used for binary numbers is shown in Figure 4-3. The most significant half-word is stored in the lower-addressed location of each pair, while the least significant half-word is stored in the other location. The most significant bit of the latter location is not used and is always set to ZERO. Thus, a double-precision word in a sixteen-bit machine is composed of thirty data bits and a sign bit. This thirty-one-bit representation is consistent with the result obtained when multiplying together two sixteen-bit numbers, each composed of fifteen data bits and a sign bit.

When adding two double-precision numbers, the least significant halves are added together first. The resulting sum, with the most significant bit set to ZERO, constitutes the least significant half of the double-precision sum. These steps are shown in Figure 4-4, as steps 1, 2, and 3. If the most significant bit is a ONE,* we provide a carry into the other half of the sum by adding the number 000...001 to the sum of the most significant halves of the two numbers. The

* To test this bit, we can treat the number in the accumulator as a single-precision number and test its sign using the instruction IF ACC = –, TRANSFER TO n. If the test indicates that the number is negative, then the sign bit, which is the most significant bit, is a ONE Otherwise, it is a ZERO.

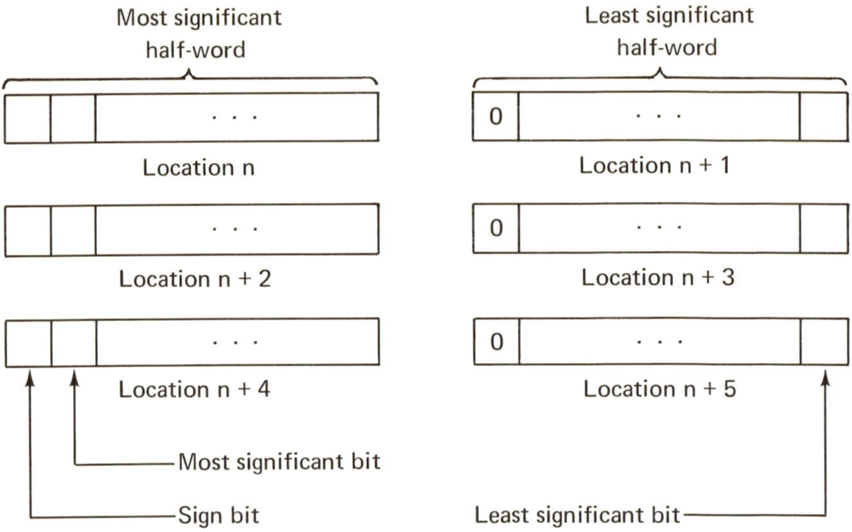

FIGURE 4-3. Storage of double-precision numbers.

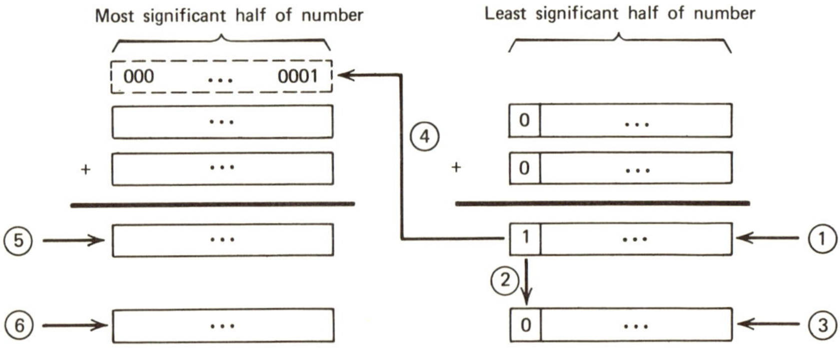

(1) Add the least significant halves of the numbers.
(2) If the most significant bit of the sum is a ONE, set it to ZERO.
(3) Store the sum as the least significant half of the double-precision sum.
(4) If the most significant bit in step 2 is a ONE, provide a carry into the other half of the sum by adding 000...0001 to the sum of the most significant halves of the numbers.
(5) Form the sum of the most significant halves of the numbers.
(6) Store the sum as the most significant half of the double-precision sum.

FIGURE 4-4. Double-precision addition.

result then constitutes the most significant half of the double-precision sum. These steps are shown in Figure 4-4 as steps 4, 5, and 6.

A sample program to add together the two double-precision numbers stored in locations n, n+1 and n+2, n+3, and to store the sum in locations n+4, n+5 is shown below. The instructions used were defined in Chapters 1 and 2. The numbers at the right refer to the steps of Figure 4-4.

```
x      LOAD ACC, n+1                 }  (1)
x+1    ADD, n+3                      }
x+2    IF ACC=-, TRANSFER TO y          (2)
x+3    STORE ACC, n+5                   (3)
x+4    LOAD ACC, n                   }
x+5    ADD, n+2                      }  (4)
x+6    STORE ACC, n+4                   (5)
.      .
.      .
.      .
y      AND, y+5                         (2)
y+1    STORE ACC, n+5                   (3)
y+2    LOAD ACC, y+6                 }
y+3    ADD, n                        }  (4)
y+4    TRANSFER TO x+5               }
y+5    0111 1111 1111 1111
y+6    0000 0000 0000 0001
```

Figure 4-5 contains a step-by-step example illustrating the execution of this program for the case when a carry is induced and also when no carry is induced.

To subtract two double-precision numbers, we first determine the complement of the number being subtracted and then add it to the first number. To form the arithmetic complement of a double-precision number, the logic complement of the least significant half is first obtained. Then 000...001 is added to it. If we assume that a carry is not generated by this step, then the sum with the most significant bit set to ZERO constitutes the least significant half of the arithmetic complement. These steps are shown in Figure 4-6 as steps 1, 2, 3, and 4. Then the logic complement of the most significant half of the number constitutes the most significant half of the arithmetic complement, as shown in steps 5 and 6 of Figure 4-6. A carry can occur during complementation only if the least significant half of the original number is all ZERO's. Its complement, 111...111, is the only number which, when added to 000...001, generates a carry. Thus, we can test for the carry condition at the outset using the

	Program	Accumulator	Location n+4	Location n+5
x	LOAD ACC, n+1	0011 1100 0011 1101	–	–
x+1	ADD, n+3	0101 0111 0001 1100	–	–
x+2	IF ACC=–, TRANSFER TO y	0101 0111 0001 1100	–	–
x+3	STORE ACC, n+5	0101 0111 0001 1100	–	0101 0111 0001 1100
x+4	LOAD ACC, n	0001 1010 1111 0010	–	0101 0111 0001 1100
x+5	ADD, n+2	0100 0000 1010 1111	–	0101 0111 0001 1100
x+6	STORE ACC, n+4	0100 0000 1010 1111	0100 0000 1010 1111	0101 0111 0001 1100

Location n	0001 1010 1111 0010
Location n+1	0011 1100 0011 1101
Location n+2	0010 0101 1011 1101
Location n+3	0001 1010 1101 1111

(a) No carry between halves of numbers

	Program	Accumulator	Location n+4	Location n+5
x	LOAD ACC, n+1	0011 1100 0011 1101	—	—
x+1	ADD, n+3	1001 1011 0101 0101	—	—
x+2	IF ACC=–, TRANSFER TO y	1001 1011 0101 0101	—	—
y	AND, y+5	0001 1011 0101 0101	—	—
y+1	STORE ACC, n+5	0001 1011 0101 0101	—	0001 1011 0101 0101
y+2	LOAD ACC, y+6	0000 0000 0000 0001	—	0001 1011 0101 0101
y+3	ADD, n	0001 1010 1111 0011	—	0001 1011 0101 0101
y+4	TRANSFER TO x+5	0001 1010 1111 0011	—	0001 1011 0101 0101
x+5	ADD, n+2	0101 1000 0100 1110	—	0001 1011 0101 0101
x+6	STORE ACC, n+4	0101 1000 0100 1110	0101 1000 0100 1110	0001 1011 0101 0101

Location n	0001 1010 1111 0010
Location n+1	0011 1100 0011 1101
Location n+2	0011 1101 0101 1011
Location n+3	0101 1111 0001 1000
Location y+5	0111 1111 1111 1111
Location y+6	0000 0000 0000 0001

(b) Carry between halves of numbers

FIGURE 4-5. Example of double-precision addition.

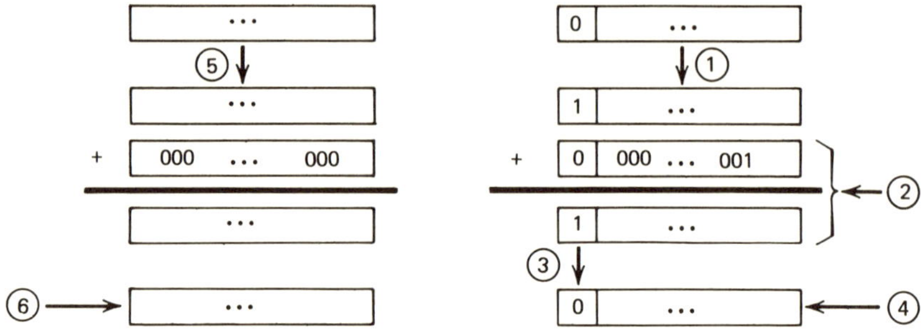

(1) Form logic complement of least significant half of number.
(2) Add 000...001.
(3) Change most significant bit to ZERO.
(4) Store result as least significant half of arithmetic complement.
(5) Form logic complement of most significant half of number.
Note: Addition of all-ZERO number is not required but is shown for completeness.
(6) Store result as most significant half of arithmetic complement.

FIGURE 4-6. Double-precision arithmetic complement if least significant half of number is nonzero.

IF ACC=0 instruction. In the case that an all-ZERO number is encountered, it is stored immediately. Then 000...001 is added to the complement of the most significant half of the number, completing the procedure. The sample program shown below forms the complement of a double-precision number stored in locations n and n+1 and stores the result in locations n+2 and n+3.

```
x       LOAD ACC, n+1
x+1     IF ACC=0, TRANSFER TO y
x+2     COMPLEMENT
x+3     ADD, y+5
x+4     AND, y+6
x+5     STORE ACC, n+3
x+6     LOAD ACC, n
x+7     COMPLEMENT
x+8     STORE ACC, n+2
 .       .
 .       .
 .       .
y       STORE ACC, n+3
y+1     LOAD ACC, n
y+2     COMPLEMENT
```

y+3	ADD, y+5
y+4	TRANSFER TO x+8
y+5	0000 0000 0000 0001
y+6	0111 1111 1111 1111

It is beyond the scope of this book to go into the details of double-precision binary multiplication and division and double-precision decimal arithmetic. We should point out, however, that a four-word product is formed in multiplication and a four-word dividend is required for division.

Double-precision floating-point operations are used when both high precision and a large range are desired. The algorithms for double-precision floating-point arithmetic are a combination of the double-precision and floating-point rules. We will not pursue this topic either.

When performing addition, subtraction, and division, it is possible for the correct result to be outside the allowable range of the number system. In fixed-point machines, this occurs whenever the result is too large for the accumulator to hold, and an **overflow** is said to have occurred. Every overflow must be detected if erroneous results are to be avoided. An overflow of the fraction during the execution of a floating-point operation is called a **temporary overflow.** This type of overflow can usually be eliminated by a process called **normalization.** An overflow of the floating-point exponent, however, cannot be corrected and must be detected. In Sections 4.5–4.7 we discuss overflow and normalization in detail.

4.5 OVERFLOW

In Chapter 3, when we introduced addition, we agreed to restrict the numbers being added so that the sum would always be in range. Thus, an overflow could not occur, and we were able to show that the carry out of the most significant digit position could be deleted and therefore ignored. Now we remove this restriction and show how the high-order carry can be used to detect an overflow.

Let us first examine all the possibilities which can occur during fixed-point binary addition or subtraction. Six examples are shown in Figure 4-7; in the examples shown in part (a), an overflow does not occur, while in the examples shown in part (b), an overflow occurs. In every example, we have shown the carry bit to the left of the sum. Referring to the examples, we can now make the following observations about addition:

1. Whenever two positive or two negative numbers are added together, and the carry bit differs from the sign bit, an overflow has occurred.
2. Whenever a positive number is added to a negative number, an overflow cannot occur; moreover, the carry bit always differs from the sign bit.

Thus, by comparing the carry bit and the sign bit and by checking the sign bits of the numbers being added, we can detect an overflow whenever one occurs. A

```
  0110 0011        +99
  0000 1010        +10
 ----------       -----
 0 0110 1101       +109
 ↑
 └──────────────── Bits similar ───→ No overflow

  1101 0000        −48
  1101 0000        −48
 ----------       -----
 1 1010 0000       − 96
 ↑
 └──────────────── Bits similar ───→ No overflow

  0110 0011        +99  ⎫
  1101 0000        −48  ⎪
 ----------       ----- ⎪
 1 0011 0011       + 51 ⎪
                        ⎬  Overflow cannot occur
  1001 1101        −99  ⎪
  0011 0000        +48  ⎪
 ----------       ----- ⎪
 0 1100 1101       − 51 ⎭
```

(a) No overflow

```
  0110 0011        +99
  0011 0000        +48
 ----------       -----
 0 1001 0011       +147
 ↑
 └──────────────── Bits differ ───→ Overflow

  1001 1101        −99
  1101 0000        −48
 ----------       -----
 1 0110 1101       −147
 ↑
 └──────────────── Bits differ ───→ Overflow
```

(b) Overflow

FIGURE 4-7. Binary integer addition. (Range of eight-bit numbers is −128 to +127.)

slight modification of the number formats can considerably simplify this test. The modification consists of increasing the word length of each number being added by appending one bit onto the left of each number. The appended bit should always be the same as the sign bit. Then, by adding the modified numbers and ignoring the carry out of the appended bit position, we obtain the results shown in Figure 4-8 for the examples previously used. Except for the appended bit, the sum is unchanged in every case. Overflow can now be detected by

```
  0 0110 0011
  0 0000 1010
  -----------
  0 0110 1101

  1 1101 0000
  1 1101 0000
  -----------
  1 1010 0000

  0 0110 0011
  1 1101 0000
  -----------
  0 0011 0011

  1 1001 1101
  0 0011 0000
  -----------
  1 1100 1101

  0 0110 0011
  0 0011 0000
  -----------
  0 1001 0011
  ↑
  └── Bits differ ──→ Overflow

  1 1001 1101
  1 1101 0000
  -----------
  1 0110 1101
  ↑
  └── Bits differ ──→ Overflow
```

FIGURE 4-8. Binary integer addition with modification to simplify detection of overflow.

comparing the appended bit to the sign bit. If the two bits differ, an overflow has occurred.

A similar approach can be used to detect overflow in a decimal computer. In this case, we set the appended digit to zero if the number is positive and to nine if it is negative. If the appended digit of the sum is zero, but the sum is a negative number, an overflow has occurred. Similarly, an overflow has occurred

0 21.462	+21.462	
0 12.367	+12.367	
0 33.829	+33.829	
9 60.379	−39.621	
9 90.846	− 9.154	
9 51.225	−48.775	
0 46.832	+46.832	
9 60.379	−39.621	
0 07.211	+ 7.211	
9 60.379	−39.621	
0 21.462	+21.462	
9 81.841	−18.159	
0 46.832	−39.621	
0 21.462	+21.462	
0 68.294 (↑ Negative number)	+68.294	Overflow
9 60.379	−39.621	
9 60.379	−39.621	
9 20.758 (↑ Positive number)	−79.242	Overflow

FIGURE 4-9. Decimal addition. (Range of allowed numbers is −50.000 to +49.999.) Numbers on the left are in tens complement notation; numbers on the right are in sign-magnitude notation.

if the appended digit is a nine, but the sum is positive. In all other cases, no overflow has occurred. Examples of the six possible cases which can occur are shown in Figure 4-9.

We stated earlier that when two numbers are multiplied together, the product contains twice as many digits as the original numbers. To allow the product to be correctly represented, a double-length accumulator is provided in the machine. As a result, overflow cannot occur during fixed-point multiplication, since the product of two numbers can always be correctly represented in the double-length accumulator. However, in division, it is possible for the quotient to exceed the range of the number system. For example, if we are performing fractional arithmetic, an overflow will occur if the dividend is greater than or equal to the divisor. In this case, the first quotient bit will be a ONE; as we pointed out in Chapter 3 in connection with binary division, if this bit is a ONE, an overflow has occurred.

A similar rule can be used to detect overflow during decimal division. In this case, if the first quotient digit is zero, no overflow has occurred; otherwise, an overflow exists.

Whenever an overflow occurs, a single bit in a memory location reserved for this purpose is set to ONE. It is the programmer's responsibility to check this bit whenever he suspects that an overflow has occurred. An instruction such as IF OVERFLOW, TRANSFER TO n can be provided to test the overflow bit. If it is a ZERO, no action is taken, and the next instruction is executed; if the overflow bit is a ONE, it is reset to ZERO, and the instruction in location n is executed next. The sequence of instructions beginning in location n allows the computer to take suitable corrective action or to terminate the execution of the program.

An alternate method of detecting an overflow is to **interrupt** the computer whenever the overflow bit is set. We will introduce the concept of a computer interrupt in Chapter 9, and describe how it is used for overflow detection.

4.6 NORMALIZATION

Normalization is used with floating-point arithmetic to ensure that maximum accuracy is maintained throughout the execution of a sequence of computations. It is also used to eliminate an overflow of the fraction of a floating-point number which we call a **temporary overflow.** We will discuss normalization using examples to illustrate how it is used in both these situations.

If we multiply the two floating-point numbers 3225,01 and 1243,01, we obtain the product 04008675,02 in the double-length accumulator. If we try to store this number as a single-precision floating-point number, we find that the number stored is 0400,02. Note that the leading zero of the fraction adds nothing to the accuracy. We can eliminate this zero by shifting the double-precision number to the left and subtracting one from the exponent. Thus, 04008675,02 becomes 40086750,01, the two representations being equivalent. Then, if we store the latter number as a single-precision number, we find that 4008,01 is stored. Thus, the accuracy of the stored result is increased significantly.

Normalization is, therefore, a process whereby the fraction is shifted as far to the left as possible without losing any significant digits or causing an overflow. In the example above, the fraction was shifted one digit position so that the most significant digit would occupy the leftmost position. An example of a number wherein the most significant digit does not occupy the leftmost position when normalized is given by 00653247,04, which becomes 06532470,03 when normalized. If we attempt to shift the fraction again, we find that the number becomes 65324700,02, which is a tens complement negative number and not equivalent to the original number, 00653247,04, which is positive. This is the overflow condition referred to above in the definition of normalization. An exception occurs when the fraction is equal to zero. Since all the digits are ZERO, we cannot normalize it according to the rule. We next consider the normalization of negative numbers.

Normalization of a negative number is accomplished by shifting out the leading 9's in the same way that the leading 0's were shifted out in the case of positive numbers. As an example, 99863245,03 becomes 86324500,01, both of which are equal to −1.36755. However, if we shift both leading 9's out of the negative number 99253876,03, it becomes a positive number, which is an overflow condition. Therefore, 92538760,02 is the normalized counterpart of 99253876,03 and both are equal to −7.46124.

In the normalization of binary floating-point numbers, the fraction is shifted until the two left-hand bits differ. This simple rule gives the same result which is obtained when the general normalization rule above is applied to binary numbers. As an example, the positive number* 0000 0101 0000 0110 becomes 0101 0000 0000 0010 when normalized. Both of these numbers are equal to +2.500, when converted to a decimal number. All the leading ZERO's have been shifted out except the last one, to avoid changing the sign of the number. Similarly, the negative number 1111 1011 0000 0110 when normalized becomes 1011 0000 0000 0010, which is equal to −2.500. Again, the number zero is an exception and cannot be normalized according to the rule.

In some computers, normalization is accomplished by the NORMALIZE instruction which we introduced in Chapter 2; in other machines, it is combined with an arithmetic or a store instruction. A common instruction in the latter group takes the format

STORE ACC NORMALIZED, n

In this case, the accumulator is normalized before being stored into location n. The two types of normalization instruction formats are equivalent. For example, the sequence

NORMALIZE
STORE ACC, n

is equivalent to the single instruction

STORE ACC NORMALIZED, n

Let us now consider the problem of temporary overflow of the fraction of a floating-point number. If we add the two numbers 0 4236,01 and 0 2376,01, we

* As in previous examples, the fraction is twelve bits long and the exponent is four bits long.

obtain 0 6612,01. Since the appended digit is a zero but the number is negative, we conclude that a temporary overflow has occurred. To eliminate this condition, a variation of the normalization procedure is used. The fraction, **including the appended digit**, is shifted by one digit position to the right, and the exponent is incremented. We thereby obtain 0 0661,02, which is the correct sum. We have lost a digit in the normalization process, but this is preferable to the overflow condition which, if uncorrected, would lead to an error.

The same procedure applies to negative numbers. Adding the negative numbers 9 6321,01 and 9 7242,01, we obtain 9 3563,01 and a temporary overflow condition. When normalized, this number becomes 9 9356,02, which is the correct sum. The appended digit is not changed during the shifting process, so that the test for temporary overflow now indicates a normal condition. A similar procedure is used for binary numbers, as illustrated in Figure 4-10.

Although an overflow always requires the attention of the programmer, temporary overflow does not. The normalization process which is used to eliminate the temporary overflow is executed automatically in a floating-point machine. If floating-point arithmetic is programmed on a fixed-point machine, however, the programmer must include this normalization procedure in his floating-point programs. This involves checking for overflow of the fraction, implementing a single right arithmetic shift, and incrementing the exponent. Once the floating-point programs are written, the computer can be used as if it were a floating-point machine. The difference between the two methods of performing floating-point arithmetic is not trivial, however, as we shall see in Chapter 12.

When we described floating-point division, we noted that the fraction of the dividend, f_1, must be less than the fraction of the divisor, f_2, to avoid an overflow. The first step in division, therefore, is to test whether f_2 equals zero since this always violates the condition that $f_1 < f_2$. If f_2 equals zero, the overflow bit is set and the division algorithm is dispensed with. If f_2 is not zero, then we normalize both the divisor and the dividend in order to ensure that the quotient will have maximum accuracy. We then proceed to the first step of the division, that of dividing f_1 by f_2. If the first quotient digit is zero, then we continue with the division algorithm to obtain the fractions of the quotient and remainder, and determine the exponents by subtraction according to the rules stated earlier. If, however, the first quotient digit is not zero, then a temporary overflow condition exists. Because the divisor and dividend were normalized, we know that if we shift the original dividend right by one digit position and increment its exponent, the temporary overflow cannot occur.* An equivalent but more efficient technique is to increment the exponent of the dividend and

* In a normalized positive binary fraction, the bit which is weighted one-half is always a ONE. Therefore, if we shift the dividend f_1 to the right by one bit position, it will take the form 01xxxx...x, whereas the divisor f_2 is of the form 1xxx...x, ignoring the sign bits. The reader can then verify that $f_1 < f_2$, regardless of what values the bits marked x take. This ensures that overflow cannot occur during the ensuing division of the fractions.

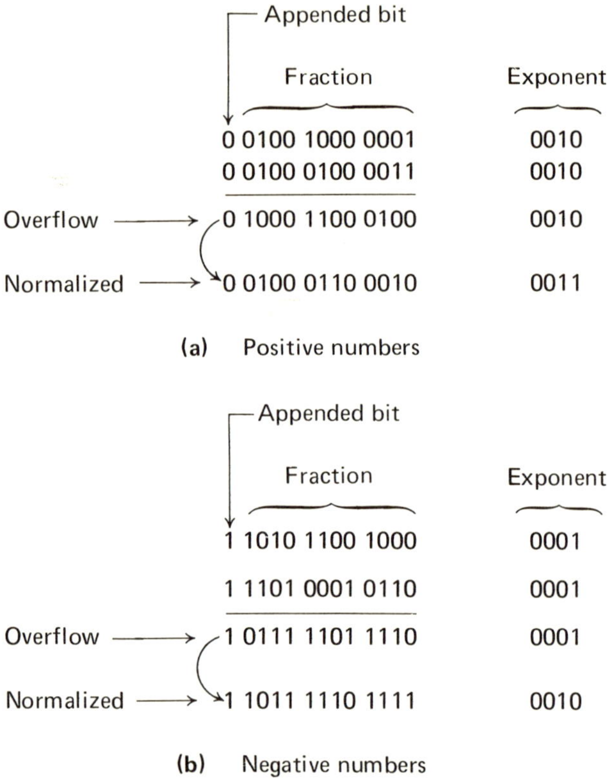

FIGURE 4-10. Normalization of binary numbers following an overflow condition.

shift the quotient right by one digit position. This moves the quotient digit already computed into the correct place in the quotient and eliminates the necessity of recalculating it. An example of the latter procedure is provided in Figure 4-11 for binary floating-point division. The rules just stated apply to both binary and decimal division without modification.

In this section, we have discussed the temporary overflow condition which occurs whenever the fraction of a floating-point result overflows. This type of overflow can be eliminated by a normalization procedure. If the exponent of a floating-point result overflows, it cannot be corrected, thereby causing a floating-point overflow. This type of overflow, which can occur during any arithmetic operation, is the subject of Section 4.7.

4.7 FLOATING-POINT OVERFLOW

During floating-point arithmetic, it is possible for the exponent to exceed its allowable range. Whenever the exponent overflows, we have a situation which cannot be corrected and must be detected in order to avoid an error. Exponent

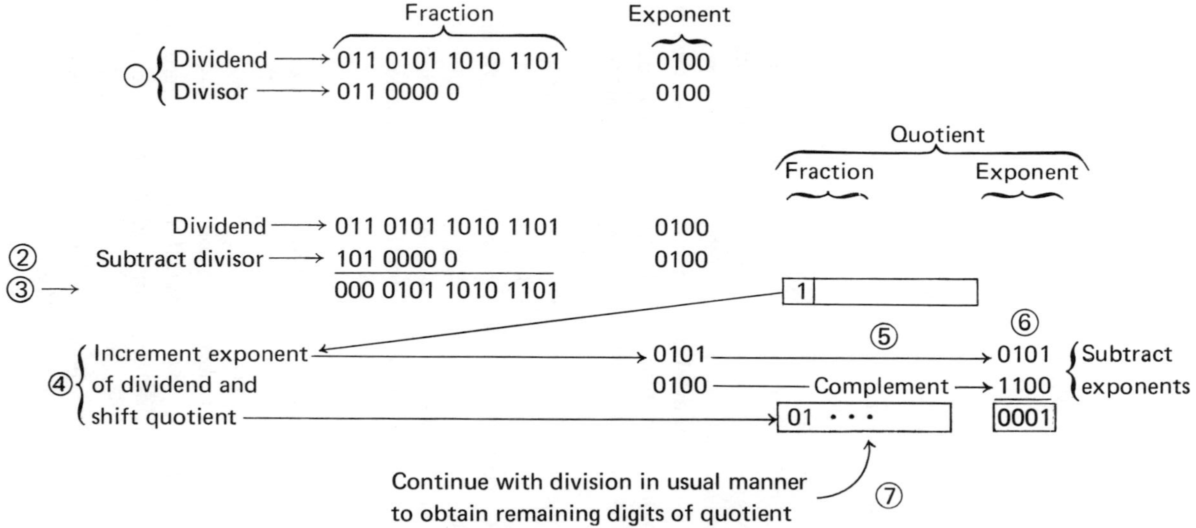

(1)	Original dividend and divisor.
(2)	Subtract divisor by adding its complement to dividend.
(3)	Positive remainder; therefore first quotient bit is not ZERO and temporary overflow exists.
(4)	Eliminate temporary overflow as shown.
(5), (6)	Compute exponent of quotient by adding complement of divisor exponent to incremented dividend exponent.
(7)	Compute fraction of quotient by continuing division in usual manner.

FIGURE 4-11. Binary floating-point division with temporary overflow.

```
                 0 3243        0 49
                +0 2640        0 49
                 0 5883        0 49
Correct
temporary
overflow
                 0 0588        0 50 <---- Exponent overflow
```

FIGURE 4-12. Example of floating-point overflow.

```
      0 2650          0 32
  x   0 4536        +0 41
0 1202 0400          0 73
```

FIGURE 4-13. Example of overflow during multiplication.

overflow can occur if the exponent exceeds either the most positive or most negative number of its allowable range. If the exponent overflows in the positive direction, the number is too large to be represented by the machine, and we have a **floating-point overflow**, or simply an overflow. If the exponent overflows in the negative direction, the number is too small to be represented by the machine, and we have a **floating-point underflow**. The overflow bit is set only if the exponent overflows in the positive direction. It is not set when a temporary overflow or an underflow occurs. We will discuss overflow first and then return to underflow.

A floating-point overflow occurs when the two numbers 3243,49 and 2640,49 are added together, as shown in Figure 4-12. During the normalization step which corrects the temporary overflow of the fraction, an overflow of the exponent is induced. Appended digits are shown for both the fraction and exponent so that both types of overflow can be detected easily.

During multiplication, the fraction of the product cannot overflow. Therefore, an overflow can occur only if the exponent overflows directly. An example of overflow during multiplication is shown in Figure 4-13. The details of multiplying the fractions together have been omitted. The overflow occurs because the sum of the exponents is out of range of the computer.

During division, overflow can occur in several ways. If the divisor is zero, the overflow bit is set directly, and the division is terminated immediately. If the difference between the exponents of the dividend and divisor should be a positive number but is out of range, an overflow is likewise indicated. The latter case is similar to multiplication overflow. Finally, the normalization procedure described in Section 4.6 for correcting temporary overflow of the fractional part of the quotient can cause the exponent to overflow in a manner similar to

Unnormalized number with appended digits	0 00327658	9 51
Normalize ⟶	0 32765800	9 49

Negative exponent overflow

FIGURE 4-14. Example of floating-point underflow.

addition overflow. The overflow bit is set whenever any one of these conditions occurs.

Although we have used decimal examples to illustrate floating-point overflow, the same rules apply to binary arithmetic. Here also, a positive exponent overflow results in the overflow bit being set.

The conditions for detecting an underflow are the same as those described above for overflow, except that the exponents are now negative numbers. In some machines, when underflow is detected, an underflow bit is set which allows corrective action to be taken. In other machines, when underflow is detected, the result is automatically set to zero. An example of underflow which occurs during execution of the NORMALIZE instruction is shown in Figure 4-14.

This completes the description of number representations and computer arithmetic. We have assumed thus far that the accumulator register can be used only as an accumulator and that the index register can be used only for indexing addresses. This is not always the case. In Chapter 5, we examine the registers of the computer to see how they are organized and how they operate.

EXERCISES

4.1 Convert the fixed-point binary number 01101000 into decimal, assuming (a) it is an integer, and (b) it is a fraction. In case (b), assume that the leading ZERO is the sign bit and that the binary point lies to its right.

4.2 Convert the decimal numbers .000635 and 635000. into the decimal floating-point format. Convert the binary numbers .0001101001 and 0110100100. into the binary floating-point format. Normalize the numbers in all cases.

4.3 Add the floating-point numbers 1350,4 and 1800,2 together. Normalize the sum, if necessary.

4.4 Add together the decimal fixed-point numbers 2571 and 0829, using the appended digit method described in the text to test for overflow. Continue by adding 0427, 1867, and 2736 to each of the sums obtained, stopping the procedure if an overflow occurs.

4.5 Add together the decimal floating-point numbers 4081,2 and 4857,3. Use the appended digit method to test for temporary overflow and normalize, if necessary. Continue by adding 4681,3 and 0812,2 to the sum, normalizing at each step, if necessary.

4.6 Every decimal number between −64 and +63 can be converted into a unique positive number by adding the decimal number 64 to it. Converting the resulting positive number into a seven-bit binary number yields the **excess 64** representation often used for floating-point exponents. Convert the decimal numbers −51, −12, 0, +22, and +43 into their excess 64 representations. Note that a procedure for converting a decimal number into binary is given in Exercise 3.10.

4.7 Convert the decimal numbers given in Exercise 4.6 into seven-bit ordinary binary numbers, using the twos complement representation for the negative numbers. Note that a procedure for converting negative decimal numbers into twos complement binary is given in Exercise 3.11. What is the difference between the excess 64 representation and the ordinary binary representation for each of the five numbers?

5

THE REGISTERS

A computer can have many registers associated with it. In a simple machine, each register is assigned a specific task, such as operating as an accumulator or as an index register, and cannot be used for any other purpose. At the other extreme, a set of general-purpose registers is provided, and the programmer is free to assign one of several tasks to each. In this chapter, we examine the computer registers further and introduce the **multi-accumulator** machine.

5.1 THE ACCUMULATOR REGISTER

As we stated in Chapter 1, a register is a fixed storage location which is not necessarily associated with the main memory. It is capable of storing a fixed number of bits of information in the same way that bits are stored in each word in the memory. However, a register may be longer or shorter than a computer word, depending on how it is used.

If the register is to be used exclusively as a fixed-point accumulator, it is built so that it can store twice as many bits as are contained in a computer word. This allows double-precision products and dividends to be stored in the accumulator. We will separate the accumulator into two parts: the most significant half will be called the A register, and the least significant half, the B register, as illustrated in Figure 5-1.

For addition, subtraction, load and store, and the logic instructions, only the

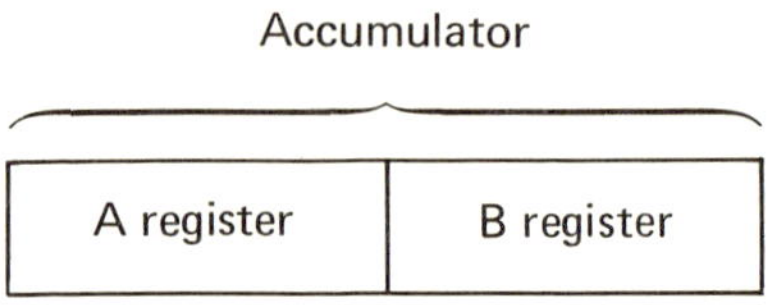

FIGURE 5-1. The organization of the accumulator.

A register is used. Thus, the program

```
LOAD ACC, n
ADD, n+1
STORE ACC, n+2
```

first causes the single-precision number stored in memory location n to be placed into the A register. Then the number stored in location n + 1 is added to the A register; and, finally, the number in the A register, which is the sum, is stored in location n + 2. Throughout the procedure, there is no need to use the B register, since only single-precision results are manipulated.

For multiplication, both the A and B registers are used. The multiplier is initially loaded into the A register; the multiplicand is obtained from the memory location specified in the MULTIPLY instruction; and, finally, the double-precision product is formed in the complete accumulator. Thus, in the program

```
LOAD ACC, n
MULTIPLY, n+1
```

the multiplier is obtained from location n and the multiplicand from location n + 1. The partial product sums formed during the multiplication can be stored to the right of the multiplier in the double-precision accumulator. To accommodate the increasing size of the partial product sums, each multiplier bit is discarded after use by a single left shift. This shift which is applied to the whole accumulator, exclusive of the most significant bit of the B register,* also shifts the partial product sum as specified in the multiplication algorithm. Thus, as the partial product sums increase in size, they extend into the part of the A register vacated by the multiplier during the shifting process. An example of binary multiplication which illustrates this procedure is shown in Figure 5-2, using the same numbers which were used in the example of Figure 3-3. As stated above, the most significant bit of the B register does not enter into the algorithm. This ensures that the product of two seven-bit numbers is a fourteen-bit number,

* The most significant bit of the B register is not used in the representation of double-precision numbers, as pointed out in Chapter 4 in connection with double-precision arithmetic. Thus, when shifting the A and B registers during multiplication, the second bit of the B register is shifted directly into the A register.

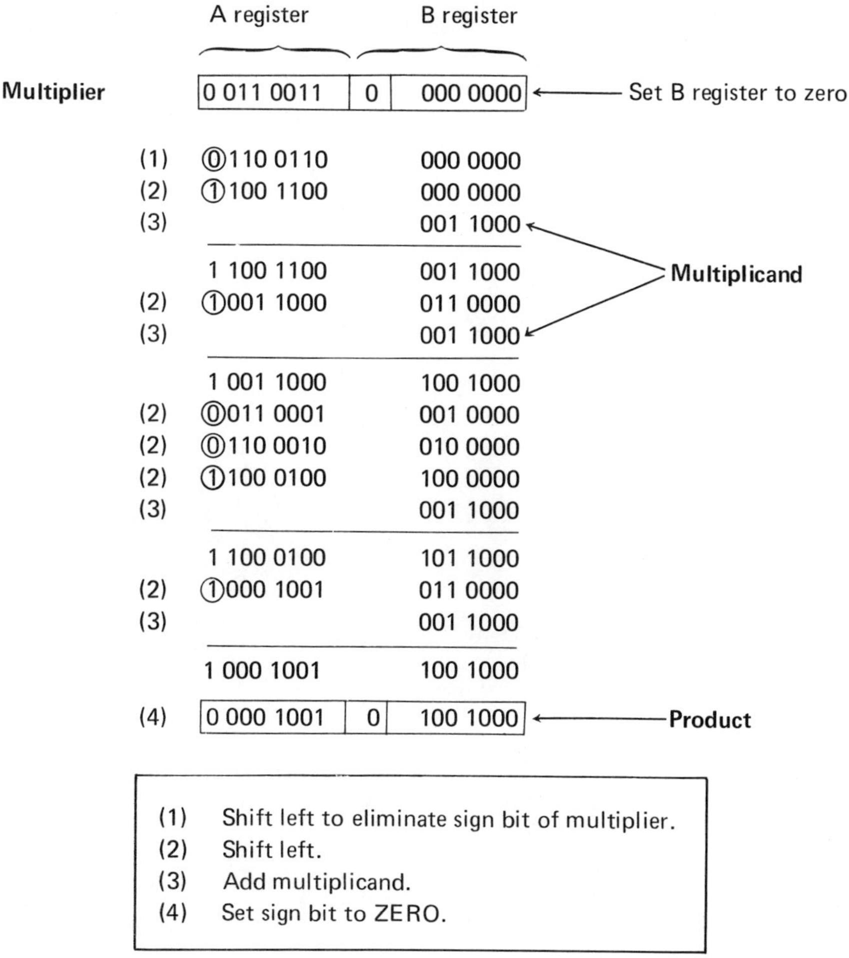

FIGURE 5-2. Example of binary multiplication in double-precision accumulator. The multiplier bit which is circled determines whether the next step is a shift or an add.

exclusive of the sign bits which are ZERO in all three numbers. The last multiplier bit is discarded by setting it to ZERO rather than by shifting, as in the previous steps. This step is consistent with the rules presented in the multiplication algorithm in Chapter 3.

In division, as in multiplication, both the A and B registers are used. In this case, the double-precision dividend is loaded into the accumulator and, as before, the most significant bit of the B register is not used. The divisor is obtained from the memory location specified in the DIVIDE instruction, and

Divisor = 0001 1000

Step	A register	B register	Quotient bit
Dividend	0 000 1001	0 100 1100	
(1)	1 110 1000		
	①111 0001	100 1100	0
(2)	0 001 1000		
	0 000 1001	100 1100	0
(3)	0 001 0011	001 1000	
(1)	1 110 1000		
	①111 1011	001 1000	0
(2)	0 001 1000		
	0 001 0011	001 1000	0
(3)	0 010 0110	011 0000	
(1)	1 110 1000		
	⓪000 1110	011 0000	1
(3)	0 001 1100	110 0001	
(1)	1 110 1000		
	⓪000 0100	110 0001	1
(3)	0 000 1001	100 0011	
(1)	1 110 1000		
	①111 0001	100 0011	0
(2)	0 001 1000		
	0 000 1001	100 0011	0
(3)	0 001 0011	000 0110	
(1)	1 110 1000		
	①111 1011	000 0110	0
(2)	0 001 1000		
	0 001 0011	000 0110	0
(3)	0 010 0110	000 1100	
(1)	1 110 1000		
	⓪000 1110	000 1100	1
(3)	0 001 1100	001 1001	
(1)	1 110 1000		
	⓪000 0100	001 1001	1
(4)	0 000 0100 (Remainder)	0 011 0011 (Quotient)	

(1) Subtract divisor.
(2) Negative result; add divisor.
(3) Shift left including quotient bit.
(4) Shift B register left including quotient bit.

FIGURE 5-3. Example of binary division. The partial remainder bit which is circled determines whether the next step is a shift or an add.

the remainder and quotient are formed in the A and B registers, respectively. The double-length accumulator can be loaded either by a double-precision LOAD instruction, if one is available, or by loading the A and B registers separately. After the dividend has been loaded into the accumulator, the instruction DIVIDE, n causes the division algorithm to be executed, using the number in memory location n as the divisor. An example of binary division is shown in Figure 5-3, using the same numbers which were used in the example of Figure 3-4. After each subtraction, the partial remainder in the A and B registers is tested for sign. If it is negative, the divisor is added to the A register, and both registers are shifted left. If the partial remainder is positive, the left shift is performed immediately. Thus, a ZERO bit is always shifted out of the left-hand end of the accumulator. At the same time, the next quotient bit is shifted into the right-hand end of the B register. Finally, after seven steps, the remainder is in the correct position in the A register. To complete the algorithm, the final quotient bit is shifted into the B register by a single left shift of the complete B register. This ensures that the quotient is in the correct position in the B register.

In a floating-point machine, the accumulator is capable of storing a double-precision fraction and an exponent. We will therefore designate the three parts of the accumulator as the A, B, and E registers. The A and B registers store the two halves of the fraction, while the E register stores the exponent of the floating-point number. As described in Chapter 4, floating-point arithmetic consists of performing fixed-point operations on both the fraction and the exponent. Thus, to multiply two floating-point numbers together, for example, the product of the fractions is formed in the A and B registers, as described above, and the sum of the exponents is formed in the E register following the usual addition rules.

The organization of the accumulator of a decimal computer is analogous to that presented above for a binary machine. Numbers are stored as sequences of four-bit BCD digits, and the decimal algorithms are implemented using rules previously described. We will not discuss the organization of the registers of a decimal computer further in this chapter, because of the similarity of the two types of machines in this respect.

We have described the operation of the registers which constitute the accumulator. We next look at the organization of the **index register.**

5.2 THE INDEX REGISTER

A register which is to be used exclusively as an index register usually contains a sufficient number of bits to enable it to store the address of any location in the memory. During the execution of a loop, the index register is used for modifying addresses and for determining when the loop should be terminated. In operation, the index register is first set to its initial value by a LOAD INDEX instruction. Then it is repeatedly incremented during the execution of the loop and tested at each step to determine when the final index value has been reached.

Although many computers have only a single accumulator, they often have several index registers. In such a machine, several index counters can be maintained at one time so that loops which are executed within other loops can be easily accounted for. It is necessary, in this type of machine, to be able to specify which index register is intended. Thus, instructions of the type LOAD INDEX k, n specify that index register k is to be loaded with data from memory location n.

As we have seen, the operations of adding, shifting, incrementing, and so on are performed by the arithmetic unit and the main control, and the accumulator and index registers are used essentially for storage. Thus, there is no reason why these registers cannot be "general-purpose" and used interchangeably. A computer which contains a set of general-purpose registers is called a **multi-accumulator** machine. In Section 5.3, we describe this type of computer and some of the features which are unique to it.

5.3 THE MULTI-ACCUMULATOR MACHINE

The organization of the registers of a multi-accumulator machine is shown in Figure 5-4. In this type of computer, data is transferred between either the main control or the arithmetic unit and one of the registers through the **register selector**. Thus, the instruction format must provide for specifying which register is to be used. A typical instruction for a multi-accumulator machine, therefore, takes the form ADD, R3, n, indicating that register 3 is to be used as an

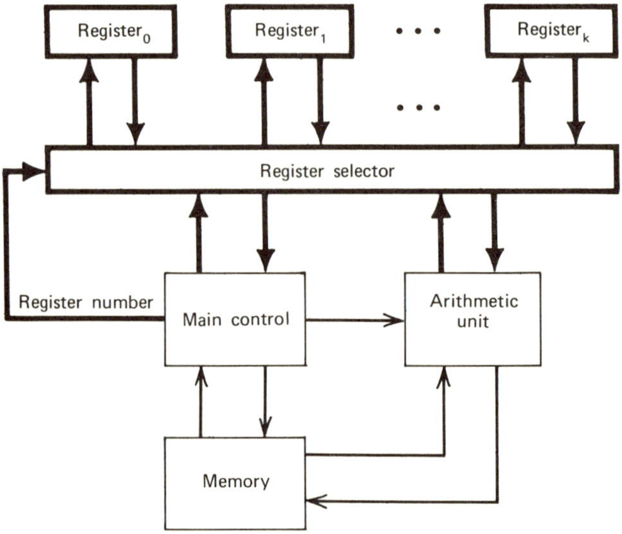

FIGURE 5-4. Block diagram of a multi-accumulator computer.

accumulator. In operation, the main control sends the register number, 3, to the register selector and the address, n, to the memory. Thus, the contents of register 3 and location n are sent to the arithmetic unit along with an ADD command. After the addition has been completed, the sum is sent to register 3, since the register selector is not altered at any time during the execution of the addition.

For multiplication and division, two registers are used together as a double-length accumulator. For definiteness, the convention that the most significant part of a double-length accumulator is always an even-numbered register is usually adopted. For example, if the instruction MULTIPLY, R2, n is executed, the multiplier is in register 2, the multiplicand is in memory location n, and the product is formed in registers 2 and 3. However, MULTIPLY, R3, n is either treated as an illegal instruction or is interpreted as if register 2 were specified.

For indexing, the main control communicates directly with the register specified. The instruction INCREMENT, R5 then causes register 5 to be incremented by one. When the instruction ADD, R1, n+R2 is executed, register 1 is used as an accumulator and register 2 is used as an index register. The operand is located in the memory location whose address is determined by adding n to the contents of register 2.

In all of the above examples, one of the operands has always been stored in the memory and the other in one of the registers. In some multi-accumulator computers, it is possible for both operands to be stored in the registers. In the instruction ADDR, 1,2, the letter R appended to the instruction signifies that the two operands are contained in registers 1 and 2. Register 1, which is specified first, is used as the accumulator. Therefore, the contents of registers 1 and 2 are added together and the sum is placed back into register 1. For this register-to-register instruction, the register selector is first set to 2, and the contents of register 2 is sent to the arithmetic unit. Then the selector is set to 1, and the addition is completed in the same manner as for the memory-to-register addition described at the beginning of this section.

In a multi-accumulator machine, one of the registers, rather than a memory location, is often used to save the address of the next instruction when a SAVE AND TRANSFER instruction is executed. As an example, let us assume that the instruction SAVE AND TRANSFER TO n,R7 is stored in memory location m. When this instruction is executed, the number m + 1 is placed into register 7, and the instruction in memory location n is then executed. When the execution of the subroutine has been completed, the instruction TRANSFER TO* R7 is executed causing the instruction in location m + 1 to be executed next. It should be noted that it is the programmer's responsibility to save the contents of register 7 by storing it in the memory and reloading it later to prevent its contents from being destroyed during the execution of the subroutine.

The multi-accumulator organization is very flexible because the programmer is not restricted to a small number of index registers and one accumulator. Moreover, it allows the roles of the registers to be changed during program execution; that is, if during execution fewer index registers are needed, then more accumulators are available, and vice versa. The availability of a large number of registers helps reduce the number of times that operands must be stored into and read out of the main memory. This, in turn, decreases the waiting time for obtaining operands, and increases the operating speed and thereby the efficiency of the computer.

In order to keep track of certain conditions which occur in a computer, a set of **status** registers is provided. The overflow and underflow bits, described in Chapter 4, for example, are located in one of the status registers. In Section 5.4, we describe the operation of the status registers and how they are used by the programmer.

5.4 THE STATUS REGISTERS

Depending on the type of computer, the status registers are connected either to the register selector or directly to the main control, or they can be located in the memory, in which case specific locations are assigned for this purpose. The number of bits in each status register varies with the computer. In addition to the overflow and underflow bits, the bits in the status registers indicate the states of interrupt conditions, error conditions, and the condition of every I/O device, indicating whether it is busy or not. In operation, whenever one of the status conditions changes, the corresponding bit in a status register is also changed. For example, if an overflow occurs, the overflow bit is set to ONE. If an error occurs, a bit in the status register which corresponds to the detected error condition is set to ONE. In these cases, the bits remain set to ONE until tested by the program and only then are reset to ZERO. A bit which indicates that an I/O device is busy, however, is automatically reset to ZERO when the corresponding device completes its assigned I/O transfer and is no longer busy.

Two methods can be used to determine the condition of a bit in a status register. In some cases, a status register bit can be interrogated directly. For example, an instruction of the type IF OVERFLOW, TRANSFER TO n would immediately test whether the overflow bit is set. However, to check a bit in the interrupt status register, the contents of the register is first transferred to an accumulator. The bits in the accumulator are then shifted until the bit in question is located in the extreme left-hand bit location. Testing the sign bit of the accumulator then indicates whether the bit is a ZERO or a ONE, the latter condition indicating that a certain type of interrupt has occurred. A similar procedure can be used to check a bit which indicates whether a particular I/O device is busy or not. In many computers, the I/O status bits can be tested

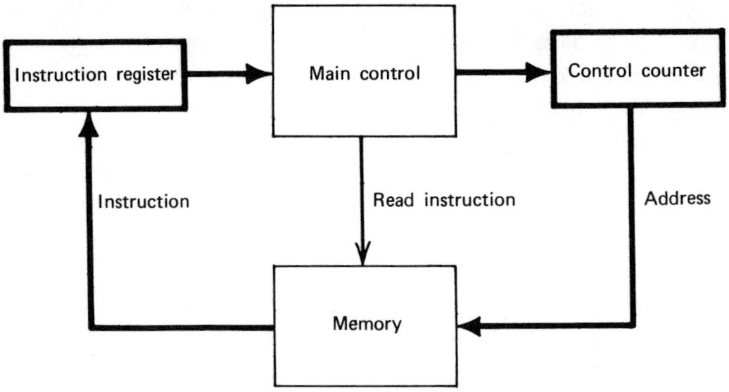

FIGURE 5-5. Block diagram showing the relationship of the control counter and instruction register to the main control and memory of the computer.

directly. For this purpose, test instructions which take the general form IF DEVICE BUSY, TRANSFER TO n are provided. We will return to these status test procedures again in Chapters 7–9 on input–output and interrupt.

During the operation of a computer, the manipulation of data in the accumulators and status registers takes place in accordance with the instructions furnished in the program being executed. There are a number of other registers in the computer which are inaccessible to the programmer. These **control registers** are used by the control systems of the computer during the execution of a program. In Section 5.5, we briefly describe the operation of two of the control registers which are used by the main control system.

5.5 THE CONTROL REGISTERS

The two registers whose operation we describe in this section are called the **control counter** and the **instruction register**. Both are associated with the main control system of the computer, as shown in Figure 5-5. The control counter contains the address of the next instruction to be executed. During the normal operating sequence, when the main control has completed the execution of an instruction and is ready to execute another instruction, it requests the memory to read the next instruction from the memory location whose address is given by the control counter. The control counter is then incremented by one, and so it always contains the address of the next instruction to be executed. When a TRANSFER TO n instruction is encountered, however, the control counter is set to n before the next instruction is read from the memory. In this way, the main control automatically proceeds from each instruction to the next with a minimum of effort. After an instruction is read from the memory, it is sent to the instruction register. This register stores the instruction so that the main control has time to decode it and thereby determine what operation is intended. Let us examine the decoding procedure to see why the instruction must be stored. First, the operation code bits are decoded to determine the type of operation which is to be executed. This step also indicates whether the associated binary number is to be interpreted literally, as a shift count, as a device code, or as an address. In the latter case, the address interpretation bits are then decoded to determine whether the address should be indexed or treated as a relative address or as an indirect address. Since the steps of the decoding procedure depend upon each other, the instruction cannot be decoded instantaneously, but must be stored and examined in a logical sequence, as described. The instruction register provides the necessary storage. Other control registers are used during the operation of the computer, and some of these registers are described in the remaining chapters of this book as they are encountered.

In Chapter 1, we introduced the memory, using a blackboard analogy. We assumed that data, instructions, and addresses, which are represented by sequences of bits, can be stored in the memory and read out when needed. In Chapter 6, we describe the internal organization of the memory and how it operates. We also describe how the memory influences the operation of virtually every other subsystem of the computer.

EXERCISES

5.1 Write a program to form three sums using a multi-accumulator computer. The first sum is to be formed by adding together the numbers stored in memory locations 100–139; the second, the numbers in locations 140–179; and the third, the numbers in locations 180–219. Use registers 1, 2, and 3 as the accumulators, and register 4 as the index register.
[Hint: Use the instruction format LOAD, R4, n or LOAD, R4, (m) to initialize the index register, and form all three sums concurrently in the accumulators using a single loop.]

5.2 What is the control counter used for?

5.3 What is the function of the instruction register?

5.4 How do the control registers differ from the general-purpose registers of a multi-accumulator computer?

6

THE MEMORY

The digital computer memory is used to store both the instructions and the data which are used during the operation of the machine. Instructions are obtained from the memory and executed sequentially by the main control. During the execution of a program, data is retrieved from the memory as needed and manipulated as specified in the program. Computed results are then stored back into the memory for later use or for use as output data. Since a great deal of the information flow in the computer involves the use of the memory, the overall computation speed and efficiency of the computer depend intimately on the speed of the memory.

In this chapter, we examine the organization of the memory to see how it influences the operation of the computer. The chapter also includes descriptions of partial word addressing, page organization, and memory sharing.

6.1 MEMORY ORGANIZATION

The computer memory is composed of a large array of binary memory cells, each of which is capable of storing a single bit of information. Each cell can be set to either a ONE or a ZERO and will remain in this state until it is reset. The cells are organized into groups which, as we have seen, are called words. The number of cells or bits which a memory word contains depends on the computer. Some common word lengths are 8, 12, 16, 18, 24, 32, and 64 bits.

We have seen how each word in the memory has an address associated with it. Using the address, we can specify the location of any word in the memory,

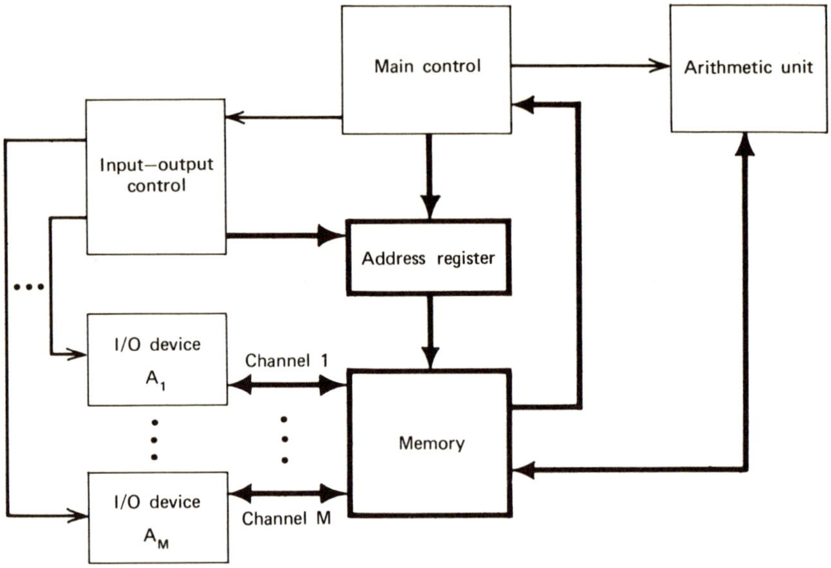

FIGURE 6-1. Computer block diagram highlighting the memory subsystem.

regardless of whether it represents an instruction, a piece of data which may be numerical or otherwise, or the address of another memory location. Let us now examine how the memory interacts with the rest of the computer subsystems.

Figure 6-1 is a block diagram of a computer similar to the one presented in Figure 1-10. It has been redrawn, however, to emphasize the central role of the memory as an information exchange. Two new features have been added to the block diagram, namely, the **address register** and the **input–output channels**. The address register is a control register which stores the address of a memory location when it is received from either of the control units. The input–output channels are used to transmit data between the memory and I/O devices A_1 through A_M. We can best illustrate the operation of the memory by specific examples.

When the main control is prepared to receive the next instruction to be executed, it sends the address of the instruction from the control counter to the address register, along with a read command. The memory then reads the word stored in the addressed location and transmits it to the instruction register of the main control. When the main control receives the instruction, it proceeds to decode the command and to execute it. If an arithmetic instruction is specified, then the address of the operand is determined from the instruction by the main control and sent to the address register. Simultaneously, the arithmetic unit is informed of the nature of the instruction and that the operand has been requested from the memory. Therefore, when the operand arrives from the memory, the arithmetic unit is prepared to use it.

The main control then requests another instruction in the same manner. Let us assume that the next instruction is STORE ACC, n. The main control instructs the arithmetic unit to send the contents of the accumulator to the memory. The address n is simultaneously sent to the address register along with a write command. When the data from the arithmetic unit arrives at the memory, it is written into location n.

The computer continues to operate as described, obtaining its instructions and operands from the memory. For the arithmetic, logic, load, and store instructions, operands are read from and written into the memory. The test and shift instructions, on the other hand, are executed without the aid of the memory. However, some of the I/O instructions, as well as the memory protection instructions described in this chapter, do involve the use of the memory. We examine memory input–output in Section 6.2.

6.2 MEMORY INPUT–OUTPUT*

As we have seen in Chapters 1 and 2, input–output operations can be performed through either the accumulator or the memory. The former operations consist of single word transfers, while the latter operations utilize the input–output channels and may consist of complete block transfers. In this chapter, we discuss only memory input–output transfers.

In order to execute a block transfer to or from the memory, the following information is needed by the input–output control: the address of the first word of the block to be used, either the length of the block or the address of the last word of the block, an identifying number which indicates which I/O device is to be used, and an indicator which specifies whether an input or output transfer is intended. Regardless of how the computer is organized, only part of the required information is contained in the input–output instruction. The rest of the information is stored either in a register or in the memory. In the latter case, either specific memory locations are reserved for this purpose or memory locations contained in the block being transferred are used. For illustration, we will describe how one particular type of system operates.

In our computer, the START I/O instruction indicates whether an input or an output operation is desired and also contains the address of the first word of

* Although we discuss input–output extensively in Chapters 6–8, it should be pointed out that in most systems the I/O instructions are contained in an input–output subroutine supplied by the computer manufacturer. This subroutine is contained in the operating monitor described in Section 11.4. Thus, it is almost never necessary for the programmer who is using the machine to insert I/O instructions in his program, and as we shall see shortly, he is usually prohibited from doing so.

Address	Contents
n	k
n + 1	ℓ
n + 2	word 1
. . .	. . .
n + ℓ + 1	word ℓ

FIGURE 6-2. Typical input–output block in memory.

a block of memory locations. The memory block itself contains the other information needed. The organization of a typical memory block which has been prepared for an I/O transfer is shown in Figure 6-2. The first location contains the identifying number k of the I/O channel. The second word of the block contains a number ℓ, specifying the length of the transfer, that is, how many words there are in the remainder of the block. Depending on whether output or input is specified, the remaining locations of the block either contain the data to be transmitted as output or store the data received as input during the transfer. We can now describe the operation of the computer during a block I/O transfer into or out of the memory.

When the main control receives a START I/O instruction, it first determines that a memory transfer rather than an accumulator transfer is desired and so notifies the I/O control. The main control then determines the address of the first word in the block and requests the memory to send the contents of both the first and second words of the block to the I/O control. It also informs the I/O control whether an input or output transfer is intended. The I/O control determines from the information that it has received that the length of the transfer is ℓ, the I/O channel number is k, and the first word is to be transferred into or out of location n + 2 in the memory. It then proceeds to transfer a block of ℓ words between the memory and I/O device A_k through I/O channel k. Because the main control is not involved in the details of the transfer, it can continue to execute the original program while the I/O transfer is taking place. In Section 6.4, we describe how the I/O control can handle multiple transfers simultaneously and how the memory is shared between the I/O control and the main control. First, however, let us introduce the concept of a **memory cycle** and show how the speed of the computer depends upon the speed of the memory.

6.3 MEMORY CYCLE

Regardless of how the memory is constructed or what kind of mechanism is used to store each bit in the memory, it takes a fixed length of time to read a word out of or write a word into the memory. The operation of reading or writing a word out of or into the memory is called a **memory cycle**; the time interval between the start of two consecutive memory cycles is called the **memory cycle time**. Usually, the memory cycle time is the same for both read and write cycles, and we shall assume that this is always so.

Let us now examine how the overall speed of the computer is affected by the memory cycle time. A simple program to add together three numbers takes the form

```
m       LOAD ACC, n
m + 1   ADD, n+1
m + 2   ADD, n+2
m + 3   STORE ACC, n+3
```

During the execution of this program, eight memory cycles are required. The instructions themselves must be read out of the memory as well as the three operands to be added. Finally, the result must be stored back into the memory. Therefore, even though the arithmetic unit may be capable of adding three numbers together in a fraction of the memory cycle time, it can accomplish no more during the execution of this program, since it cannot obtain any more instructions or operands from the memory. As a result, the time that it takes to add together three numbers stored in the memory and store the result back into the memory takes eight memory cycle times.* If indirect addressing is used, the execution time is increased even more.

Multiple memories are often used to increase the overall speed of the computer. In a dual memory machine, one memory contains the even-numbered locations and the second memory contains the odd-numbered locations. This arrangement results in a shorter overall execution time, because the cycle times of the two memories can be overlapped. Figure 6-3 illustrates one way in which the program to add three numbers together is executed in a dual-memory machine.

Figure 6-3 is divided into three columns representing the operations performed by the first memory, the computer, and the second memory. In the figure, operations take place in sequence from top to bottom. First, the

* In many computers, the execution times of the ADD and LOAD instructions are much shorter than the time needed to read the data from the memory. We will therefore assume that the memory cycle time includes the execution time of these instructions.

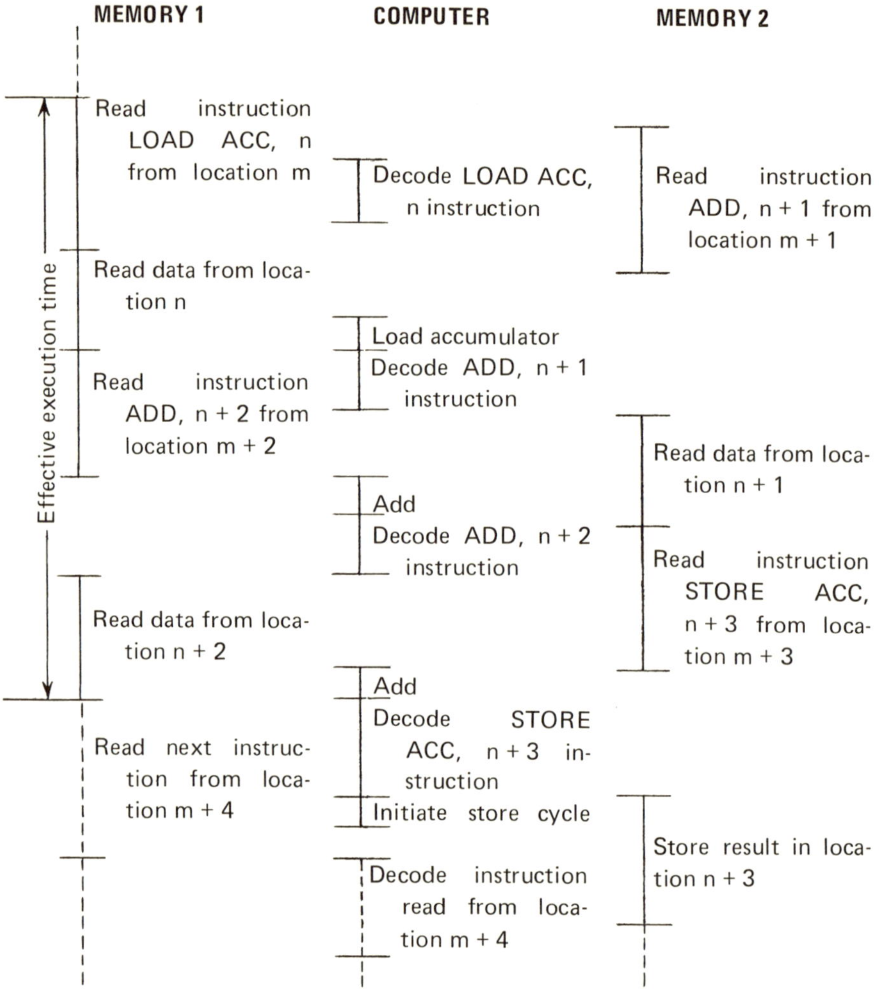

FIGURE 6-3. Execution of sample program in a dual-memory computer showing overlapping of the memory cycles.

instruction LOAD ACC, n is read from memory 1 and decoded. Then, the data stored in location n is read from the same memory. While these operations are taking place, the instruction ADD, n + 1 is read from memory 2. After the accumulator is loaded, the ADD, n + 1 instruction is decoded. Then, while data is being read from location n + 1 of memory 2, the instruction ADD, n + 2 is read from memory 1. The remaining steps of the program also result in an overlapping of the operation of the two memories, as shown in Figure 6-3. The effective execution time of the program in a dual-memory machine is therefore less than five memory cycle times. The time needed to complete the STORE ACC, n + 3 operation by the second memory is not included in the effective execution time, since it overlaps the reading of the next instruction from memory 1, as shown. Thus, we see that it is possible for a dual-memory computer to operate almost twice as fast as a comparable machine with a single memory. Additional advantages in speed, albeit at high cost, can be obtained by using more than two memories.

We have shown how the speed of the computer depends on the speed of the memory. Now we describe how the memory is shared between the main control and the input–output control and how multiple input–output transfers are executed.

6.4 MEMORY SHARING

As we have stated, each I/O block transfer, once initiated, continues autonomously without further intervention from the main control. The main control is free, therefore, to continue executing programs stored in the memory. Moreover, additional input–output block transfers involving other I/O devices can be initiated by the main control without waiting for the completion of any transfers which are in progress. Whenever several block transfers are taking place concurrently, they compete for memory cycles, since a single memory is capable of reading or writing only one word at a time. The I/O control is responsible for **lining up** the I/O requests and requesting memory cycles for each in turn. But since the main control continues to function, the I/O control must in turn compete with the main control for the memory. The memory is shared, therefore, among the I/O devices which are executing block transfers and the main control.

Every I/O device connected to the computer has associated with it a device **cycle time**, which is the time it takes to transfer a single word to or from the device. A device with a short cycle time is capable of transferring data at a rapid rate, whereas one with a long cycle time operates at a slower rate. An I/O device is considerd to be **fast** or **slow**, depending on whether its cycle time is short or long, respectively. Let us assume that every I/O device which is connected to the computer can operate at any rate up to the maximum rate determined by its cycle time. When a block transfer is in progress, the I/O control must wait until after each word transfer has been completed before it initiates the transfer of the next word in the block. In this system, the I/O control need only form the I/O devices into a simple **queue**, or line-up, to assure correct operation. After the completion of every word transfer to or from a device, the device reenters the queue and awaits its turn to use the memory. This procedure guarantees that the main control and all of the I/O devices share the memory in a reasonable manner. When both controls are repeatedly competing for memory cycles, the main control obtains one-half of the cycles, whereas the I/O devices share the remaining cycles. Because a fast device has a shorter cycle time than a slow device, it will reenter the queue more often, thereby obtaining more memory cycles.

As we shall see in Chapter 7, many I/O devices do not operate in the manner described above. Data is transferred to and from these I/O devices at a predetermined fixed rate, or **synchronously**. A word must be read from or written into the memory by a synchronous device within the allotted time interval, or it is missed. Thus, if the time spent in a queue by a synchronous device is excessive, a word transfer will be missed, causing an error. To avoid transfer errors, the I/O devices are assigned priorities which are used to change the ordering of the queue. For example, let us assume that a particular I/O device has a cycle time which is exactly four times as long as the memory cycle time. In this case, the device must receive at least one-fourth of the total memory cycles. The main control can obtain one-half of the memory cycles. Therefore, if the I/O device in question obtains one-half of the remaining memory cycles, a transfer error will not occur. The I/O device will receive the required memory cycles if the priority assigned to it ensures that it is either first or second in line whenever it reenters the queue. It should be noted that the assignment of queue priorities is dependent upon the characteristics of the I/O devices. Thus, the assignment is generally made by the computer manufacturer before the machine is installed. Only if an I/O device is added or removed from the machine is it necessary to change these priorities.

If several synchronous devices are executing concurrent block transfers, the operating speeds of the nonsynchronous I/O devices may be reduced significantly. This reduction of I/O rates occurs because the synchronous devices repeatedly enter the queue in the middle and thereby slow the movement of the nonsynchronous devices in the queue. For the fast nonsynchronous devices, the resulting reduction of operating speed must be accepted. However, if a slow nonsynchronous device is slowed down further, it could be rendered virtually useless. To prevent this situation from occurring, the slow nonsynchronous devices are usually assigned higher priorities than the fast ones. As a result, the slow devices will operate at their maximum rates, but since they do not require many memory cycles per second for operation, they will have little effect on the speed of the fast I/O devices.

In some computers, the main control is treated as if it were a nonsynchronous I/O device. It must then enter the queue and await its turn to access the memory. In most cases, this mode of operation does not affect the speed of the machine to a great extent. However, if many I/O block transfers are in progress, the main control can be slowed down considerably in this type of computer. If the main control is assigned a high priority in the queue to avoid slowing it down, then the machine behaves in a manner similar to the computer described above.

After initiating a block transfer, the main control continues to operate while the transfer is taking place. Until the block transfer has been completed, however, the program being executed must avoid using the memory block involved in the transfer. Otherwise, there is a possibility of destroying data which is waiting to be transferred out of the memory, or of using incorrect data because the input data has not yet arrived from the input device. If the main control waits idly for each I/O transfer to be completed before continuing to execute the program, it will not destroy data or use incorrect data. However, this method of operation is inefficient, since the main control is unproductive during block transfers. Two methods are commonly used to keep the main control productive during a block transfer.

In the first method, at least two distinct programs are maintained in the memory. Then, while an I/O transfer associated with one program is in progress, the main control can execute instructions from another program. This method is known as **multiprogramming** and is discussed further in the chapter on time-sharing (Chapter 10).

The second method makes use of a technique called **buffering** and is described in Section 6.5.

6.5 BUFFERED BLOCK TRANSFERS

We describe the concept of a buffered block transfer for the output case first. Assume that two memory blocks, A and B, are reserved by the programmer for the output device being used. As the output data is generated by the main control, it is stored sequentially into the memory in block A. As soon as block A is filled, an output transfer is initiated from block A, and the main control then continues to generate further data which is stored in block B. When block B is filled, an output transfer is initiated from block B, and block A is again used to store the output data. Since it generally takes longer to generate a new block of data than to complete the block transfer, no time is wasted waiting for the output transfer to be completed. In this way, the main control avoids using whichever block is being used for the output transfer, and operates on a **buffer** block instead. Thus, when block A is being used for output, block B is acting as the buffer block, and vice versa. The logic for a buffered output transfer is shown in Figure 6-4 in the form of a **flow chart**. Not shown in the figure is the test for determining when to terminate the loop and to continue with another part of the program.

For input transfers, let us designate the two blocks to be used as C and D. The first input transfer is made to block C in advance of when it is needed. When the transfer to block C is completed, a block transfer is initiated to block D, and

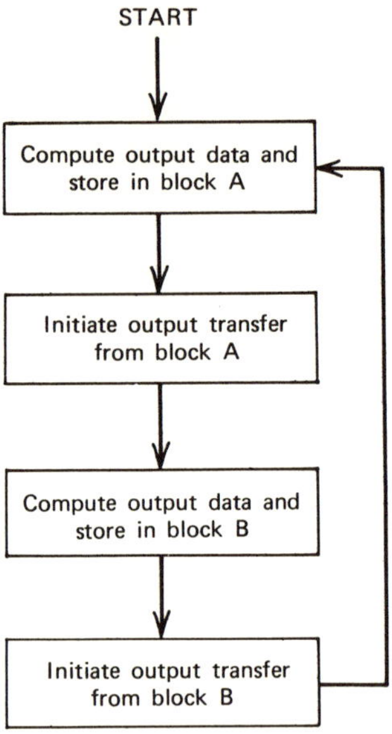

FIGURE 6-4. Flow chart for buffered output transfers.

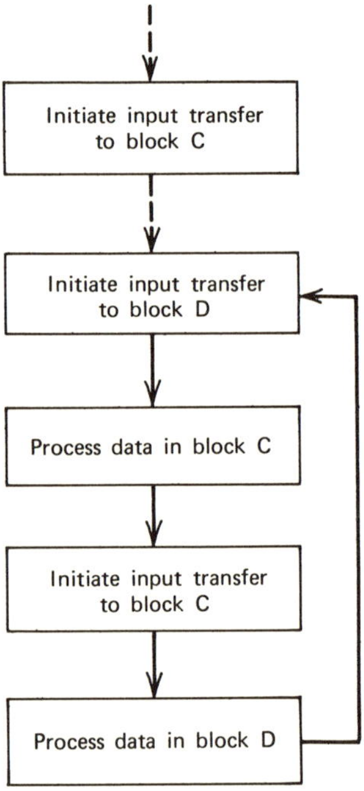

FIGURE 6-5. Flow chart for buffered input transfers.

while the latter transfer is taking place, the data in block C is used by the main control. When the data in block C has been processed, a new transfer can be initiated to block C and the data in block D used, and so on. This procedure is shown in flow chart form in Figure 6-5. Again, the test for determining when to terminate the loop is not shown in the flow chart.

The buffering procedure we have just described can also be used when multiple block transfers are taking place simultaneously. Let us assume that data is to be read into the memory from an input device, processed internally by the main control, and then transferred out via an output device. For consistency, we will use blocks A and B for output and blocks C and D for input. The flow chart illustrating multiple block transfers is shown in Figure 6-6. As before, an input transfer to block C is initiated and completed in advance. Then while an input transfer to block D is in progress, the data in block C is processed and the results stored in block A. Then block A is transferred out and block C is refilled while the data in block D is processed and the results stored in block B. During the next interval, the data in block B is transferred out and block D is refilled while the data in block C is being processed and the results stored in block A. This

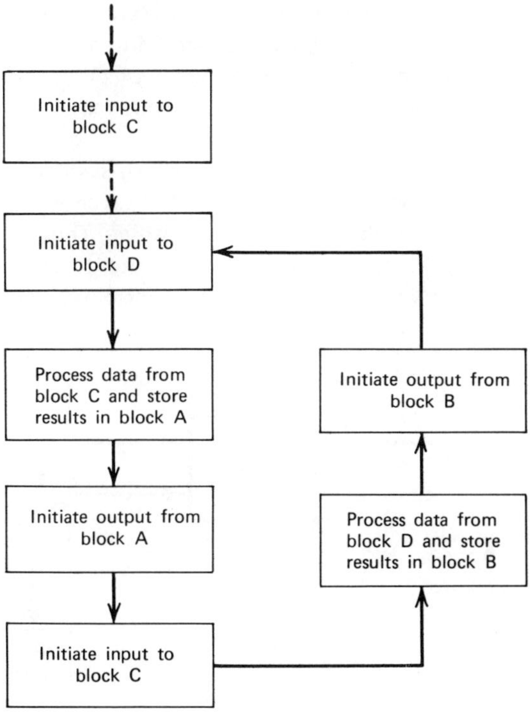

FIGURE 6-6. Flow chart for multiple buffered input–output transfers.

procedure is continued until it is terminated by a suitable test instruction. It should be pointed out that all four blocks are used simultaneously: two for I/O and two for processing. The latter two are the buffer blocks.

In Section 6.4, we described how the memory subsystem is shared among the I/O devices and the main control. A special case of memory sharing, called **multiprocessing**, occurs when a single memory is shared by several computers. In Section 6.6, we examine multiprocessing in detail.

6.6 MULTIPROCESSING

In many cases, the computational requirements of a computer facility can be fulfilled by using either one large machine or several smaller ones. Since the latter approach may often be more economical, we find that many computer facilities contain more than one computer. If more than one of these machines require frequent access to a single set of data or if the data produced by one machine is to be used by another machine, then a multiprocessing system can be used to advantage. In the case where several machines need access to a single set of data, the common data set can be stored in a shared memory, thereby reducing the total memory requirements. In the second case, the data produced by one machine for use by another can be stored in a common memory. It is unnecessary, therefore, to transfer the data out of one computer and into a second computer, thus reducing the input—output requirements. Let us now examine how a multiprocessing system operates.

A simplified block diagram of a multiprocessing system incorporating two computers is shown in Figure 6-7. In this system, each computer has its own memory which is not accessible to the other machine. Thus, each computer is a complete entity in itself. In addition, each computer has access to a common memory and treats it as an extension of its own memory. Let us assume, as an example, that each computer contains m words of memory and that the

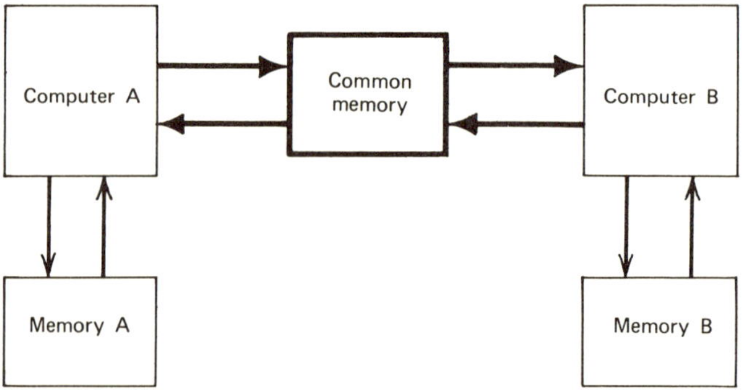

FIGURE 6-7. Two-computer multiprocessing system.

common memory contains n words. Then any address from 0 to m − 1 refers to the main memory of the respective computer, whereas any address from m to m + n − 1 refers to the common memory. The opposite convention, wherein any address from 0 to n − 1 refers to the common memory and any address from n to m + n − 1 refers to the main memory of the respective computer, can also be used. Thus, the common memory is accessible to either computer as if it were a direct extension of its own memory.

Since the common memory can be used for I/O through either machine, a queuing procedure must be established to ensure that it is properly shared by the main controls and the I/O controls of both computers. This procedure requires only a simple extension of the principles described in Section 6.4.

A more important problem is that of preventing data from being incorrectly used. For example, if computer A is generating data and storing it in the common memory for use by computer B, then B must not attempt to use the data before it has been generated. This difficulty can be avoided by using buffer blocks for all data being stored into and retrieved from the common memory.

In a multiprocessing environment, it is often necessary to prevent one of the computers from inadvertently destroying information which has been written into the common memory by the other computer. The **memory protection** feature which we describe next and which is available on most computers can be used to prevent overwriting information in the memory of both conventional and multiprocessing systems.

6.7 MEMORY PROTECTION

To prevent information which has been written into the memory from being destroyed, it is necessary to prevent new data from being written into the same memory locations. Using the instruction PROTECT MEMORY, which is provided in a machine having the memory protection feature, we can prevent a computer from writing into certain locations of the memory. In operation, a special register is used which contains one bit for each block of words in the memory.* This bit is set to a ONE by the PROTECT MEMORY instruction and to a ZERO by a similar UNPROTECT MEMORY instruction. Whenever the bit corresponding to a particular block is a ONE, information cannot be written into any location of the block. If an attempt is made to write into a protected location, an interrupt occurs so that suitable corrective action can be taken. We discuss this aspect of the memory protection feature further in Chapter 9.

In a conventional single-computer system, memory protection is used to

* Unlike data and input–output blocks, the blocks used for memory protection are fixed in size and cannot be altered by the programmer.

prevent a programmer from destroying other programs which are located in the memory. An example of a protected program is the supervisory program which reads each user's programs into the memory, allows them to be executed, and then proceeds to read the next user's programs into the memory for execution. Supervisory programs are dealt with in Chapter 11. In a time-sharing system, several users' programs may be located in the memory at one time, and memory protection is used to prevent these programs from inadvertently destroying each other. We deal further with time-sharing systems in Chapter 10.

In a multiprocessing system, memory protection is used to ensure that data written into the common memory by one of the computers is not overwritten and destroyed by one of the other computers. It should be noted that the common type of memory protection only prevents data from being overwritten. Information can be read out of a protected memory location at any time. Therefore, to prevent the use of incorrect data from the common memory, the data being written into the memory should be buffered and then memory protection applied to prevent its destruction. When the data in a protected block is no longer needed, the protection can be removed and the memory block reused.

We have assumed thus far that a fixed-length computer word is read from or written into the memory in a single memory cycle. In some computers, the memory is organized into eight-bit bytes, and we can specify the number of bytes which can be read out of or written into the memory during a single cycle. In Section 6.8, we describe how a byte-oriented memory is addressed.

6.8 BYTE-ORIENTED MEMORY

We assume in our description of byte-oriented memory that a word consists of thirty-two bits, so that a half-word is two bytes long and a full word is four bytes long. Figure 6-8 illustrates the relationship of bytes, half-words, and full words in a byte-oriented memory. Each byte is assigned an address in the usual manner. Then the bytes are combined into half-words so that the most significant byte of each half-word is even-numbered. Similarly, half-words are combined into full words so that the most significant half-word of each full word is even-numbered. The general relation between the three entities is that full word n consists of half-words 2n and 2n + 1, which, in turn, consist of bytes 4n, 4n + 1, and 4n + 2, 4n + 3, respectively.

In a computer which has a byte-oriented memory, instructions exist which manipulate bytes, half-words, or full words. For example, the instruction LOAD BYTE, R2, k causes byte k to be read from the memory into register 2. Since register 2 will generally be a full-word register, the instruction causes only one of the four bytes to be changed. If byte k corresponds to the most significant part of a full word in the memory, such as byte 4, then the most significant byte of

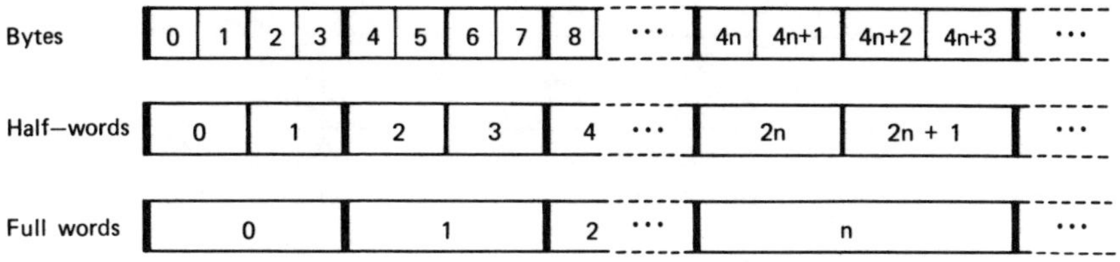

FIGURE 6-8. Organization of the byte-oriented memory.

register 2 is changed. Similarly, if bytes from any of the other three possible positions are loaded, they change the corresponding byte in the register. The instruction LOAD HALF, R2, k causes half-word k to be read from the memory and causes the corresponding half-word of register 2 to be changed. Finally LOAD, R2, k causes register 2 to be loaded with the full word from location k in the memory. In a similar manner, the instruction STORE BYTE, R2, k causes only one byte to be read from register 2 and stored in byte location k in the memory. Since only one of the four bytes contained in register 2 can be stored, the one to be used is determined by the location of byte k in the memory. Let us now examine the interpretation of the address part of the instruction in a byte-oriented machine.

Assume that a sixteen-bit address is used to specify a location in the memory. For byte-oriented instructions, the address can be interpreted in any of three equivalent ways, as illustrated in Figure 6-9. In part (a), the most significant fourteen bits are used as a word address and the remaining two bits as a byte indicator which specifies one of the four bytes. As an example, the most significant fourteen bits of address 0000 0000 0011 1000 specify word location 14, while the least significant bits, which are ZERO's, indicate that the most significant byte is to be used. If the least significant two bits are 01, 10, or 11, then the second, third, or least significant byte, respectively, is used.

In part (b) of Figure 6-9, the most significant fifteen bits are used as a half-word address and the least significant bit as a byte indicator. For the example, 0000 0000 0011 1000, the half-word location 28 is specified by the most significant fifteen bits, while the least significant bit indicates that the most significant byte is to be used. Similarly, 0000 0000 0011 1011 indicates that the least significant byte of half-word location 29 is to be used. Referring to Figure 6-8, the reader can verify that the two definitions are equivalent to each other and to part (c) of Figure 6-9, where the full sixteen bits are used as a byte address. Using the same examples as above, byte locations 56, 57, 58, and 59 are specified. In general, a sixteen-bit address is used to specify a particular byte in the memory, while the two-bit byte indicator is adequate to specify one of the four bytes in a register.

A similar equivalence exists for the interpretation of the address of a

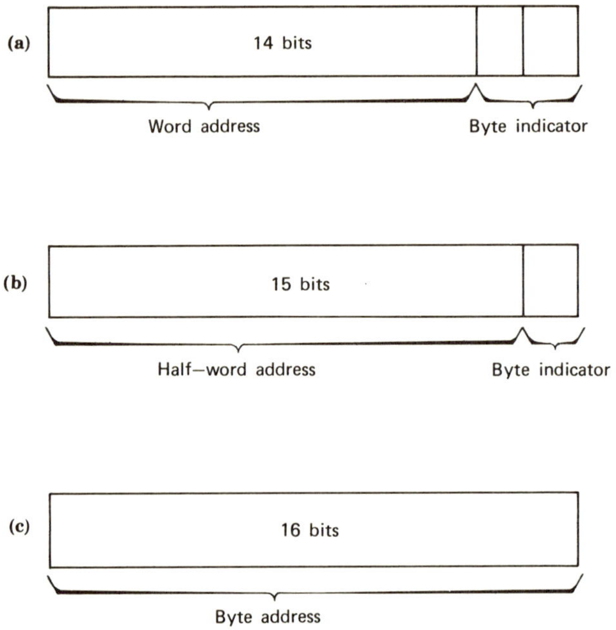

FIGURE 6-9. Interpretation of an address for a byte-oriented instruction.

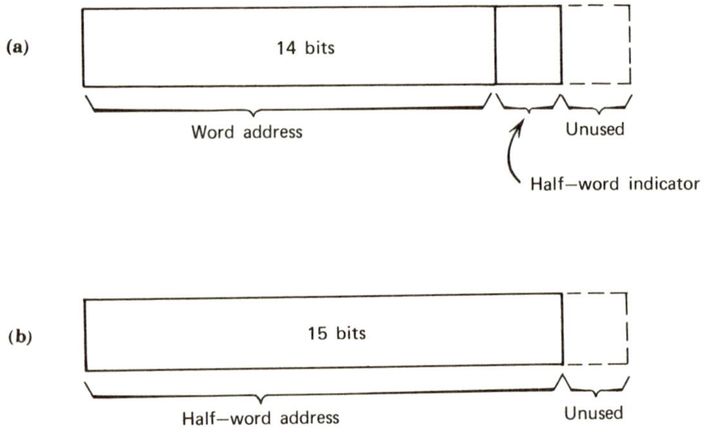

FIGURE 6-10. Interpretation of an address for a half-word instruction.

half-word instruction, as shown in Figure 6-10. In both cases, the least significant bit of the address is unused. When the most significant fourteen bits are used as a word address, then the remaining bit indicates which half-word is specified. Thus, the address 0000 0000 0011 1000 refers to the most significant half-word of word location 14. Alternatively, the most significant fifteen bits can be used as a half-word address. Then the example refers directly to half-word 28. In general, a fifteen-bit address is used to specify a half-word in the memory, while the half-word indicator is used to specify one of the half-words of a register.

Finally, for full-word instructions, only one interpretation is possible: The two least significant bits are unused and the remaining bits are treated as a full-word address.

The reader will recall that a technique called "relative addressing" was described in Section 2.7. A similar procedure called **page addressing** is often used in place of relative addressing. We describe the **page organization** of the memory needed for this type of addressing in Section 6.9.

6.9 PAGE ADDRESSING

In small computers, page addressing is often used in place of relative addressing. It is also used in many large time-sharing systems, where it simplifies keeping several programs in the memory at one time. In either type of machine, the memory is divided up into blocks, called **pages**, and each page contains exactly the same number of computer words. Thus, pages differ from data and input–output blocks because their size cannot be altered by the programmer.

Let us first describe the features of page addressing which are common to all computers using the page format. An example of the organization of a page-oriented memory is shown in Figure 6-11. In the example, there are a total of 64 pages in the memory, and each page contains exactly 256 words. Thus, it is necessary to specify both a page address from 0 through 63 and a word address from 0 through 255. For example, word 105 in page 2 is in memory location 617, whereas word 105 in page 62 refers to location 15,977. The page address is stored in a special **page register**, which is associated with the address register, as shown in Figure 6-12. In operation, the page register is set by an instruction such as SET PAGE, (2), which is included in the instruction repertoire of every page-oriented computer. Once the page register has been set by this instruction, until it is changed, every instruction which specifies a page address uses page 2. Thus, the instruction* ADD, *+105 is interpreted as ADD, 617. When a page instruction is encountered by the main control, the address

* The same notation is used for page addressing as for relative addressing, since both schemes would never be implemented in a single computer.

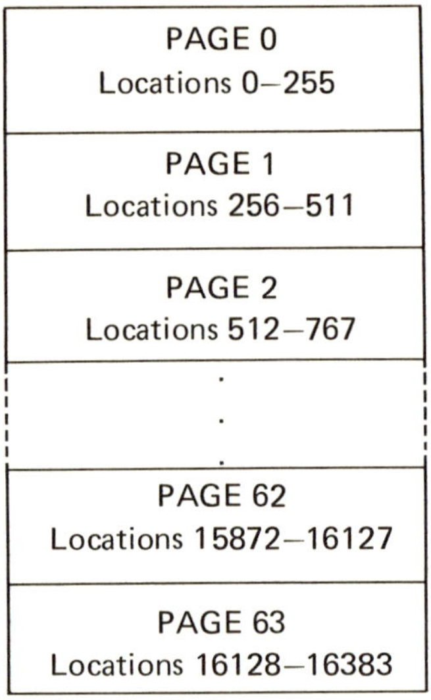

FIGURE 6-11. Page organization of a computer memory.

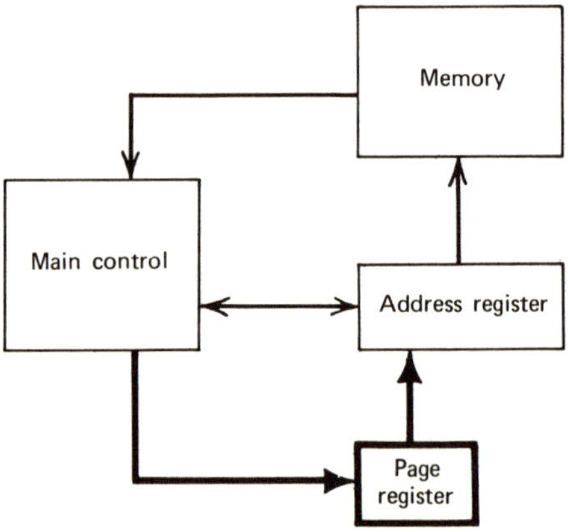

FIGURE 6-12. Partial block diagram of memory subsystem showing the page register.

associated with the instruction is loaded into the least significant part of the address register. The page number is simultaneously loaded into the most significant part of the address register from the page register. For the example given above, the address 105 is 0110 1001 in binary and the page number 2 is 0000 0010 in binary. Combining these in the address register as described above, we obtain the address 0000 0010 0110 1001, which is the number 617. The size of the pages is always chosen to be a power of 2 so that no computation is required to determine the actual address from the page address. An example of a program using page addressing follows:

```
--    SET PAGE, (3)                       ---
 .     .                                   .
 .     .                                   .
 .     .                                   .
908   LOAD ACC, (0)                       (3) 140
909   LOAD INDEX, (-80)                   (3) 141
910   ADD, 181+INDEX                      (3) 142
911   INCREMENT INDEX                     (3) 143
912   IF INDEX=-, TRANSFER TO *+142       (3) 144
913   STORE ACC, 100                      (3) 145
```

This program is essentially the same one used in Section 2.7 to illustrate relative addressing. When the program is executed, the numbers stored in memory locations 101–180 are added together and stored in location 100. For convenience, we have also shown the equivalent page address for each location used, with the page number shown in parentheses.

To show how flexible page addressing can be, we have modified the above example so that the data to be added together is located in word addresses 101–180 of any arbitrary page n. For simplicity, **indirect addressing** is used for the test instruction.

```
2     910
 .     .
 .     .
 .     .
--    SET PAGE, (n)
 .     .
 .     .
 .     .
908   LOAD ACC, (0)
909   LOAD INDEX, (-80)
910   ADD, *+181+INDEX
911   INCREMENT INDEX
912   IF INDEX=-, TRANSFER TO* 2
913   STORE ACC, *+100
```

Note that the address of the ADD instruction is sent to the address register, where it is combined with the page address. The resultant address is then indexed to determine the actual address to be used. This procedure allows us to change the location of the data by changing the value of n, the page number. In a program with many instructions, being able to change the data location in such a simple way may reduce the programming effort substantially.

In a small computer, page addressing provides us with one more method for addressing any location in the memory. We will not attempt to compare relative addressing, page addressing, and indirect addressing any further, since the relative efficiency of each method is strongly dependent on application.

In a time-sharing system, page addressing can lead to a simple way of manipulating programs. Although we elaborate on this further in Chapter 10, a few points can be made here. Because it is a simple matter to change page numbers, it is not necessary to assign these numbers in advance. Thus, a complete program can be written using page addressing but with the actual page numbers left unspecified. Then, when the program is read into the memory, the page numbers are inserted to correspond to the pages which are assigned to the program at that time. As a result, a program can be placed anywhere in the memory as long as a sufficient number of pages are available for its proper execution.

In this chapter, we described the computer memory and how it operates. As part of the discussion, we introduced the input–output subsystem of the computer as well as those aspects of I/O which are associated with the memory. In Chapter 7, we further describe the input–output subsystem and we describe, in detail, the more commonly used I/O devices and how they operate.

EXERCISES

6.1 How are the control counter and the address register related?

6.2 Set up an output block to transfer 372 words to output device 21. What is the format of the START I/O instruction needed to initiate a block transfer from this block? Assume that the block is located in the memory starting in location 2476.

6.3 How many memory cycles are needed to execute the following program in a single memory computer?

```
LOAD ACC*, 2
ADD*, 2+INDEX
INCREMENT INDEX
STORE ACC*, 2+INDEX
```

6.4 What is the purpose served by the I/O queue?

6.5 Why is it necessary to buffer block transfers in a computer?

6.6 What is a multiprocessing system?

7

INPUT–OUTPUT

I

As we pointed out in Chapter 1, the input–output subsystem of a computer provides for communication between the machine and its environment. Without the ability to receive data from and transmit results to the environment, a computer would serve no useful purpose. Moreover, the speed at which data can be transferred into or out of the machine is often the limiting factor which determines the speed of computation. As a result, a great deal of emphasis has been placed on the input–output portion of the computer, and this emphasis has led to the development of a large variety of sophisticated I/O devices.

In this chapter, we first review the I/O subsystem, including descriptions of the buss I/O and multiplexor I/O. Then we describe a few of the more common input–output devices and the different ways in which they are used. In this connection, we include a brief description of the codes which allow alphabetic and special symbols to be manipulated by the computer. In Chapter 8, we continue the description of input–output devices and include descriptions of several devices which are primarily used for auxiliary storage.

7.1 ORGANIZATION OF THE INPUT–OUTPUT SUBSYSTEM

The input–output subsystem of the computer consists of the input–output control, the I/O buss, I/O channels, and a number of I/O devices. In the block diagram of the computer reproduced in Figure 7-1, the input–output subsystem of the machine is emphasized.

The **input–output control** supervises all the input–output operations of the

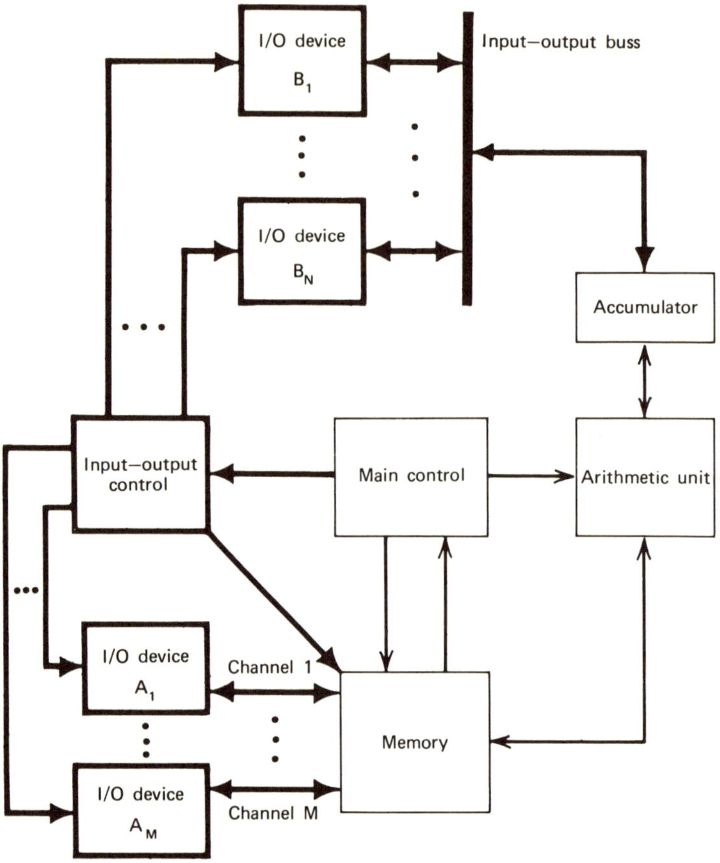

FIGURE 7-1. Computer block diagram highlighting the input–output subsystem.

computer. It receives instructions from the main control and can communicate directly with all the I/O devices and the memory.

The **input–output buss** is used to transfer the contents of the accumulator to one of the I/O devices $B_1 - B_N$ or data from an I/O device to the accumulator. All these devices are connected to the buss and are capable of receiving data from it or transmitting data to it. However, the I/O control prevents all but one of these I/O devices from using the buss at any given time.

The **input–output channels** provide data paths for block transfers between the memory and I/O devices $A_1 - A_M$. Because a channel is provided for each device, several block transfers can take place concurrently. The I/O control completely supervises each of the devices and its channel during a block transfer.

The START I/O instruction is used to initiate all input–output transfers. The details of memory block transfers were described in Section 6.2. Once started, a block transfer proceeds without further intervention from the main control. However, for each word transferred, a memory cycle must be used either to obtain the word from or to store the word into the memory. Thus, the main control continues to operate but is slowed down during input—output, since it must share the memory with the I/O channels.

To transfer a sequence of words between the computer and one of the devices connected to the I/O buss, it is necessary to use a START I/O instruction for each word transfer. The START I/O instruction, in this case, contains a number which identifies the I/O device to be used. For input, a word is read from the specified device and transferred to the accumulator via the buss, overwriting the previous contents of the accumulator. For output, the accumulator contents are transmitted to the selected device via the I/O buss. In this case, the data which is to be transferred out must be loaded into the accumulator before the START I/O command is given.

The START I/O instruction along with the other instructions needed for manipulating each word of an accumulator transfer are usually written in the form of a subroutine. This subroutine is executed whenever a transfer is to take place between the accumulator and one of the I/O devices connected to the buss. Between transfers, the main control can continue to operate. Thus, the computer is slowed down by accumulator input—output, because a subroutine must be executed for each word transferred. An example of a typical subroutine which requires about twelve memory cycles for each input transfer is shown in Figure 7-2. The computer, therefore, is slowed down more by a device connected to the buss than if the same device were connected to a channel.

It would therefore appear to be logical to attach every I/O device to a channel and use only memory input—output. Unfortunately, it is economically unsound to do so. It is more expensive to provide a channel for an I/O device than to connect it to the I/O buss. A compromise must be sought between the cost of a channel and the speed of the computer. Since a slow I/O device cannot transfer many words per second, an I/O subroutine need not be executed very often. Therefore, even though a slow device connected to the buss slows the machine down more than when connected to a channel, the overall decrease in speed is negligible. For example, let us assume that we have a machine capable of operating at a rate of one million memory cycles per second, and an input—output device which can transfer one hundred words per second. Then, in one second, this device will require about 1200 memory cycles when attached to the buss. This leaves 998,800 memory cycles for other purposes. In this example, the computer is slowed down to 99.88% of its maximum operating speed, which is not a significant change.

Fast I/O devices, on the other hand, would definitely slow the machine down by an intolerable amount if connected to the buss. It is common, therefore, to connect slow devices to the I/O buss and provide channels for the fast devices.

Instruction	Comments	Memory cycles used
m — — —	Return address is stored in this location by a SAVE AND TRANSFER TO m instruction	2
STORE ACC, k	Save accumulator contents in location k	2
START INPUT, ACC, n	Read word from DEVICE B_n into accumulator	1
STORE ACC*, ℓ	Store accumulator in location whose address is stored in memory location ℓ	3
LOAD ACC, k	Restore accumulator to original contents	2
TRANSFER TO* m	Return to original program	2

FIGURE 7-2. Example of a subroutine for executing an input transfer from DEVICE B_n via the accumulator.

There is no universal way of distinguishing between a slow and a fast device. For every system, an evaluation must be made as to how a given I/O device would affect the overall speed of operation and a decision must be made as to whether to attach the device in question to the buss or to a channel.

An exception arises if a large number of similar slow I/O devices are to be connected to the computer. In this case, it is often preferable to provide them with a single channel which they share. This technique, which is known as **multiplexing**, is more efficient than a direct connection to the I/O buss. Moreover, because a single channel is shared among a large number of slow I/O devices, it is economical, as well.

7.2 THE MULTIPLEXOR CHANNEL

The multiplexor channel provides a technique for sharing a single input–output channel among a large number of slow I/O devices. The block diagram of a typical multiplexor channel is shown in Figure 7-3. From the diagram, we see that, as far as the memory is concerned, a single channel, ℓ, is involved regardless of what is actually connected to the other end of the channel. Switch A, which is usually an electronic switching device, causes one of the multiplexed I/O devices to be connected to the channel at a time. At the same time, an I/O control signal is sent to the selected device through switch B, causing a word to

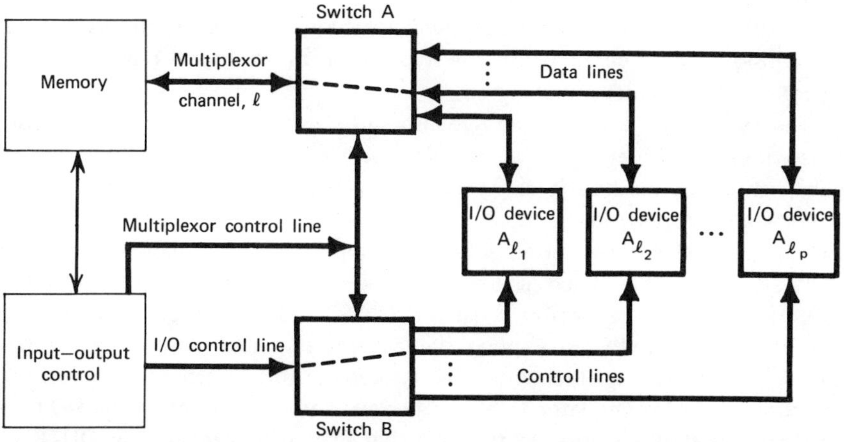

FIGURE 7-3. The multiplexor channel. (The switches are shown as blocks. In operation, the data line from one of the I/O devices is connected to the multiplexor channel through switch A. The control line from the same device is connected to the I/O control line through switch B. The dashed lines in the blocks show the switches in the position which connects device A_{ℓ_2} to the computer.)

be transferred by the device. The position of the switches is controlled by the multiplexor control signal, which is sent to the switches from the input–output control unit.

Although the multiplexor can be operated in several different modes, we will describe only one mode of operation. In this mode, which is very common, the switches are actuated and move one step after each word of input or output. Thus, the first word of a block transfer is sent to or received from device ℓ_1, the second word, device ℓ_2, and so on. For continuous operation, ℓ_1 is assumed to follow ℓ_p, so that the procedure is repeated. The advantage of this mode of operation is that it is unnecessary to determine which device is to be used next, as the devices are sequenced automatically.

In Chapter 1, we introduced input–output using the typewriter and its associated paper tape reader for illustration. Let us now examine the typewriter as an I/O device in more detail.

7.3 THE TYPEWRITER

An electric typewriter is the simplest and least expensive device which can be connected to a digital computer for performing input–output. Typewriters are therefore widely used on computing systems of all sizes. On a small machine, a typewriter often serves as the primary input–output device. On a large system, it can be used to provide a convenient method of communication between the operator and the machine. In many time-shared systems, typewriters serve as input–output terminals for the users who are sharing the system. In this section, we consider the operation of the typewriter as an input–output device, regardless of its intended application.

The typewriter is a slow nonsynchronous device. It is slow because most typewriters can type no more than five or ten characters per second. It is nonsynchronous because it can type at any speed up to its maximum rate. Therefore, the typewriter is usually connected to the I/O buss rather than to an I/O channel. Data is transferred out of the computer through the typewriter one character at a time. Each character to be typed is first loaded into the accumulator from the memory.* Then a START I/O instruction of the format OUTPUT ACC, TYPE, specifying the accumulator and the device number corresponding to the typewriter, is executed. This instruction causes the character in the accumulator to be transferred to the typewriter via the I/O buss and instructs the typewriter to type the character. After executing an OUTPUT ACC, TYPE instruction, the computer cannot execute another one until the

* Each character is represented in the computer as a sequence of bits. The typewriter interprets each bit sequence as an **alphanumeric** character, that is, as a letter of the alphabet, a numeral 0–9, or a symbol such as a period or a comma. The interpretation of a binary code as an alphanumeric character is the subject of Section 7.5.

typing of the character has been completed. Since this typically takes more than one-tenth of a second, and the computer can execute 100,000 or so instructions during this time, it can execute other parts of the program or other programs while waiting.

In order to keep the typewriter operating at its maximum rate, each OUTPUT ACC, TYPE instruction should be executed as soon as the typing of the previous character has been completed. One of the bits in an I/O status register* can be used to determine when the typing of a character has been completed. This typewriter output status bit is a ONE whenever the typewriter is busy. That is, it is a ONE during the fraction of a second while the character is being typed. This status register bit can therefore be tested periodically to determine when the typewriter is free to type a new character. As soon as it has been ascertained that the typewriter is free, the next character to be typed can be loaded into the accumulator and transferred to the typewriter. Alternately, when the typewriter becomes free, the change of the status register bit from a ONE to a ZERO can be made to automatically interrupt the computer which can then proceed to transfer the next character to be typed. We discuss the use of interrupt as it applies to input–output in Chapter 9.

When the typewriter is being used for input, it appears to the person using the device that it is operating in a manner similar to an ordinary electric typewriter. However, unlike an ordinary typewriter, depressing a key on the computer typewriter keyboard would cause nothing to happen if it were not for a sequence of instructions which the computer executes each time one of the keys is depressed. This instruction sequence includes an INPUT ACC, TYPE instruction for transferring the character corresponding to the depressed key from the typewriter to the accumulator, and an OUTPUT ACC, TYPE instruction for transferring the same character back to the typewriter to be typed. If the latter step were omitted, the typist would not see what he is typing, despite the fact that the information was being transferred into the computer. A typewriter input status bit is provided in a status register to inform the computer whenever a typewriter key is depressed. This bit changes from ZERO to ONE whenever a typewriter key is depressed. Thus, it can be tested periodically, and if a ONE is detected, an input sequence as described above can be initiated. Note that testing the status bit, in this case, automatically resets it to ZERO, preparing it for another input cycle from the typewriter keyboard. Alternately, the change of the status bit to a ONE can be used to interrupt the computer, which would then proceed to transfer the character into the accumulator.

In Chapter 1, we described a typewriter which had a device attached for reading punched paper tape. Paper tape readers and punches can be used in

* See Section 5.4.

conjunction with the typewriter or as completely independent input–output devices. Both modes of operation are described in Section 7.4.

7.4 PAPER TAPE INPUT–OUTPUT

Another common input–output medium is punched paper tape. Paper tape readers and punches are relatively inexpensive and are often used as a convenient substitute for the typewriter. Many readers and punches are faster than the typewriter and can therefore transfer data into and out of the computer more rapidly. Thus, the computer equipped with high-speed paper tape equipment can operate more efficiently than with typewriter I/O.

The paper tape commonly used is in the form of a one inch wide strip of paper. A character is punched as a series of holes across the tape, as shown in the example of Figure 7-4. Up to eight holes can be punched across the width of the tape in addition to the small sprocket hole which is always punched and used as a guide. Each hole punched into the tape represents a binary ONE; the absence of a hole is interpreted as a binary ZERO. In the figure, we have shown the interpretation of the holes as binary digits. The relationship between the binary digits of each character and its alphanumeric counterpart is presented in Section 7.5.

As stated above, an advantage of paper tape equipment over the typewriter is that paper tape equipment can operate more rapidly. Paper tape readers are available which can read over 1000 characters per second, and punches are available which can punch over 100 characters per second. A tape can be prepared by a typist in advance of when it is needed and read into the machine at a much faster rate than is possible with a typewriter alone. Also, it is easier and faster to reread a tape into the computer, when necessary, than to retype the information on the typewriter keyboard. With these points in mind, we examine the operation of the paper tape reader and punch.

The paper tape reader which is attached to a typewriter generates binary codes which are indistinguishable from the codes generated by the keyboard. Thus, if the user starts the tape reader, it appears to the computer as if someone were typing on the keyboard. Just as for typewriter input, after each character is read, a status register bit is changed to a ONE. This change is sensed either by testing the bit directly or by causing an interrupt to occur. In either case, an INPUT ACC, TYPE instruction transfers the character to the accumulator from the device. If desired, it can be typed by an OUTPUT ACC, TYPE instruction. The data from the tape reader is therefore processed in exactly the same manner as data produced by the typewriter keyboard. Readers which are attached to typewriters are fairly slow devices and operate at about five to ten characters per second. This rate is equivalent to a fast typing speed.

The paper tape punch which is connected to a typewriter receives the same binary codes which are sent to the typewriter. When the punch is turned on, however, the codes are punched onto a paper tape instead of being printed. Since the punch operates at the same speed as the typewriter, it is possible for the data to be punched onto paper tape and printed by the typewriter at the same time. This type of reader and punch is very slow and is used more for convenience than to increase the speed of operation of the computer.

High-speed readers and punches are treated as completely independent input–output devices. The high-speed punch operates in the manner we have described above. When a character is transmitted to the device, it proceeds to punch that character onto the paper tape. As soon as the punching of each character is completed, a status register bit changes, and the computer can either test it or be interrupted by the change. In either case, the transfer of the next character is then initiated, thus maintaining a high data rate to the punch.

The operation of the high-speed reader differs slightly from the operation of the reader described above. The operator inserts the tape into the reader but does not start it. When the computer is prepared to read a character from the tape, it must first start the reader, which then proceeds to move the next character on the tape into the correct position to be read. The computer starts the reader by transferring a special character to the punch which is interpreted as a start command for the reader rather than as data for the punch. After the reader has been started and the next character on tape has been read by the reader, a status register bit is changed. The computer can either test for the change or be interrupted by it. In either case, a suitable START I/O instruction transfers the character from the tape reader into the accumulator. After reading the character, the tape reader stops moving the tape until another start command is given. Therefore, to read a sequence of characters from the tape, the sequence of steps described above must be repeated for each character.

A high-speed reader which reads 1000 characters per second may appear fast to an observer when it is in operation. However, to the computer, it is a relatively slow device, since the machine can execute about 1000 instructions while a single character is being read. Thus, even high-speed paper tape equipment is commonly connected to the I/O buss rather than to a channel.

The BCD system, described in Chapter 3, provides a simple way of encoding decimal digits using sequences of binary digits. As described in Chapter 2, sequences of bits can also be interpreted as binary numbers or as instructions by the computer. In Section 7.5, we describe the type of code used by the computer for representing the letters of the alphabet and other characters which are commonly used by the computer.

7.5 CHARACTER CODES

Data is commonly fed to a computer in the form of decimal numbers; therefore, the computer must be able to manipulate the numerals 0–9. Moreover, it must be able to print its output in a format suitable for easy interpretation by the user of

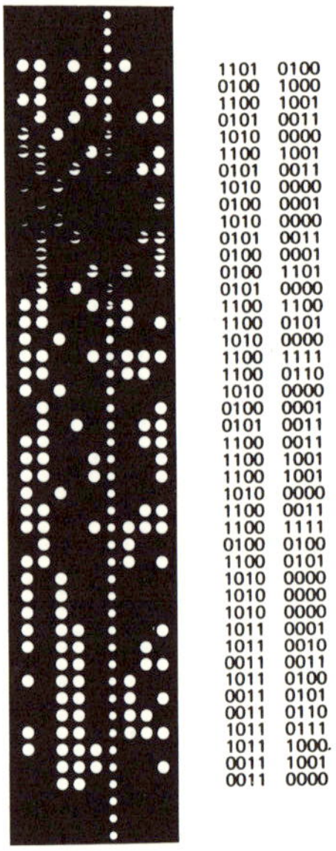

FIGURE 7-4. Example of a punched paper tape.

the machine; this requires the printing of alphabetic characters as well as numerals. Special symbols such as the **period** are important, since it is used as a decimal point in the printed data. In this section, we examine the codes used to represent alphanumeric characters.

A common code is the **American Standard Code for Information Interchange** (ASCII), which is used with teletype machines for sending data over telephone lines. The characters shown on the tape in Figure 7-4 are examples of the ASCII code. Table 7-1 shows the binary equivalent for each character in the ASCII teletype code. The bit corresponding to the left-hand column of the tape has been omitted from the table. This bit is a check bit or **parity** bit which is used to determine if an error has been made by the reader or punch. If there are an odd number of ONE's in the code, the parity bit is a ONE; otherwise it is a ZERO. Thus, including the parity bit, there must always be an even number of ONE's in each character. For example, in the codes for 1 and 2, the parity bit is a ONE; for 0 and 3, a ZERO. If a code is read which does not have an even number of

TABLE 7-1. American Standard Code for Information Interchange

@	100 0000	0	011 0000
A	100 0001	1	011 0001
B	100 0010	2	011 0010
C	100 0011	3	011 0011
D	100 0100	4	011 0100
E	100 0101	5	011 0101
F	100 0110	6	011 0110
G	100 0111	7	011 0111
H	100 1000	8	011 1000
I	100 1001	9	011 1001
J	100 1010	:	011 1010
K	100 1011	;	011 1011
L	100 1100	<	011 1100
M	100 1101	=	011 1101
N	100 1110	>	011 1110
O	100 1111	?	011 1111
P	101 0000	Space	010 0000
Q	101 0001	!	010 0001
R	101 0010	"	010 0010
S	101 0011	#	010 0011
T	101 0100	$	010 0100
U	101 0101	%	010 0101
V	101 0110	&	010 0110
W	101 0111	'	010 0111
X	101 1000	(	010 1000
Y	101 1001	)	010 1001
Z	101 1010	*	010 1010
[	101 1011	+	010 1011
\	101 1100	,	010 1100
]	101 1101	–	010 1101
↑	101 1110	.	010 1110
←	101 1111	/	010 1111
Line feed		000 1010	
Carriage return		000 1101	
Bell		000 0111	
Delete		111 1111	

ONE's, this indicates that a reader or punch error has been made.* Note that the use of a parity bit for detecting errors assumes that no more than one bit of each character is altered whenever an error occurs.

As we see from Table 7-1, the ASCII code is formed in a very straightforward way: @ and the letters of the alphabet A–Z are represented by the binary codes 100 0000 through 101 1010, arranged in order as if they were binary numbers. The numbers 0–9 are represented by the binary codes 011 0000 through 011 1001; note that the least significant four bits form the equivalent BCD code for each number. The remaining codes in each column of the table represent the special characters, as shown. Finally, the three typewriter carriage control characters are represented by the codes 000 1010, 000 1101, and 000 0111. The delete code is merely a character with a ONE punched in each position. A character punched in error on a paper tape is erased by converting it to the delete code. If the delete code is sent to the typewriter, it is ignored, whereas the other nonprinting codes, such as the line feed code, cause the typewriter carriage to move.

Several codes other than the ASCII code are in use, but they are not described here because there is no fundamental difference between paper tape codes. Each code assigns a bit sequence for each alphanumeric character, and as long as each bit sequence is correctly interpreted, the details of the code are relatively unimportant.

In this section, we described the ASCII alphanumeric code with specific reference to the paper tape reader and punch, and the typewriter. An alphanumeric code is used whenever alphanumeric characters must be transmitted between the computer and an I/O device. The line printer and the card reader and punch are I/O devices which use alphanumeric codes extensively. These devices are described in Sections 7.6 and 7.7.

7.6 THE LINE PRINTER

The typewriter and paper tape equipment manipulate a single character at a time. A line printer, however, prints a complete line of characters in a single operation. Thus, printed information can be produced at a much faster rate than with a typewriter. For example, a 600 line per minute printer prints 10 lines per second. If 120 characters can be printed in a line across the page, then 1200 characters per second can be printed by the line printer, as compared to five to ten characters per second for a typewriter.

In operation, all of the characters for a complete line of print plus suitable

* The opposite convention is sometimes used. In this case, an odd number of ONE's constitutes a correct character. If the number of ONE's in each character is an even number, then it has **even parity**; otherwise, it has **odd parity**.

carriage control characters are transferred to the printer either via the buss or through a channel. The characters are automatically stored in a buffer register associated with the printer until a complete line has been received. Then, all the characters in the buffer are printed in one operation of the printer. When the printer is ready to receive the next line to be printed, a status register bit changes and is used to inform the computer of the status of the printer. The control characters are used to provide proper spacing between lines and pages of the printed material. Whether the buss or a channel is used for the printer is determined by the speed considerations mentioned in Section 7.1.

Punched card equipment can also manipulate more than one character at a time. However, card readers and punches operate in a different manner than the line printer, as we see in Section 7.7.

7.7 PUNCHED CARDS

Of the different types of punched cards which are in use, the Hollerith card is one of the most common. An example of a Hollerith card is shown in Figure 7-5. Each card is divided into twelve rows and eighty columns; each character is punched as a series of up to three small rectangles or holes in a column, as shown in the example. The numerals are represented by a single punch in a column; the letters of the alphabet by two punches; and all but three of the remaining characters are represented by three punches, one of which is a punch in row 8. The & and – characters are represented by single punches in the 12 and 11 rows, respectively, and the / character by a double punch in rows 0 and 1.

Hollerith cards can be punched and read either row-by-row or column-by-column. The latter method of reading is similar to reading paper tape. For each character, a twelve-bit code is read from the card and transmitted to the computer through the I/O buss. For example, the code for the letter A is

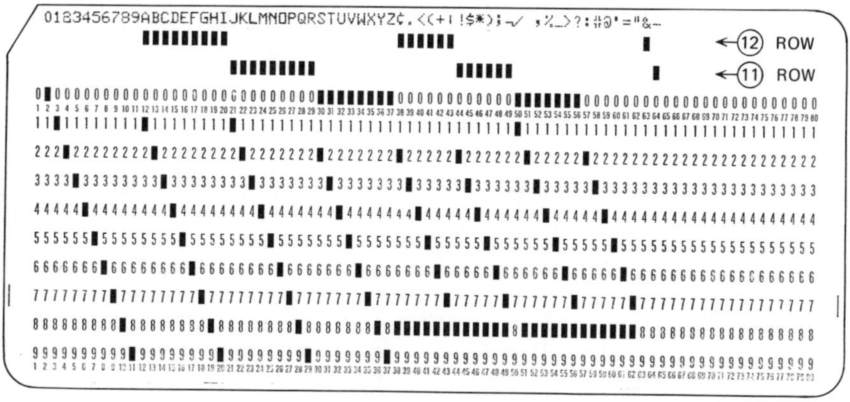

FIGURE 7-5. An example of a Hollerith punched card.

1001 0000 0000. When reading row by row, however, an eighty-bit code is generated for each row. This code is stored in a buffer memory in the reader and transmitted to the computer as a sequence of byte or word transfers either via the buss or a channel. After all twelve rows are read and stored in the computer memory, the machine must translate the data into character codes. The execution time of the program which performs this translation is not negligible, because a significant amount of data must be manipulated. However, a card reader which reads rows operates much faster than one which reads columns. Therefore, the additional time needed to translate the codes is usually justifiable, because the overall operating speed of the system is increased.*

Since the twelve-bit character code is not an easy one to manipulate, a further translation can be performed which converts the twelve-bit code into ASCII, BCD, or some other convenient code. This conversion procedure, which is described in Section 7.8, takes a negligible amount of computer execution time when compared to the row—column translation described above.

For punching cards, the data to be punched is first converted into the twelve-bit column code. Then, if a column card punch is used, the data is transferred to the punch via the buss or a channel in the usual way. If a row card punch is used, the data must first be translated from the column code to the eighty-bit row code by the computer. It is then transferred to the punch as a sequence of bytes or computer words and reassembled into an eighty-bit code in the buffer memory of the punch. When the complete code has been assembled, it is punched into the card.

It is apparent that quite a few different codes are used in a single computer. For example, the row card reader reads data as eighty-bit row codes, and this data must be converted into twelve-bit column codes. For processing numerical data, the twelve-bit column code is converted into BCD or binary.† To print out numerical results, the binary or BCD codes are converted into one of the codes used by the typewriter or line printer. Thus, code conversion is a very important aspect of input—output and is the next topic presented.

7.8 CODE CONVERSION

By executing suitable programs, the digital computer can convert data from one alphanumeric code into another. In this section, we describe several sample

* An alternate method of operation is to use a **peripheral computer** to perform the row—column translation, as described in Section 8.3.

† The conversion from the twelve-bit code to the BCD code is a code conversion. However, the conversion into binary also involves a conversion from the decimal number system to the binary number system. The latter conversion involves more than a single character and is therefore more complex than a simple code conversion. The reader may prefer to think of the twelve-bit-to-binary conversion in two steps: (a) the conversion to BCD (b) the conversion from BCD to binary.

programs which are illustrative of the principles involved in converting codes in the computer.

Of the code conversions presented above, the most complex is the conversion between the eighty-bit row code and the twelve-bit column code for Hollerith card data. Let us assume that the eighty-bit codes received from the card reader are stored in the input memory block illustrated in Figure 7-6; that a sixteen-bit computer, such as the one described in Chapter 2, is being used; and that the other block shown in the figure is used to store the twelve-bit column codes generated by the conversion program. Each eighty-bit code is stored in five consecutive sixteen-bit words, such as x through x + 4, in the input block. Since a complete card consists of twelve row codes, the block of sixty computer words, x through x + 59, serves to completely store a single card. Because the data is transferred in the form of row codes, each of the bits from a single column on the card is stored in a different word in the block. For example, the twelve bits constituting the column code for the character punched in column 1 of the card are stored in the most significant bit positions of words x, x + 5, . . . , x + 55. The bits constituting each of the other seventy-nine column codes are similarly stored as corresponding bits of different words, as shown in detail in Figure 7-6 for the first four columns. The column code block consists of one computer word for each column, or the eighty words, y through y + 79. Only the least significant twelve bits of each word are used to store each character. To illustrate how the formats of the two blocks are related, the first four column codes of the card are shown stored in the column code block as twelve-bit column codes.

To carry out the conversion, each bit of each word of the column code block is first set to ZERO. Then each word of the input block is examined bit-by-bit, and whenever a ONE is encountered, the corresponding bit of the column code block is changed. Since the first bit examined in the first word of the example is a ONE, a ONE is placed into bit position 5 of word y, as shown. The next bit of word x is a ZERO. If it were a ONE, bit 5 of word y + 1 would be changed. Similarly, the remaining bits in words x through x + 4 affect only bit 5 of words y + 2 through y + 79. Words x + 5 through x + 9 affect only bit 6 of the words in the column code block, and so on for the remaining data. A program to perform this conversion is presented in Exercises 7.4–7.7.

The conversion from a twelve-bit column code to BCD is simplified because each code is stored in a single computer word. Moreover, a simple shifting and counting sequence is all that is required for this conversion. We assume that only the decimal digits 0–9 are encountered, although it is not too difficult to test for this situation. Table 7-2 lists the twelve-bit column codes as well as the BCD equivalent codes for each of the numerals. Figure 7-7 is an example of a program which executes the conversion between the two codes. The program, which is in the form of a subroutine, is entered by placing the twelve-bit column code to be converted into the accumulator and executing a SAVE AND TRANSFER TO 10

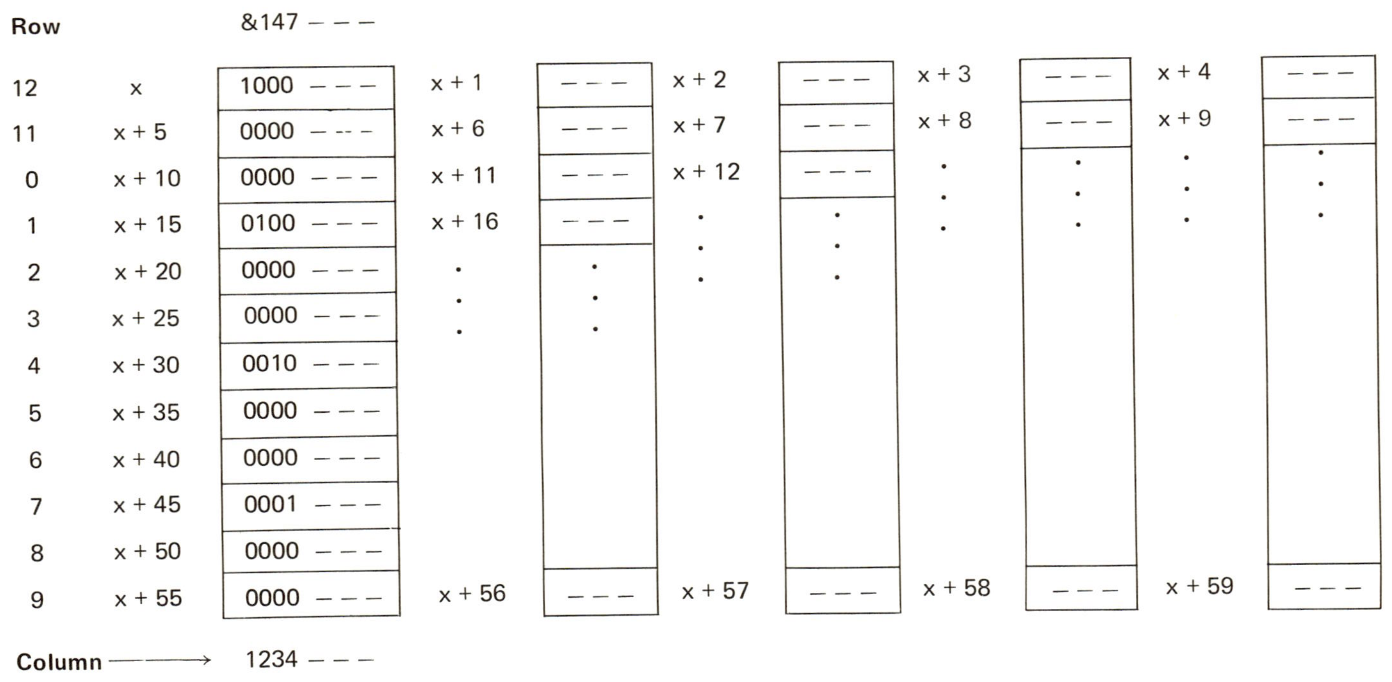
Row
&147 — — —
12
11
0
1
2
3
4
5
6
7
8
9
x
x + 5
x + 10
x + 15
x + 20
x + 25
x + 30
x + 35
x + 40
x + 45
x + 50
x + 55
1000 — — —
0000 — — —
0000 — — —
0100 — — —
0000 — — —
0000 — — —
0010 — — —
0000 — — —
0000 — — —
0001 — — —
0000 — — —
0000 — — —
x + 1
x + 6
x + 11
x + 16
x + 56
x + 2
x + 7
x + 12
x + 57
x + 3
x + 8
x + 58
x + 4
x + 9
x + 59
Column
1234 — — —

(a)

y	0000 1000 0000 0000	&
y + 1	0000 0001 0000 0000	1
y + 2	0000 0000 0010 0000	4
y + 3	0000 0000 0000 0100	7
y + 4	— — —	.
y + 5	— — —	.
y + 6	— — —	.
.	.	
.	.	
.	.	
y + 76	— — —	
y + 77	— — —	
y + 78	— — —	
y + 79	— — —	

(b)

FIGURE 7-6. Organization of memory blocks used for storing (a) input data from cards, and (b) converted column codes.

TABLE 7-2. Comparison between Twelve-Bit Column Code and BCD Code for the Numerals 0–9

Numeral	Twelve-bit column code	BCD code
0	(0000) 0010 0000 0000	0000
1	(0000) 0001 0000 0000	0001
2	(0000) 0000 1000 0000	0010
3	(0000) 0000 0100 0000	0011
4	(0000) 0000 0010 0000	0100
5	(0000) 0000 0001 0000	0101
6	(0000) 0000 0000 1000	
7	(0000) 0000 0000 0100	0111
8	(0000) 0000 0000 0010	1000
9	(0000) 0000 0000 0001	1001

```
10   - - - -                          Store return address
11   LOAD INDEX, (-10)                Set index
12   SHIFT LEFT, 6                    Eliminate leading ZERO's
13   IF ACC=-, TRANSFER TO 18         Test for leading ONE
14   INCREMENT INDEX                  Count ZERO's
15   IF INDEX=0, TRANSFER TO* 10      Test for end
16   SHIFT LEFT, 1                    Eliminate leading ZERO
17   TRANSFER TO 13
18   LOAD ACC, 30+INDEX               Load BCD data
19   TRANSFER TO* 10                  Return
20   0000 0000 0000 0000  )
21   0000 0000 0000 0001  |
22   0000 0000 0000 0010  |
23   0000 0000 0000 0011  |           BCD numbers 0–9
24   0000 0000 0000 0100  }           stored in least significant
25   0000 0000 0000 0101  |           four bits of each word
26   0000 0000 0000 0110  |
27   0000 0000 0000 0111  |
28   0000 0000 0000 1000  |
29   0000 0000 0000 1001  )
```

FIGURE 7-7. Example of a program which converts the twelve-bit column code into the BCD code.

instruction. The subroutine instructions proceed to shift the bits of the accumulator to the left, searching for a ONE bit as determined by satisfying the test instruction in location 13. When a ONE bit is found, the count in the index register is used for determining the address of one of the BCD codes stored in locations 20–29. The appropriate code is thereby loaded into the accumulator. Thus, on returning to the main program via the TRANSFER TO* 10 instruction, the correct BCD code is located in the least significant four bits of the accumulator. If no ONE bits are found, the subroutine automatically leaves zero in the accumulator. The subroutine shown in Figure 7-7 is not the most efficient possible, but it is very straightforward and illustrates the principles involved in code conversion.

The conversion from BCD into ASCII for the numerals is very simple. It involves only the addition of the bits 011 to the left of the BCD code. The direct conversion of the twelve-bit column code into ASCII for any alphanumeric character is very useful. It is a logical extension of the program shown in Figure 7-7. Both of these conversion programs are presented as problems for the reader in Exercises 7.8 and 7.9.

In this chapter, we described the input–output subsystem and some of the more common input–output devices. The magnetic tape, drum, and disk, described in Chapter 8, are examples of devices which are attached to the I/O subsystem but are used primarily for auxiliary storage of large data files. Also included in Chapter 8 are brief descriptions of a number of other I/O devices which are primarily used for the transfer of information between the computer and its users and operators.

EXERCISES

7.1 What is the difference between a block transfer executed via an I/O channel and a block transfer executed via the I/O buss? Under what circumstances is each of these two types of transfers preferred?

7.2 What is a multiplexor channel? Under what circumstances is a multiplexor channel preferred over the I/O buss or an ordinary I/O channel?

7.3 Decode the paper tape message used as an example in Figure 7-4.

The solutions to Exercises 7.4–7.7 together constitute a program to perform the row-to-column conversion for Hollerith card data.

7.4 Write a program to set the bits of each word of the column code block of Figure 7-6(b) to ZERO's.

7.5 Write a program to load each word of a single row of the input block of Figure 7-6(a) into the accumulator and test whether each bit is a ZERO or ONE.

7.6 Write a program to change to a ONE the bit in the column code block corresponding to each ONE bit found in the program of Exercise 7.5.

7.7 Write a program to set all counters to their initial values and to correctly sequence the programs of Exercises 7.4–7.6.

7.8 Write a program to convert the BCD numeral codes into ASCII.

7.9 Write a program to convert a column code into its corresponding ASCII code. Assume that only the numerals 0–9 and the alphabetic codes for A–Z will occur.

8
INPUT—OUTPUT II

In this chapter we conclude the description of the input—output subsystem. The auxiliary storage devices which are connected to the I/O system are described in detail. Then, brief descriptions of a number of miscellaneous input—output devices, such as the plotter and CRT, are presented. Finally, we describe how it is possible for certain I/O devices to communicate directly with one another in some of the more sophisticated computers.

8.1 AUXILIARY MEMORY DEVICES – MAGNETIC TAPE

The magnetic tape, drum, and disk are each capable of storing a large quantity of digital data. This data can consist of programs which are waiting to be executed, input data needed for the operation of the computer, output data produced by programs which have been executed, or intermediate results which have been generated by the computer and are being saved for later use. These storage devices are fast synchronous devices and so are generally connected to the computer via suitable I/O channels rather than to the I/O buss. Magnetic tape is described below; the drum and disk are the subjects of Section 8.2.

The magnetic tape device uses a strip of polyester tape which is coated with a magnetic recording medium. ONE's and ZERO's are recorded as magnetic patterns on the tape. The common one-half inch wide tape can record eight data tracks, a parity track, and a clock track, simultaneously. Thus, data can be recorded on tape as a sequence of bytes in much the same way that data is

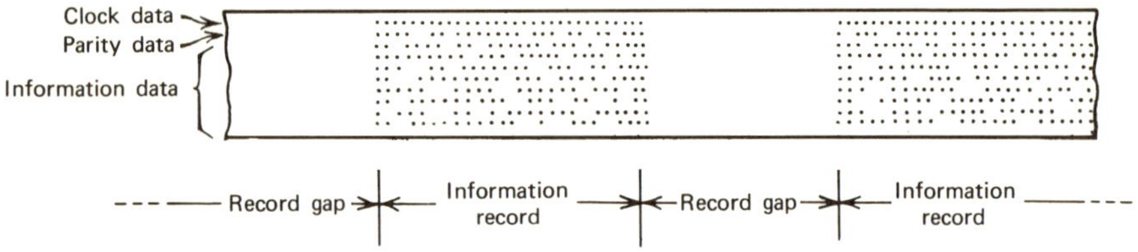

FIGURE 8-1. Illustration of format used to record data on magnetic tape.

punched onto a paper tape. Information read from the clock track is used to inform the I/O control each time a byte is read from the tape.

High-speed magnetic tapes cannot be started and stopped between individual characters. Therefore, information is recorded in blocks of characters, called **records**, with gaps between the records, as illustrated in Figure 8-1. No information is recorded in the record gaps which are provided to allow the moving tape to slow down to a stop and to start up again. Let us assume that the tape is initially stopped with the reading device, which is called the read head, in contact with the tape at a record gap. Then, in order to read information from the tape, the following sequence of events takes place. When the computer is ready to read a record from tape, it executes a START I/O instruction. This instruction specifies a block transfer and contains a block address. From the memory block itself, the length of the transfer and the I/O channel number are determined by the I/O control. The control then sends a start tape command to the magnetic tape reader. The tape starts to move and shortly attains the correct speed for reading data. When an information record starts to pass over the read head, the clock track generates signals which are sent to the I/O control to inform it that a record is being read. The data from the tape record is then stored character-by-character into the memory block specified by the START I/O instruction. When the transfer from the magnetic tape reader is completed, a stop tape command is sent to the device and a braking mechanism is actuated. The tape slows to a halt with a record gap under the read head and remains there until another tape instruction is executed by the computer.

Since the record being read contains a predetermined number of characters, it is necessary that the memory block size specified in the computer conform to the size of the record stored on the tape. Otherwise, either insufficient memory space is allocated for the transfer or insufficient data is read from the tape to fill the memory block. In either case, a transfer error exists and a bit in a status register is set to ONE; if desired, an interrupt is also generated.

Errors can occur while writing information onto or reading it from a magnetic tape. An error can be caused by the presence of dust, dirt, or a worn-out spot on the tape surface. In either case, if a bit is written as a ONE but read as a ZERO, or vice versa, an error condition exists and must be detected. A parity bit, written on the tape along with each character, is used to check for tape errors in the same manner as it is used for checking errors on paper tape. For example, if odd parity is used, then any character read from tape which contains an even number of ONE's has been incorrectly written or read. A bit in a status register is set to ONE to inform the computer of the error condition so that corrective action can be taken. For example, the tape can be backspaced and a second attempt made to read the record. If the error is caused by dust on the tape, then the record is often read correctly the second time. If repeated tries at reading the record fail, then either the record can be skipped over and ignored or program execution can be terminated. The programmer must anticipate the potential error conditions and any desired corrective action he may wish the computer to take and include instructions for this purpose in his program.

It should be noted that, while the tape record is moving past the read head, the rate at which characters are being read is determined by the tape speed and the spacing between characters. Since both of these parameters are fixed for a given machine, the magnetic tape reader is a synchronous device and must be assigned a suitable priority in the I/O queue to avoid a transfer error. A typical transfer rate for a magnetic tape reader is 100,000 characters per second.

A similar sequence of events takes place when information is written onto a magnetic tape. When a START I/O command is executed by the computer, the I/O control sends a start tape command to the magnetic tape device. Writing of the data is delayed, however, until the tape has attained its operating speed, at which time a special circuit associated with the tape control system begins to generate clock pulses. These clock pulses are sent to the I/O control, which transmits a byte from an output block in the memory to the magnetic tape system for each pulse received. Each byte is written on the tape along with the clock pulses which, when recorded on the tape, form the clock track whose use was described earlier. When the block transfer is completed, a stop tape command is given and the tape is slowed to a halt. A record gap is thereby automatically created during the stopping and starting of the tape. A block size error cannot occur during a tape writing operation, since the record size is determined solely by the size of the block being transferred.

During writing, a parity bit is generated and written on the tape along with the character information. A check is performed by simultaneously reading the characters while they are being written, and if the parity of any character is not correct, an error signal is generated. The lack of an error signal thus provides an indication that the information is being correctly written on the tape. If an error is detected during the write operation, the information can be rewritten immediately while it is still stored in the computer memory. To rewrite a record on a magnetic tape, the tape is backspaced until the record gap is again under the

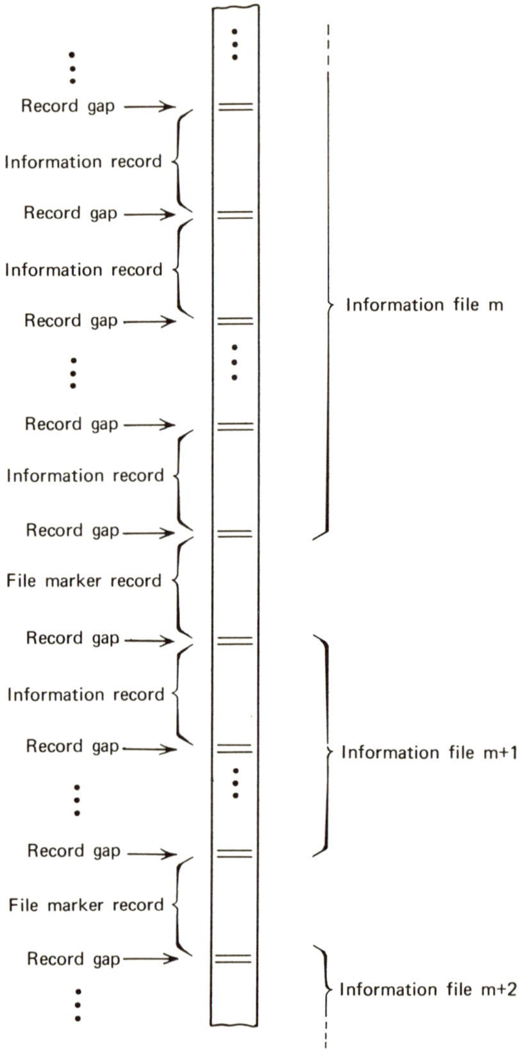

FIGURE 8-2. Example showing formatting of records into files.

read head. Then, by executing a block transfer from the same block of the memory to the tape, the old record is erased and a new record is written in its place. If no further parity errors are detected, the new record is deemed to be correctly written on the tape.

It is impractical to write an extremely large record or **data file** onto the tape as a single record. Such a file is divided into a number of smaller information records which constitute the data file on the tape. To separate the records of one file from those of another, a record containing a **file marker** is written following the last information record of each file, as shown in Figure 8-2. If a file marker record is encountered when a tape is being read, a status bit is changed and can be tested or used to cause an interrupt.

In a computer equipped with magnetic tape, it is common for several tape handling mechanisms to be connected to a single channel in a multiplexing type of arrangement. In such a machine, a method is provided whereby the programmer can select a particular tape handler prior to initiating a block transfer through the channel. Depending on the computer, the number of the tape unit to be selected is either loaded into a special register, stored in the memory, or sent directly to the I/O control by the execution of an output transfer which specifies a device code reserved for this purpose. Then, when the START I/O instruction is executed, the I/O control uses this number to select the appropriate tape handler and connect it to the channel. The transfer then proceeds between the memory and the selected tape unit as described above.

Several control options are available to the programmer in a machine which is equipped with magnetic tape. These options are usually specified in the same manner that the tape unit number is specified. The control options allow the programmer to skip a record or a complete file without reading the data into the computer, or to backspace a record or a complete file so that the data can be reread or rewritten. These options are useful for searching and editing the information stored on the tape without the need to read each record into the machine. Finally, a control option is provided to allow the automatic rewinding of the tape at high speed without extensive backspacing. This option is used when a tape is to be completely rewritten or if it is to be removed from the machine by the operator and saved for later use.

The magnetic drum and disk systems are other examples of mass storage media and are described in Section 8.2.

8.2 AUXILIARY MEMORY DEVICES – MAGNETIC DRUM AND DISK

The magnetic drum and disk systems are quite similar in operation. Both consist of high-speed rotating surfaces which are coated with a magnetic recording medium. The active surface of the drum is the surface of a cylinder, as shown in Figure 8.3(a). The disk, on the other hand, consists of one or more round flat plates whose upper and lower surfaces are both coated with magnetic material and used as storage surfaces. An example of a disk assembly, with three disks shown, is sketched in Figure 8-3(b). The prime advantage of the disk over the drum is that for a given physical size system, the active area of the disk is greater than that of the drum. Therefore, a great deal more information can be stored on a disk than on a comparably sized drum.

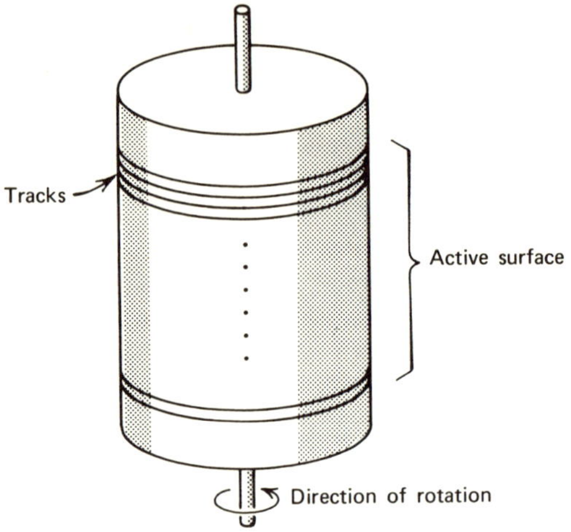

(a) Magnetic drum

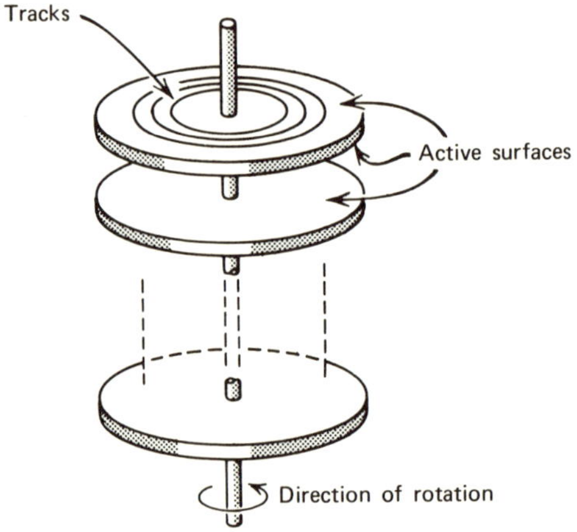

(b) Magnetic disk

FIGURE 8-3. Sketches showing active surfaces of the magnetic drum and disk and indicating locations of tracks on these surfaces.

The active surfaces of both devices are divided into tracks, as shown in Figure 8-3. By writing a group of tracks simultaneously, bytes or words can be stored in a simple manner. As with tape, parity tracks and clock tracks are provided. However, the clock tracks are prerecorded and arranged so as to divide the disk or drum into sectors, as illustrated in Figure 8-4. Thus, to write or read data corresponding to a particular part of the disk or drum, an **address** which denotes a particular group of tracks, and a **sector number** are both necessary. In general,

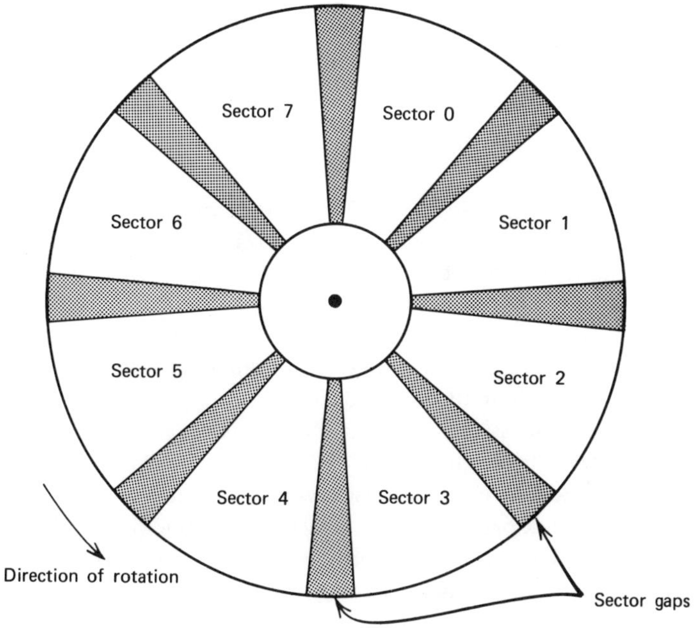

FIGURE 8-4. Surface of disk shown divided into sectors.

for a system with n groups of tracks and k sectors, the programmer assumes that the disk or drum can store k x n blocks of data and simply specifies a record address from 0 to (k x n) – 1. The machine then automatically assigns both a track address and a sector number to each record address.

To write a record onto the disk or drum, the record address is either loaded into a special register, stored in the memory, or sent directly to the I/O control via an output transfer. Then, when the START I/O instruction is executed, the I/O control determines the track address from the record address and uses it to route the data to the write heads which correspond to the tracks to be written. The I/O control also evaluates the sector number and uses it to determine when the desired sector is passing under the write heads, at which time the block transfer is executed. The prerecorded clock tracks provide the necessary synchronizing signals for transferring each word of the block being transferred. A similar set of events takes place during the read operation when a block of data is read from the device.

Errors can occur in disk and drum systems in the same way that they occur in magnetic tape systems. Thus, parity must be checked during every read operation to detect errors. However, since it is much less likely for worn-out spots to occur on a disk or drum, the latter systems have higher reliability than a magnetic tape system. As a result, it is unnecessary to check parity during write operations. Transfer errors occur if the memory is unable to keep up with the device or if the block reserved in memory is not the same size as the disk or drum record being transferred. The detection and elimination of these error conditions are accomplished in the same manner as in a magnetic tape system, as described earlier.

In many disk systems, a single set of read–write heads is used for each disk surface. In this type of system, the track address is used to move the heads into a position adjacent to the correct tracks before reading or writing. In a typical system, over 200,000 bytes per second are transferred when data is actually being written onto or read from a disk or drum. Thus, both the drum and the disk are fast synchronous devices. However, the time between the command to read or write information on the disk and the actual transfer is much longer for a single-head disk system as compared to a drum whenever the heads must be moved from one track to another.

A variation of the disk is the disk-pack, which is functionally identical to the disk. However, the disk-pack controller which rotates the disks and houses the electronic circuitry and read–write heads is physically separate from the pack which contains the disks. Thus, disk-packs can be removed, interchanged, and stored in much the same way as magnetic tapes. The disk-pack therefore has many of the advantages of the magnetic tape system as well as the higher reliability of the disk as compared to tape.

In some disk systems, a separate set of read–write heads is provided for each track of each surface. This type of system has all the advantages of both the drum and disk systems. It is more expensive than either, however, and, as a result, it is found only in large computing systems where the cost can be justified.

Other types of mass storage devices are available for use with the computer. Regardless of the physical mechanism used for storage, such devices generally appear to the machine as if they were drums or disks. An example of such a device is the **optical memory**, which uses a laser beam to read and write a large amount of data in a relatively small area of a suitable storage medium. Detailed descriptions of such devices are beyond the scope of this book.

In Chapter 7, we described the operation of the typewriter, line printer, punched card, and paper tape input–output equipment. Many other I/O devices can be connected to the computer. In Section 8.3, we briefly describe some of these devices to emphasize the versatility of the digital computer.

8.3 MISCELLANEOUS INPUT–OUTPUT DEVICES

In the miscellaneous category we include direct I/O, modems, analog I/O, plotters, CRT and light pen devices, digitizers, character readers, and peripheral computers.

Direct Input–Output. A digital computer can be used to control a highly specialized piece of equipment such as a machine tool or an industrial assembly line. For such applications, a method must be provided for sending control signals to and accepting status signals from the device being controlled. The control signals are provided by connecting an output register to the I/O buss and connecting the external control lines to the output register. Then, whenever a word is transferred to the output register via the I/O buss, it is also transferred to the device being controlled. Similarly, if an input register is connected to the buss and to the external device, data can be transferred from the device to the computer. Of course, suitable control lines are needed to ensure that the data transfers to and from the computer are correctly synchronized with the external device being controlled.

For controlling many devices simultaneously, a multiplexor can be used with the buss or with an I/O channel. This mode of operation has the advantage that one device number can be used to collectively designate all the direct I/O registers which are connected to the multiplexor.

Modems. It is often desirable to provide communication between the computer and a remotely located device via telephone lines. A modem is a device which converts data transferred to it from the computer into signals which are suitable for transmission over the telephone network. A modem connected to the other end of the line translates the telephone signals back into machine-usable data. Since a modem can operate in both a transmit and receive mode, two-way transmission of data can be carried out using a single modem at each location. Typewriters, display devices, printers, or other computers can be attached to the remote modem and can communicate with the computer as if the two were physically tied together in the same location. High-speed operation is possible by using special telephone lines and a high-speed modem which can be connected to an I/O channel rather than to the I/O buss.

Analog Input-Output. Although we have dealt exclusively with digital quantities in this book, it should be pointed out that most physical variables are analog rather than digital in nature. These variables are able to assume any value in a continuous range of allowable values. For example, the speed of an accelerating automobile does not suddenly change from 30 to 31 to 32 miles per hour, but actually passes from 30 to 32 miles per hour in a continuous manner. The speedometer is, therefore, an analog measuring device, since the needle moves continuously between the numbers and can indicate any speed between zero and 120 miles per hour.

It is often necessary to perform digital calculations involving an analog variable. It is necessary, therefore, to convert the analog variable into a sequence of digital quantities which approximate it in value. This conversion usually involves a two-step procedure. First, the analog variable is fed to a transducer whose output is an electrical voltage whose value is proportional to the value of the original analog variable. Then the voltage is fed to an electronic analog-to-digital converter, which is connected to the computer. The output of the converter is a sequence of binary or BCD numbers which are then transferred into the computer via the I/O buss.

To generate an analog variable, a sequence of digital approximations are first calculated by the computer. The digital numbers are then transferred to an electronic digital-to-analog converter via the I/O buss and produce a varying electrical voltage waveform at the output of the converter. A suitable transducer is then used to convert this voltage into the desired analog variable. The digital-to-analog converter therefore provides an analog output signal, while the analog-to-digital converter provides analog input capability. The transducers are not usually supplied with the computer but are attached externally to the analog input- output lines.

Multiplexing is often used with analog I/O equipment. For input, each of the analog voltages is sampled and sequentially converted by the analog-to-digital converter. For output multiplexing, an analog storage device is provided for each output voltage. The output of the digital-to-analog converter is then fed to each of the storage devices in turn, thereby generating a complete set of analog voltages. In a multiplexed system, it is often possible to use a single analog-to-digital converter for input, and a single digital-to-analog converter for output, thereby reducing the cost of the system over one using multiple converters.

Plotters. A plotter can be used to provide a graphic representation of the results produced by the computer. Plotters are available for producing records on either microfilm or paper. On some plotters, the output is recorded as a set of points, while on others, it is recorded as a set of short lines. Thus, a graph produced by a digital computer is approximated either by a large number of points or by a large number of short line segments. In the former case, the x and y coordinates are sent to the plotter with a command to plot a single point at that location. In the latter case, the plotter is commanded to move the plotting stylus by one increment in one of eight directions, as shown in Figure 8-5. As it moves, a short line segment is produced by the stylus. The graph of a waveform produced by the latter type of machine is shown in Figure 8-6.

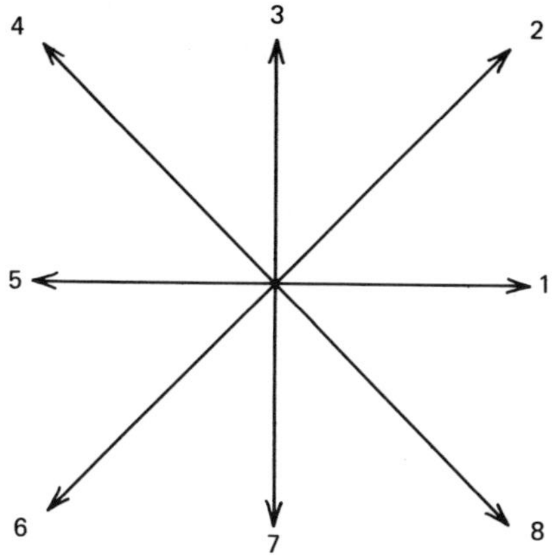

FIGURE 8-5. Eight directions in which the stylus of an incremental plotter can be moved.

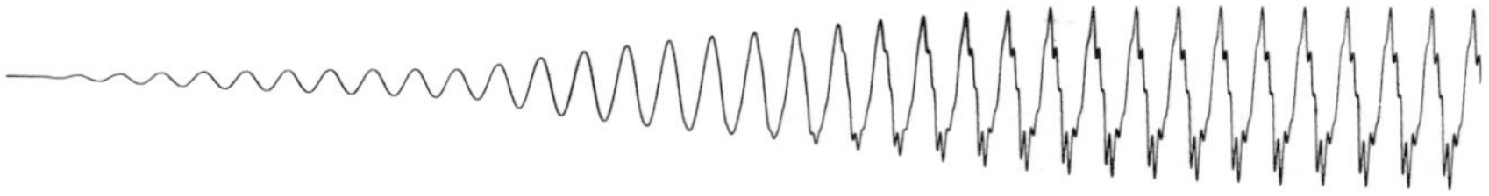

FIGURE 8-6. Example of the graph of a waveform produced on an incremental plotter.

Many standard curves as well as alphanumeric characters for labeling graphs can be traced by providing suitable sequences of commands to the plotter. Programs which automatically produce such command sequences are usually supplied by the plotter or computer manufacturer. These programs are written in the form of subroutines whose input is a code for the curve or character to be plotted. For example, if the input to the subroutine indicates that a circle is to be plotted, the location of the center of the circle and its radius must also be supplied. The subroutine then generates a complete set of commands to direct the plotter to plot the desired circle. For alphanumeric characters, a code for the desired character, its size, and location are provided to the subroutine, which then generates the correct command sequence to trace the character on the graph. The programmer can plot arbitrary curves by writing a subroutine to generate suitable commands for the plotter.

Most plotters are relatively slow devices and are therefore connected directly to the I/O buss. Graphs can be produced by a computer plotter more rapidly and more accurately than by hand. Thus, when accurate graphic information is required, a plotter is an indispensable input–output device.

The CRT and Light Pen. At most major airports, flight arrival and departure information is provided to the passenger by means of a television type of display. In some cases the information is merely photographed by a television camera and displayed on closed-circuit television monitors. In other cases, the information for the display devices is generated by a computer. Since the picture tube used in the display devices is a cathode-ray tube, the devices are called CRT's. In addition to being used to disseminate computer-generated information to large crowds, CRT's are used as substitutes for typewriter terminals and to provide communication between the operator and the machine. The major advantage of the CRT over the typewriter is that the complete display can be changed very rapidly. Thus, it is more like reading the pages of a book than is the typewriter output, which is produced one character at a time.

To avoid flicker in a CRT, the display is regenerated or renewed about 60 times per second. Therefore, in the simplest form of CRT terminal, the computer must send the information for a complete image to the CRT each time the display is renewed. The display information is stored in the computer memory and is repeatedly transferred to the CRT via a high-speed I/O channel. This mode of operation is very inefficient, since the information displayed by the CRT is changed only once every few seconds, at most. Thus, in some systems, a buffer memory is provided along with each CRT. The display information is transferred from the computer memory to the CRT buffer memory via either the I/O buss or an I/O channel whenever the display information is updated. The CRT display is then repeatedly renewed from the information stored in the buffer memory.

The information which is transferred to the CRT from the computer generally consists of one bit of data for every point on the display screen. If the bit is a ONE, the corresponding point on the screen is illuminated; if it is a ZERO, the point remains dark. If the CRT is used primarily for the display of alphanumeric characters, a so-called **character generator** can be used. In the latter system, the computer transfers a sequence of character codes to the CRT system. The CRT character generator then automatically translates these codes into the bit information corresponding to each character and stores the bits in the buffer memory. The information in the buffer memory is then transferred to the CRT, as described above, in order to produce the display. This system has the advantage that the computer need not compute the bits for each point, nor does it have to transfer a complete image to the CRT system. Thus, both the computing and I/O requirements for the computer are greatly reduced by using a character generator and buffer memory with the CRT display.

By using a CRT and a light pen, information can be entered into the computer. The light pen is a device built in the shape of a pen whose tip is sensitive to light. When the pen is pointed at a character or other lit-up portion of the CRT, the computer is able to determine the location of the light pen tip on the CRT face. The operation of the light pen can be described briefly as follows: The information from the computer or buffer memory is fed to the CRT and displayed in a bit-by-bit manner at high speed. If the light pen is pointed at a lit-up spot and actuated, then the next time that the character located under the tip of the light pen is renewed, it is sensed by the light pen, which informs the computer by causing a status bit to change, thereby producing an interrupt. Since the computer can determine which character is being transferred to the CRT at the time of the interrupt, it can deduce what the light pen user is trying to communicate to the computer. For example, let us assume that the numerals from 0 to 9 are displayed on the CRT screen and that the operator is to enter a three-digit number into the computer. If he points the light pen first at the 2, then at the 5, and finally at the 6 and actuates the pen in each case, the computer will interpret his actions as if he actuated the keys 2, 5, and 6 on a typewriter keyboard.

Other types of information can also be transferred into the computer via the light pen. If the computer has completed an assigned task, it must be instructed to proceed to another task. One way of doing this is to list all possible tasks on the face of the CRT. By pointing to the one desired and actuating the light pen, the operator can instruct the computer to execute the program corresponding to the selected task. The CRT is therefore an important output device for the computer. In conjunction with the light pen, the CRT provides a simple and natural input–output interface for communication between the computer and its users.

Digitizers. The plotter and the CRT are both used to provide graphic output from the computer. The plotter, however, is far more accurate than the CRT and is therefore used to produce graphs and drawings which require high accuracy. In comparison, graphic information plotted on the CRT is used for quickly displaying rough graphs for rapid evaluation by the user.

The digitizer and the light pen are likewise both used to provide graphic input to the computer. Although the light pen only provides approximate graphic input information, the digitizer provides highly accurate graphic input data to the machine. A cursor or stylus is used to trace over a drawing or photograph, and accurate x–y coordinates are produced for each point the cursor touches. Two modes of operation are commonly used: in one mode, the x–y coordinate information is transferred to the computer only when the user actuates the digitizer. Thus, the operator can digitize only selected points of a photograph such as the end points of a road. In the other mode of operation, points are periodically transferred to the computer as the cursor is being moved. This mode of operation allows continuous curves to be accurately digitized without the need for repeatedly actuating the digitizer.

One application for the digitizer is the production of maps from photographs.

Pertinent artifacts in the photograph, such as roads and buildings, are carefully traced over with the cursor. The computer modifies this information to correct for known distortions in the photograph and traces the results on a plotter, thereby producing a highly accurate map of the region. Names of roads and other alphanumeric information can be fed into the computer via any convenient alphanumeric input device, such as a typewriter keyboard, and added to the map.

Thus, the digitizer is useful for accurately transferring graphic information into the computer. Together with a plotter, the digitizer can be used to produce maps, blueprints, and other drawings which require accurate scaling of dimensions.

Character Readers. As we have seen, a variety of devices are available for providing input data to the computer. Of these devices, the punched-card reader is the most widely used for reading source material into the computer at high speed. Most punched cards are prepared by keypunch operators who read the data from written or typed sheets of paper and type the information onto cards. The keypunch used for this operation is similar to an ordinary typewriter except that it punches holes in a Hollerith card. The preparation of the cards in this manner is slow and costly and is often the biggest bottleneck associated with the operation of a large computer installation.

A device for automatically reading hand-printed or typed information directly into the computer is called a **character reader.** Character readers have been built which optically scan a hand-printed or typed page and convert each character into its corresponding machine code. Most of these devices require that the characters be printed in a particular typewriter print style or that they be printed according to very specific rules, if printed by hand. In the latter case, boxes are usually provided, and each character must be printed inside a separate box.

The computer can be used to control the character reader so that only desired information is read into the machine. For example, the reader may be instructed to read a specific line of printing from the page while completely ignoring the remainder of the page.

Currently available character readers are highly complicated and expensive devices whose use is therefore limited to large-scale computing systems. Great strides are being made in the design of character readers, which should make them less expensive. Their use as input devices can therefore be expected to increase as they are perfected.

Peripheral Computers. The larger a computer system is, the more important it is to maintain a high operating efficiency so that the cost of maintaining the machine is justified. One way that the efficiency of a large machine can be improved is to relieve it of most of its input– output equipment. The I/O devices

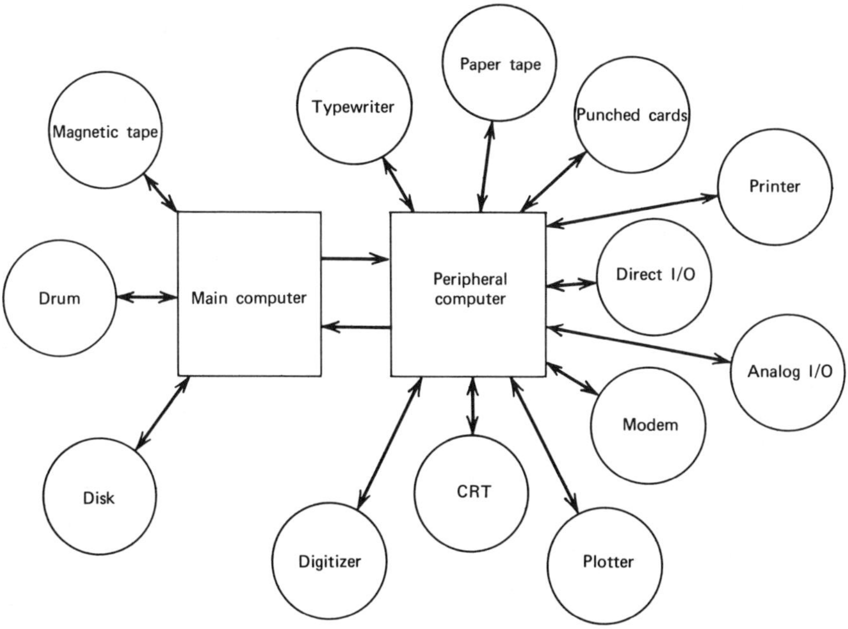

FIGURE 8-7. Division of input–output tasks between a large machine and its peripheral computer.

are instead connected to a small peripheral computer which is then connected to one of the I/O channels of the large machine. A typical configuration for a system incorporating a peripheral computer is illustrated in Figure 8-7. The division of the input–output tasks shown in the figure indicates that the only I/O devices which remain connected to the main computer are the magnetic tape, drum, and disk systems, and the peripheral computer.

In operation, under the supervision of the main computer, the peripheral machine executes I/O transfers to and from the I/O devices. It also transfers data to, and receives data from, the main computer. The data transfers between the two computers take place at a much higher speed than the I/O devices themselves are capable of. Thus, the peripheral computer acts as a buffering device which communicates at slow speed with the I/O devices and at high speed with the main computer.

Since the peripheral computer is capable of performing other tasks in addition to input–output, it can also be used to execute the code conversion routines, thereby increasing the overall efficiency of the system even further. As an example, the eighty-bit row code received from the card reader can first be converted into a twelve-bit column code. Then the twelve-bit code can be further converted into a byte-oriented code, such as ASCII, before being transferred to the large machine. For output, the code received from the main computer can be converted, if necessary, before being sent to its designated output device.

The magnetic tape, disk, and drum systems are connected to the large computer, since they are primarily high-speed devices used for auxiliary storage. Thus, data from the main computer memory is transferred to the auxiliary memory devices more efficiently if they are connected directly to the main computer. If the peripheral computer has need for auxiliary storage, it can transfer the data to one of the devices via the main computer memory. This procedure is very inefficient, since it ties up a portion of the main memory and also slows the operation of the large computer. An alternate method of transferring data between the peripheral computer and the auxiliary storage devices is by the use of the **channel-to-channel transfer.**

8.4 CHANNEL-TO-CHANNEL TRANSFERS

A peripheral computer which is connected to a large system may itself have need for an auxiliary storage device. However, it may not be economical to provide such a device for the peripheral computer, since adequate storage capacity is usually available in the auxiliary storage system of the large computer. The peripheral computer can therefore transfer data to or from the auxiliary storage device via the main computer memory. As pointed out earlier, this procedure is not very efficient. A method to bypass the large computer memory is provided for in some of the larger computers and is known as the channel-to-channel transfer.

In a machine which is able to implement this type of transfer, the channel serving the peripheral computer can be connected directly to another channel. A block transfer from the peripheral computer then proceeds directly to the device connected to the second channel. The main memory is bypassed in this mode of operation. Block transfers from the auxiliary storage device to the peripheral computer can be made to bypass the main computer memory in the same manner.

In operation, the peripheral computer sends its requests for a channel-to-channel transfer to the main computer. The large machine connects the channels together, and its I/O control supervises the complete transfer. Other than acting as a supervisor for the transfer, the main computer is not involved. Thus, it continues to operate in a manner which is virtually unaffected by the channel-to-channel transfer.

As we have seen, efficient operation of the input–output subsystem requires that the I/O devices be able to inform the computer of their current status. The simplest way to inform the computer of any change is to **interrupt** its operation whenever the change occurs. In Chapter 9, we describe the interrupt concept and show how it is implemented in the computer.

EXERCISES

8.1 Compare the merits of magnetic tape, disk, and drum systems. For what type of usage would each be preferred?

8.2 What is the difference between direct input–output and modem input–output?

8.3 Compare the plotter to the CRT as graphic output devices.

8.4 Compare the digitizer to the CRT light pen as graphic input devices.

8.5 What advantages does a character reader have over other input devices such as punched-card readers?

8.6 When is it advantageous to use a peripheral computer?

8.7 How does the ability to perform channel-to-channel transfers enhance the operation of a computer system?

9

INTERRUPT

During the execution of a program by the computer, many situations arise which require prompt attention. To ensure that such situations are dealt with efficiently, the execution of the current program is interrupted. The computer then proceeds to execute a program which determines the condition which caused the interrupt and deals with it accordingly. Unless a computer error or a programming error caused the interrupt, the execution of the original program can be resumed at the point of the interruption.

In this chapter we describe the interrupt system and how it operates. Methods for dealing with an interrupt which occurs while another interrupt is being serviced are also considered. In this connection, it is necessary to examine how the execution of an interrupted program can be resumed so that no errors are generated by the interruption procedure. We also describe some of the situations which occur and which are most easily taken care of by the interrupt procedure.

9.1 THE INTERRUPT SYSTEM

The interrupt system is implemented by the main control in conjunction with the interrupt status registers. Before executing each instruction of a program, the main control examines the interrupt status registers to determine if a situation exists which calls for an interrupt. If none exists, the instruction is executed in the usual manner. If an interrupt condition does exist, the main control instead executes a series of steps which are similar to a SAVE AND TRANSFER TO n instruction, where n is a predetermined fixed memory location. This procedure transfers control to a subroutine which is stored in the memory starting in location n. Either location n or a register is used to store the address of the instruction which would have been executed had the interrupt not occurred. The interrupt subroutine contains instructions which first save the contents of the accumulator and any other registers which contain data which is needed when the computer resumes the execution of the interrupted program. The subroutine then proceeds to examine the bits of the interrupt status registers to determine the cause of the interruption. Once the cause is isolated, another subroutine is executed which performs the tasks required to service the interrupt request. When these tasks are completed, the registers whose contents were saved are reloaded with the saved data. The execution of the original program is then resumed using the address which was saved when the interrupt occurred.

To determine the cause of an interrupt, the interrupt subroutine examines the bits stored in the interrupt status registers. The most convenient method of examining these bits is to load the contents of each of the interrupt status registers into the accumulator, and, if the accumulator is nonzero, locate the ONE bit corresponding to the interrupt condition by applying a shift and test procedure. An alternate procedure is to have each interrupt source cause a different interrupt subroutine to be executed by having the main control transfer to a different location in the memory for each interrupt. In the latter case, each interrupt source has its own service routine which is entered directly; thus, it is unnecessary to examine the interrupt status bits each time the computer is interrupted. As a result, a machine which incorporates this type of interrupt system operates more rapidly than a machine in which the interrupt status bits must be tested.

Many computers have interrupt systems which use a combination of the two interrupt systems just described. In these machines, the interrupt sources are divided into groups. Each group has its own interrupt subroutine, and, if more than one interrupt source belongs to a particular group, the corresponding interrupt status register bits are tested to determine the exact source of the interrupt. This type of interrupt system is a compromise; interrupt sources requiring rapid attention can be treated individually, while those with lower priority can be grouped together.

In many situations, the computer can be interrupted while it is servicing an interrupt. This type of operation allows interrupt requests which have a high priority to be serviced ahead of those with lower priority, regardless of which interrupt occurs first. We examine multiple interrupts and interrupt priority next (in Section 9.2). In Section 9.3, we discuss the interrupt sources themselves and point out which have need for high interrupt priority.

9.2 MULTIPLE INTERRUPTIONS

Whenever an interrupt occurs, we must ensure that the program being executed will be correctly resumed after the interrupt is serviced. For this purpose, it is necessary to save the address of the interrupted instruction, as well as the contents of the accumulator and any other registers containing data needed to resume the execution of the original program. If the interrupted program is itself an interrupt subroutine which is servicing a lower-priority interrupt, sufficient information must be saved so that the execution of the latter subroutine, and ultimately the execution of the original program, can be resumed. The same argument holds regardless of the number of interrupts which occur while an interrupt is being serviced.

In a computer where a different subroutine is used to service each interrupt source, it is a simple matter to ensure that the return addresses and the contents of the saved registers are stored in different memory locations so that they will be available when needed. In a machine where all the interrupt sources are serviced by a single subroutine, additional programming is required to ensure that the interrupted subroutines are correctly resumed. Provision must be made by the programmer to store the address of the interrupted instruction and the contents of the saved registers in different locations for each level of a multiple interrupt. This procedure ensures that the saved information will not be destroyed if another interrupt occurs during the execution of the interrupt subroutine.

In a computer where interrupt sources are grouped together, the subroutine which services the interrupt requests for a particular group cannot be interrupted by another interrupt request from the same group. This type of interrupt system is therefore similar to the system wherein each interrupt request is serviced by a different subroutine. To see why an interrupt request which is being serviced cannot be interrupted by another request from the same interrupt group, we must examine the priority scheme used with the interrupt system of a computer.

The priority interrupt system determines which interrupt sources are permitted to interrupt the machine while an interrupt is being serviced. Each interrupt source is assigned to a priority level; only interrupt requests from sources assigned to a higher priority level can interrupt the servicing of a particular interrupt source. Since sources which are grouped together are all assigned to the same level and have equal priority, they are not allowed to interrupt one another as we noted above. High-priority interrupt levels are assigned to requests, which, if delayed or interrupted, could have serious consequences. Several examples where high-priority interrupt requests are required are presented in Section 9.3.

While an interrupt is being serviced, all interrupt requests of equal or lower priority are lined up in a queue according to priority. As soon as the current interrupt request has been serviced, the highest-priority request in the queue is permitted to interrupt the machine.

A priority interrupt system can be implemented on a machine which uses a single subroutine to service all the interrupt requests. In this type of machine, the priority of each interrupt source determines the order in which the bits of the interrupt status registers are tested. The interrupt status bit corresponding to the device with the highest priority is tested first. Then, the bits corresponding to all lower-priority devices are tested sequentially in order of priority. Once an interrupt source is identified, all lower-priority interrupts are disabled so that they are not able to interrupt the machine. The method of disabling interrupts is described further in Section 9.4. Thus, a computer which uses a single subroutine to service all the interrupt requests requires a great deal more programming than either of the other machines described. Since delays can be encountered in the interrupt system of this type of machine, it is not used if rapid response by the interrupt system is needed.

The assignment of interrupt priorities can be made in several ways. In some computers, the priority of each interrupt source is wired into the machine by the manufacturer and cannot be changed by the programmer. To change the interrupt priorities in this type of machine, wiring changes must be made. In a machine with a single interrupt subroutine, the programmer can change the priority assigned to each interrupt source by changing the order in which the interrupt status bits are tested. Finally, there are some sophisticated computers which use different interrupt subroutines for each group of interrupt sources and still allow the programmer to change the priority of each interrupt source. In the latter type of machine, the interrupt priority is established by storing interrupt control information in a special register which has the same effect as wiring the priorities into the machine. To change the interrupt priorities, it is only necessary to change the control information.

We have described how the interrupt system operates. We now turn to the interrupt sources, themselves, and describe some of the conditions which require that the computer be interrupted.

9.3 SOURCES OF INTERRUPT REQUESTS

In this section, we include brief descriptions of several interrupt sources. The descriptions are not in order of priority, since the priority of a particular interrupt source is not the same for every computer system.

Power Failure. The electricity needed to operate the computer is usually supplied by the local power company via its existing power distribution system.

As a result, the computer is affected in the event of a local power failure. In a computer without provision for an orderly shutdown procedure during a power failure, data can be lost, erroneous information can be written into the memory, and other malfunctions can occur in the fraction of a second while power is being lost. To protect against such an occurrence, the voltage being supplied by the power company can be monitored continuously. If it drops to about 85% of its nominal value, the assumption is made that a power failure is occurring and an interrupt request is generated. If the power failure interrupt request is assigned the highest interrupt priority, there will be sufficient time for the computer to save the contents of all of its registers and shut itself down before a malfunction can occur. Then, when power is restored, the contents of the registers can be reloaded and operation resumed where it was interrupted. The restart procedure can be initiated by the operator or, in a computer provided with an automatic restart feature, it can take place automatically as soon as power is restored to the machine.

Real-Time Conditions. Computers are often used for control and monitoring of real-time industrial processes. A condition which is potentially costly or dangerous can often be averted if it is detected sufficiently far in advance of its occurrence for corrective action to be taken. A potentially dangerous situation can occur during the heating of a volatile chemical solution. The temperature of the solution is measured and the computer is interrupted if the temperature exceeds a preset level. The computer can then take suitable action to lower the temperature or perhaps even stop the process. By quickly reducing the temperature in this way, the risk of an explosion is minimized.

A potentially costly real-time situation can occur during the control of a machine tool by a computer. If an expensive part is being machined and the cutter breaks, both the part and the machine can be damaged. By detecting that tool breakage has occurred and putting the equipment in a standby mode, damage to the part and the machine can be prevented.

Input–Output. In the chapters on input–output (Chapters 7 and 8), we noted that the input–output devices provide the computer with status information. This information, which indicates that some form of input–output activity has taken place, can be used to interrupt the computer in order to expedite the necessary follow-up action required. When an output device which is connected to the I/O buss generates an interrupt request, the computer is informed that a previously initiated output transfer is complete and that the device is prepared to accept another output transfer. For an input device which is connected to the buss, an interrupt request signifies that a character has been transferred into the device and is waiting to be transferred to the accumulator. For an input–output device which is connected to an I/O channel, an interrupt signifies that a block transfer has been completed and another transfer can be initiated.

Other interrupt requests from the input–output subsystem inform the computer of error conditions. Both transfer and parity errors can occur during input or output, as described in Chapters 7 and 8. One type of transfer error results from the inability of the computer memory to supply data to or accept data from a synchronous device at a sufficiently high rate for correct operation. This type of error can often be eliminated by executing the block transfer a second time. The subroutine which services the transfer error interrupt request contains the necessary instructions for repeating the transfer. If repeated attempts to complete the transfer prove futile, the subroutine generates an error message for the programmer and terminates the execution of the program. For the magnetic tape, disk, and drum systems, another type of transfer error can occur wherein the length of the block in memory is not equal to the length of the record being transferred. This type of error is usually a programming error, and it is futile to attempt to correct it by repeating the transfer.

During an input or output transfer, a parity error occurs if a character or byte does not have correct parity. For some output devices, each character is read back and checked for correct parity immediately after being written. For parity errors which are detected during a write operation to one of these devices, no information is lost, and if the transfer is repeated by the interrupt subroutine, it will most likely be completed successfully. If a parity error occurs during a read operation, the transfer can be repeated by the interrupt subroutine in an attempt to read the data correctly.

Errors. Other errors which sometimes occur during the execution of a program are memory parity errors, system errors, and overflow. For detecting memory errors, a parity bit is provided for every word in the memory. When a memory malfunction occurs, one of the bits of a stored word is written into or read from the memory incorrectly. Thus, a ONE bit may inadvertently become a ZERO, or vice versa. In the event that this type of error occurs, the word read from memory will not have the correct parity. In this case, an interrupt is generated which causes the execution of the program to be terminated. If the program were not terminated, either incorrect data would be used in a calculation, or an instruction which differs from that intended by the programmer would be executed.

An error which occurs in a subsystem, such as the arithmetic unit, can also be detected and used to generate an interrupt request. The subroutine servicing this interrupt request either terminates the execution of the program or attempts to correct the error, if possible. Most system errors do result in termination of program execution.

An overflow error can also generate an interrupt request. Usually an overflow occurs because the programmer did not anticipate that a computed result would exceed the range of the machine. The overflow interrupt subroutine either terminates execution or provides a transfer to a user-supplied subroutine so that the execution of the program can be continued despite the overflow condition.

Clock. Two types of clocks are used in computer systems. One is a real-time clock which can be read by the computer to determine the actual time of day. This clock is used to keep a log of the time each job is started and completed. The other clock is an interval timer which can be used to interrupt the computer when a specified interval of time has elapsed. Both clocks are connected to the I/O buss. When an input transfer is executed from either type of clock, a number representing the clock setting is transferred into the accumulator. To set the interval timer, a number indicating the desired interval is loaded into the accumulator and transferred to the interval timer by an output transfer.

Both clocks can interrupt the computer. The real-time clock generates an interrupt request at a specific time of day. For example, if a particular program must be executed at approximately 4:30 in the afternoon, the clock is set to generate an interrupt at that time. The program to be executed at that time is then read in and executed by the computer. The interval timer, on the other hand, is set to a specific time interval, and generates an interrupt when the specified interval of time has elapsed. The interval timer is used when an operation must be performed for a specific length of time. For example, let us assume that during a chemical heating process, a chemical solution is to be held at a certain temperature for one minute. Once the required temperature is reached, the interval timer can be set to one minute and started. One minute later an interrupt informs the computer to proceed to the next processing step.

Protected Memory Violation – Privileged Instructions. In Section 6.7, on memory protection, we described how a programmer is prevented from writing information into that part of the memory which is reserved for supervisory programs and other users' programs. If an attempt is made by any program to write into a protected memory block, an interrupt request is generated, execution of the program is terminated, and an error message is produced.

A memory block is protected by executing a PROTECT MEMORY instruction, and protection is removed by executing an UNPROTECT MEMORY instruction. Provision must be made for allowing these instructions to be executed only by the supervisory programs of the computer. Otherwise, a programmer could arbitrarily remove protection from a memory area assigned to another user. Instructions in this category are called **privileged instructions** and cause the computer to be interrupted whenever they are used. The subroutine servicing the interrupt request must determine whether the privileged instruction is being executed by a supervisory program or a user program. In the latter case, program execution is terminated and an error message is sent to the programmer. We will see how the supervisory programs are able to execute privileged instructions in Section 9.4.

9.4 INTERRUPT CONTROL

While an interrupt request is being serviced, only requests of higher priority are permitted to interrupt the machine. To indicate that the servicing of an interrupt request has been completed, the request is turned off and an ENABLE INTERRUPT instruction is executed before the computer returns to the interrupted program. The request is turned off by setting the corresponding ONE bit in the interrupt register to a ZERO, using an instruction provided for this purpose. The ENABLE INTERRUPT instruction then restores the interrupt system to the state it was in before the machine was interrupted. If the computer is to resume servicing a lower-priority interrupt, only the interrupt levels above the one to be serviced should be enabled. To enable a particular set of interrupt levels, a binary code which specifies the levels to be enabled is included as part of the ENABLE INTERRUPT instruction. Thus, with suitable programming, it is possible to completely restore the status of the computer following an interrupt.

Whenever a program attempts to execute a privileged instruction, an interrupt request is generated. If the subroutine which services this interrupt request determines that the interrupt was generated by a supervisory routine, it returns control to the program without executing the ENABLE INTERRUPT instruction. The privileged instruction can then be executed without causing further interrupts. However, if the interrupt subroutine determines that the request was generated by a user's program, execution is terminated and an error message to the programmer is generated. This procedure allows the supervisory programs to execute privileged instructions, but prevents the users' programs from doing so. As a result, the supervisory programs have complete control over all operations involving privileged instructions and can prevent unauthorized use of the system by the user.

A DISABLE INTERRUPT instruction is provided to allow the supervisory programs to disable a specified interrupt level, thereby preventing devices connected to that level from generating interrupt requests. This instruction is also a privileged instruction and therefore cannot be executed by a user's program. The DISABLE INTERRUPT instruction is executed to prevent the computer from being interrupted by a request of lesser importance while executing a program which has a high priority in the system. It is sometimes necessary, however, to disable the interrupt requests from some sources but not from others which are connected to the same interrupt level. For this purpose, the computer is equipped with one or more **interrupt mask registers**. Each bit in an interrupt mask register corresponds to one of the interrupt sources. If a bit in the mask register is ZERO, the respective source is "masked out" and cannot interrupt the computer. If it is a ONE, it can cause an interrupt request if the priority level to which it belongs is enabled. A bit in a mask register is set to a ONE or a ZERO by a privileged instruction provided for that purpose.

We have described how memory blocks are protected and how tampering with the interrupt system is prevented. To protect data files stored in an auxiliary memory device and to prevent input and output data from being inadvertently destroyed, the START I/O instruction must be a privileged instruction, so that all input and output operations are controlled by the supervisory programs. The method whereby a user requests a supervisory program to execute an input or output transfer in its behalf is described in Chapter 11.

By proper use of the interrupt system, a computer can postpone the execution of one task to execute another. In one mode of operation, a clock interrupts the computer periodically so that the computer can divide its time among many tasks. Many users' programs are stored simultaneously in the computer, and the available execution time is shared by these programs. A system which implements this type of operation is known as a **time-sharing system**, which is the subject of Chapter 10.

EXERCISES

9.1 Describe the steps which occur during and immediately following a computer interrupt, including the steps which must be taken to ensure that the execution of the interrupted program is correctly resumed.

9.2 Why is it necessary to assign priorities to interrupt requests from different devices?

9.3 What is a privileged instruction, and why is it necessary for some instructions to be privileged?

9.4 What is the interrupt mask register, and how is it used?

10

TIME-SHARING SYSTEMS

There are several ways to operate a computing system. In the simplest case, the user has complete control over the machine and interacts with it through a typewriter, CRT, or other terminal. The major advantage of this type of operation is that output information is available to the user as soon as it is generated. The major disadvantage is that a high-speed computer may be restricted by how fast the user is able to feed it information.

Batch processing of computer programs overcomes this disadvantage. Programmers submit their programs and data, which are batched together and loaded onto a magnetic tape or disk. A small computer which is either a peripheral computer or a completely separate system is used to load the tape or disk. The computer then reads the programs from the tape or disk at high speed and executes them much more efficiently than in the simple case described above. Output data is written onto a tape or disk by the computer and printed using the same machine which was used to load the input. The batch processing system has the disadvantage that a user is unable to interact with the system. He must wait for the output to be printed to evaluate the results, and then completely resubmit the program and data in order to make even a simple change in either the program or the input data. Errors take much longer to correct in this type of system than in the single-user system.

In a third mode of operation, a single high-speed computer is connected to a number of input–output terminals, each consisting of a CRT or a typewriter, and is shared among the users of the terminals. If interrupt procedures are used to ensure that each user obtains a reasonable share of computer time, it can be made to appear to each user that he has complete control of the machine. Thus, the approach of **time-sharing** a single computer among many users possesses all the advantages of both the single user and the batch processing systems.

The time-sharing system just described is an **interactive** system, because the users interact directly with the machine. We use this type of time-sharing system as an example to illustrate how a time-sharing system operates. Descriptions of other time-sharing systems are also included in this chapter as are several related topics, such as program updating and system saturation.

10.1 OPERATION OF A TIME-SHARING SYSTEM

In a time-sharing system, the users' programs are stored in an auxiliary memory device such as the disk, and are transferred to the main memory for execution. To avoid delay while programs are being swapped between the main memory and the disk, a buffering procedure, such as described in Section 6.5, is employed. In the simplest case, the memory is divided into two parts. Program A, stored in one part of the memory, is executed until its execution is interrupted by the interval timer. Then program B, stored in the other part of the memory, is executed while program A is swapped for program C. During the swapping operation, program A is transferred to the disk and program C is transferred from the disk to the main memory. After another interval timer interrupt, execution of program C is initiated and programs B and D are swapped. This type of operation continues indefinitely, with each program being executed in turn. If another type of interrupt occurs during the execution of a program, it is processed in the usual manner, as described in Chapter 9. Thus, in a time-sharing system, the programs are actually executed piecemeal. This fact is not apparent to the user, however, since he obtains the same results regardless of how many times the execution of his program is interrupted. The interval timer is set so that execution of each program is resumed sufficiently often to ensure that the user actually has the sensation of interacting with the machine.

Several variations of this simple time-sharing system are in use. In the **multiprogramming** system, many users' programs are stored simultaneously in the main memory. In the **multiprocessing** system, more than one computer is used to process the users' programs. These two systems are described in Sections 10.2 and 10.3.

10.2 MULTIPROGRAMMING

In a multiprogramming system, many users' programs are located simultaneously in the main memory of the computer. A program whose execution is interrupted usually remains in the main memory until its execution is resumed. The amount of swapping which takes place between the main memory and the disk is therefore minimized, thereby increasing the overall efficiency of the system. As a result, more user terminals can be serviced by a multiprogrammed computer than by a similar-size time-sharing system of the type described in Section 10.1.

Each user's program requires a different amount of storage space in the main memory. Thus, if a memory block of fixed length were reserved for each user, short programs which did not use up their allocated block would cause memory space to be wasted, while long programs would not always fit into the allocated space. One easy way to solve this problem is to divide the memory into pages, as described in Chapter 6. Then we are free to use as many pages as necessary to store a program in the memory. At most, no more than one page is wasted in storing a program. Furthermore, in a program which uses page addressing, the actual page numbers can be left unspecified when the program is written. Then, when the program is loaded into the memory, the page numbers are automatically assigned, regardless of where the program is stored. As a result, a program can be stored in pages which are not adjacent to one another in the memory and still be executed correctly. One restriction must be placed on this system: At the time when a program is being loaded into the main memory, a sufficient number of unused pages must be available to store the program in its entirety.

10.3 THE TIME-SHARING MULTIPROCESSOR

In Chapter 6, we introduced the concept of a multiprocessing system and described its operation. When used as a time-sharing system, each of the computers within the multiprocessor system can be used to execute a particular program. In fact, it is possible for different parts of a single program to be executed by different computers. For example, after a segment of a program has been executed by computer A and interrupted by the interval timer, the program may be transferred to the disk. At some later time, the same program can be transferred from the disk to computer B and its execution resumed on the latter machine. In this type of multiprocessor, the auxiliary memory and I/O devices which are connected to the system can be used to transfer data to any of the main memory systems under the supervision of a common input–output control system.

As described in earlier chapters, memory protection in a time-sharing system is used to prevent a user program from accidentally writing into a region of the memory which is allocated to another user. Moreover, all input–output transfers are executed by a supervisory program, so that data files stored in the disk during a swapping operation are not accidentally destroyed. The protection of I/O files in a multiprocessor environment is complicated by the fact that several computers have access to each auxiliary storage and I/O device. A form of file protection is needed which is recognized by each of the computers. One way of providing positive file protection is to assign all I/O supervision to one of the computers. Transfers between one of the other computers and an auxiliary memory or I/O device is then initiated by the supervisory machine. The input–output system in this type of multiprocessor operates in a manner similar to the one described in Section 8.4 on channel-to-channel transfers. There, a peripheral computer was able to transfer data directly to or from an auxiliary memory device of the main computer under main computer supervision.

In an interactive time-sharing system, the programmer communicates with the computer via a **time-sharing terminal**, which usually consists of either a CRT or a typewriter. In Section 10.4, we describe how the terminal is used to communicate with the computer. We also describe the operation of the remote terminal and the communications processor which is used in many systems.

10.4 THE TIME-SHARING TERMINAL

Many time-sharing terminals can be connected simultaneously to a single time-sharing system. However, when a terminal is not in use, it is completely ignored by the system. When a programmer wishes to use a terminal, he initiates a sign-on procedure which interrupts the computer and activates the terminal. A typical sign-on sequence takes place as follows: The programmer turns on the power to the terminal and then depresses a special control character key which causes an interrupt request to be generated. When interrupted, the computer proceeds to execute a subroutine which initiates a series of input–output transfers to the terminal. These transfers constitute a brief interrogation of the programmer by the computer. He is asked to type an identification number which identifies him to the machine. If the identification number is not a valid one, the terminal is turned off. If it is a valid identification number, the programmer is allowed to proceed. After identifying his program and the programming language* he is using, the user can type or read his program into the system and request that the computer execute it. After execution, the results are printed or displayed and the programmer can make changes in the program and run it again, if necessary, or he can read in and execute another program. After he has completed using the system, he can request that his program be saved as a file stored on the disk. This procedure allows the programmer to use the program at a later date without the necessity of reading it into the machine again. He can request that the terminal be deactivated by typing a suitable phrase, such as GOOD-BYE, which the computer has been programmed to interpret as a sign-off message.

The operation of a remote terminal is similar to one which is connected directly to the machine. If a telephone line is connected permanently to each

* We describe programming languages in Chapter 11.

terminal, then operation is the same as described above. A modem is provided at each end of the line to properly connect the equipment together. If the connection between the terminal and the computer is via a dial-up telephone line, the sign-on procedure differs slightly. To sign-on, the telephone number assigned to the computer system is dialed by the user. The "ringing" causes the computer to be interrupted, and when the computer "answers the phone," the terminal is automatically connected to the system. The action of answering the phone consists of activating the modem which is connected to the line receiving the incoming call. The remainder of the sign-on and operating procedures are the same for this type of system, except that when the computer receives the message GOOD-BYE, it deactivates the modem. This has the effect of "hanging up," thereby freeing both that telephone line and its associated modem to accept a call from another user terminal.

Although the terminals can be serviced directly by the time-sharing computer, this mode of operation is very inefficient. Each input or output transfer consisting of a single character causes the computer to be interrupted. With a large number of terminals connected to the system, the number of interrupts can increase to the point where the system is significantly slowed down by the input—output and interrupt subsystems. To prevent such a situation from occurring, a peripheral computer called a **communications processor** is used. The task of the communications processor is to accept the character-by-character input transfers from each terminal and assemble them into blocks of data. The assembled blocks are then transferred at high speed to the time-sharing system. For output, blocks of data are transferred from the large system to the communications processor, which transfers the data in a character-by-character mode to the terminals. Thus, the time-sharing computer is virtually relieved of the responsibility of performing input—output transfers to the terminals and can concentrate on executing the programs themselves.

10.5 LARGE-SCALE TIME-SHARING SYSTEMS

In a large-scale time-sharing system, other programs are executed by the system in addition to those which originate at the interactive terminals. For example, the computer may also control a real-time process such as the operation of an assembly line or chemical plant. For this application, a higher priority is assigned to the real-time process than to the interactive terminals. This high priority ensures that the needs of the real-time process are fulfilled as quickly as possible even if the programmers using the interactive terminals experience a delay in the execution of their programs. Batch processing of programs can also be implemented on a time-sharing system. In this case, the program being executed in the batch mode can be treated as if it originated from a terminal. As before, if a real-time process is controlled by the system, it is assigned a higher priority.

In an interactive time-sharing system, the computer can often complete all of its current tasks. The machine then executes a **wait loop** until it is interrupted to execute a program. The wait loop consists of one or two instructions which accomplish nothing. For example, a suitable wait loop is provided by the instruction

m TRANSFER TO m

which is executed continually until an interrupt occurs. The interrupt causes control to be transferred to a subroutine which determines the cause of the interrupt and proceeds to service it. In a system which includes batch processing, the computer executes programs in the batch mode while waiting for a task to originate from the interactive or real-time parts of the system. Thus, only if no batch programs remain to be executed, does the computer enter the wait loop. As a result, this type of system is more efficient than one without provision for batch processing.

Since a time-sharing system must always be available for use, the computer cannot be stopped to make procedural changes. Provision must therefore be made for changing or **updating** the system while it is operating. It is also important that the system not require that the user of an interactive terminal wait an excessive length of time for a response from the machine. Excessive delays occur whenever the work load presented to the computer is so great that the system becomes saturated. The problems associated with updating the system and saturation and how they are solved are presented in Section 10.6.

10.6 MAINTAINING A TIME-SHARING SYSTEM

The user of a time-sharing system should not be concerned with the scheduling of computer time. The machine should be available for use around the clock. As a result, updating of the supervisory programs should not require the operation of the machine to be curtailed in any way. Let us consider how an interrupt service subroutine can be updated without disrupting the system.

We assume that the computer manufacturer has supplied the system operator with an improved version of an interrupt subroutine and that the new program is thoroughly tested and operates properly. Using an updating program, the subroutine is first transferred to the disk or to another auxiliary memory device. Then the program notifies the supervisory programs of the pending change. The computer is interrupted, but before proceeding to make the change, the status of all interrupt sources is checked. If the subroutine being changed does not affect any current interrupt requests, then the new subroutine is transferred into the machine from the disk. The machine is then restored to its previous state so that it can continue to serve its users. The complete updating procedure need take only a fraction of a second so that the users are unaware of its having been executed. Other system changes are made in a similar manner.

In order for the programmer to interact with the system as if he were the only user, he should not have to wait long for its response. If the number of users is large compared to the capability of the system, it can become saturated. In this case, no matter how the jobs are divided, the users will always have to wait. To improve the response of the system, a communications processor can be used to reduce the input–output load on the main machine. If the system is still saturated, a second computer can be added to the system, converting it into a multiprocessing system. Either the computers can share the work load evenly, or, if one is larger than the other, the larger computer can execute the users' programs while the smaller one performs the supervisory functions. If the system still remains saturated, then the number of terminals can either be reduced, or an additional computer added to the multiprocessing system.

Throughout the book, we have discussed the programs which are executed by the computer. In contrast to the machine itself, which consists of electronic **hardware**, the programs are called **software**. The software associated with a particular computer installation consists of the supervisory routines, the users' programs, and a number of other types of programs commonly used during the operation of a computer. We describe computer software in Chapter 11.

EXERCISES

10.1 Compare batch processing with interactive time-sharing. What advantages do each of these methods of operating a computer system have?

10.2 What is the difference between multiprogramming and multiprocessing?

10.3 What is a communications processor, and how is it used?

10.4 How does a time-sharing system become saturated? What are the symptoms of a saturated system? What can be done to a time-sharing system to prevent it from becoming saturated?

11

SOFTWARE

The software provided by the manufacturer as part of a computer system is as important to the user as the hardware. A typical software "package" consists of a set of translation programs, library subroutines, and supervisory programs. The user prepares programs in a programming language as described in Section 11.1, and a translation program automatically converts the program into the binary machine language used by the computer. If a program requires the computation of a commonly used function, such as a square root or a sine, a library subroutine is automatically incorporated into the program. The user is therefore not required to write the programs to calculate square roots, sines, or other such functions. The supervisory programs completely oversee every operation performed by the computer. Under the control of supervisory programs, the user's program is translated, loaded into the computer, and executed. In a time-sharing system, the computer is automatically shared among the users under the control of a supervisory routine. Finally, in the event of an error condition, the interrupt subroutines, which are part of the supervisory programs, determine what corrective action should be taken. If the error is caused by the user, the execution of the program can be terminated.

In this chapter, we first describe the types of programming languages which are available to the user. Then, the system software used during the operation of a computer is presented.

11.1 PROGRAMMING LANGUAGES

We have introduced two types of computer languages in this book: **machine language**, which consists of a sequence of bits for each instruction; and **assembly language**, which is more like English, and consists of a complete phrase for each instruction. For example, as presented in Chapters 1 and 2, LOAD ACC, 22 is an assembly language instruction whose corresponding machine language instruction is

011 000 00 0001 0110

Other programming languages which use simple algebraic or English language **statements** have been devised. These languages, which are called **compiler languages**, are procedure-oriented rather than machine-oriented. For example, the algebraic statement

$$A = B + C$$

causes the numbers stored in memory locations B and C to be added together and stored in location A. Three assembly language instructions,

```
LOAD ACC, C
FLOATING ADD, B
STORE ACC, A
```

are required to implement the single statement A = B + C in a compiler language. The relative simplicity of writing a program in a compiler language can be better appreciated by noting that the single statement

```
A=B+C/D–F*G+H**5–J*M
```

which is of moderate complexity, requires at least nineteen assembly language instructions for implementation. This statement, which is typical of an arithmetic statement in a compiler language, computes the function

$$A = B + \frac{C}{D} - (F \times G) + H^5 - (J \times M)$$

Thus, it is far simpler for the programmer to write an algebraic statement in a compiler language than to write the equivalent set of assembly language instructions. A detailed description of even a single compiler language is beyond the scope of this book. However, for illustration, we will describe the equivalent of the test instruction as well as how to set up a loop in the FORTRAN compiler language.

In FORTRAN, the test statement takes the general form

$$\text{IF (EXPRESSION) } m_1, m_2, m_3$$

When this statement is encountered, the EXPRESSION within the parentheses is first evaluated. Then, statement* m_1, m_2, or m_3 is executed next, depending on whether the EXPRESSION is negative, zero, or positive, respectively. For example, the statement

```
IF(20*Z-5*X+Y) 120, 180, 250
```

transfer control to statement 120 if $20Z - 5X + Y < 0$, to statement 180 if $20Z - 5X + Y = 0$, or to statement 250 if $20Z - 5X + Y > 0$. In assembly language, it is necessary to explicitly write the instructions to form the function $20Z - 5X + Y$ and to test it. The assembly language program

```
LOAD ACC, Z                  Z
FLOATING MULTIPLY, (4)       4Z
FLOATING SUBTRACT, X         4Z - X
FLOATING MULTIPLY, (5)       5(4Z - X)
FLOATING ADD, Y              20Z - 5X + Y
IF ACC=-, TRANSFER TO a
IF ACC=0, TRANSFER TO b
IF ACC=+, TRANSFER TO c
```

is therefore equivalent to the single compiler test statement

IF(20*Z–5*X+Y) m_1, m_2, m_3

The contents of the accumulator, after the completion of each step of the program, is shown alongside the instructions in the example.

To set up a loop in FORTRAN, a DO statement is used. An example of such a statement is DO 200 I=1, 80. In this example, I is first set to 1, and each statement following the DO statement, up to and including statement 200, is executed. Then I is tested, and if it is less than 80, I is incremented, and the statements following the DO statement are again executed. When the test indicates that I = 80, the statement following statement 200 is executed next. An example of a DO loop which computes the sum of the eighty numbers stored in locations† A(1), A(2), . . ., A(80) is

```
      S=O
      DO 200 I=1, 80
200   S=S+A(I)
```

To avoid adding the previous contents of memory location S to the sum, S is first set to zero. Then for each value of I, the number stored in location A(I) is

* In FORTRAN, an arbitrary number can be assigned to a statement for identification. This number is not related to either a memory address or the number of statements in the program.

† The FORTRAN notation A(1), A(2), A(3), . . ., A(79), A(80) defines the memory locations A, A + 1, A + 2, . . ., A + 78, A + 79, respectively.

added to the contents of location S, and the result is stored back in location S. When the DO loop is completed, memory location S contains the correct sum.

Regardless of whether a program is written in assembly language or in one of the many compiler languages, it must be translated into machine language before it can be executed. This task is accomplished by a translation program, as described in Section 11.2.

11.2 TRANSLATORS

A **translator** is a program which converts an assembly language or a compiler language program into machine language instructions. The two types of translators are respectively called **assemblers** and **compilers**. When the user wishes to have a program translated, he must tell the computer which language he used when he wrote the program. The corresponding translation program is then read into the machine from an auxiliary storage device and executed.

Under the control of the translation program, the program to be translated is read into the computer and analyzed. Memory locations are assigned to variables; instructions and statements are converted into suitable binary codes;

```
A      VAR                        1   ---
B      VAR                        2   ---
C      VAR                        3   ---
D      VAR                        4   ---
.       .                         .    .
.       .                         .    .
.       .                         .    .
       LDA   C                   50   6003
       ADD   B                   51   2002
       STA   A                   52   6801
       IAP   NEXT                53   8437
       STA   D                   54   6804
NEXT   LIX   A         ILLEGAL   55   ---
```

```
VAR   VARIABLE ASSIGNMENT
LDA   LOAD ACC
ADD   ADD
STA   STORE ACC
IAP   IF ACC= +, TRANSFER TO
LDX   LOAD  INDEX
```

FIGURE 11-1. Example of the output of an assembler.

and, certain types of errors are found and noted. An example of the printed output of an assembler is shown in Figure 11-1. The first three columns are directly reproduced from the user's program by the computer. The remaining columns are supplied by the assembler program. Note that the machine language code is printed in hexadecimal rather than in binary. Mnemonics, such as LDA, are used to reduce the amount of typing which is required of the programmer. The instruction which is equivalent to each mnemonic used is shown in the figure. The VAR mnemonic is used to assign memory locations to the variables A, B, C, and D. For the IAP instruction, the programmer has used the symbolic address NEXT rather than an absolute address. The assembler automatically inserts the binary code for the address of the instruction identified by the symbolic address NEXT into the IAP instruction when it is translated. The use of symbolic addresses, such as NEXT, simplifies the writing of programs in assembly language. Since LIX is not a valid mnemonic, LDX being intended, the assembler prints the error message ILLEGAL.

The machine language instructions produced by the assembler are stored in an auxiliary storage device until the translation of the program is completed. It can then be punched onto cards or paper tape and saved for later use. If desired by the programmer, it can also be read into the computer and executed. Execution is attempted only if no errors are found during the translation. If, when the program is executed, it does not operate properly, the programmer can use the assembler printout as an aid in locating his programming errors.

The printed output produced by a compiler does not usually contain the machine language code for each instruction. These codes are not meaningful to a programmer who is not familiar with the assembly language or machine language of the particular computer being used. The printout does contain error messages and a listing or **map** of key storage locations. The map is helpful when a programmer is attempting to find a fault in his program which caused an error during its execution. The supervisory program which terminates execution of the user's program in case of an error prints the location of the instruction which caused the error. By referring to the map, the programmer can narrow down the cause of the error to at most a handful of statements. Moreover, if he requests a printout of the memory whenever an error occurs, he can determine the values of all variables at the time of the error, since the map tells him where each variable is stored. As in the case of the assembler, the machine language cade produced by the compiler is stored in an auxiliary storage device as it is generated. When the complete program has been compiled, the programmer can request that it be executed if there are no errors. He can also request the computer to punch the machine language cade onto cards or paper tape so that it can be saved for later use.

The program which reads the machine language code produced by an assembler or compiler into the computer for execution is called a **loader**. The loader also reads **library subroutines** into the computer if they are needed by the program being loaded. The loader is the subject of Section 11.3, which includes a description of how the computer library is used.

11.3 THE LOADER AND LIBRARY

The loader reads the machine language code produced by the translator into the computer for execution. In so doing, the loader must store each instruction in its intended memory location. A **loading address** is included with each block of machine language code produced by the translator to inform the loader where each instruction should be stored. After the program is loaded, the loader transfers control to the program, causing it to be executed. Since the first instruction to be executed need not be stored in the first memory location occupied by the program, the loader is supplied an **execution address** by the translator. The format of a program which has been translated into machine language and is ready for loading is illustrated in Figure 11-2.

In the example shown in Figure 11-2, the first two words supplied to the loader are the loading address 16 and the block size 32, respectively. Thus, the next thirty-two words are stored by the loader in memory locations 16–47. Examining the next two words, the loader obtains a loading address of 512 and a block size of 512. Thus, the next 512 words are stored in memory locations 512–1023 by the loader. The most significant bit of the next word of the program is a ONE bit, which tells the loader that the remaining fifteen bits of this word should be used as the execution address and not as another loading

Program	Explanation
0000 0000 0001 0000	Loading address (16)
0000 0000 0010 0000	Block size (32)
– – – – – – – – – – – –	Machine language instructions to be stored in memory locations 16–47
0000 0010 0000 0000	Loading address (512)
0000 0010 0000 0000	Block size (512)
– – – – – – – – – – – –	Machine language instructions to be stored in memory locations 512–1023
1000 0010 1000 0000	Leading ONE signifies execution address (640) instead of loading address

FIGURE 11-2. Format of a machine language program which is ready to be loaded into the computer for execution.

address. The loader then executes a TRANSFER TO 640 or equivalent instruction so that the loaded program is executed by the computer.

In Chapter 2, we described the use of the SAVE AND TRANSFER instruction for transferring control to a user-supplied subroutine. Library subroutines are usually stored in an auxiliary memory device and read into the computer by the loader when needed. Therefore, the location of a library subroutine in the memory is not known until after the program and the subroutine are loaded. As a result, the assembler cannot supply the address for the SAVE AND TRANSFER instruction when it translates the instruction into machine language. A method has been devised whereby the address of a library subroutine can be supplied by the loader immediately after the program and the subroutine are loaded into the computer. When writing a program in assembly language, the programmer requests a transfer to a library subroutine by inserting the **name** of the subroutine into the program as part of a SAVE AND TRANSFER instruction. An example of a request for the SIN subroutine is given by SAVE AND TRANSFER TO* SIN. As described in Chapter 2, the use of the asterisk indicates that an indirect address is intended. During translation, the assembler assigns an address in the memory to the SAVE AND TRANSFER instruction, but leaves the contents of the corresponding memory location blank. Instead, it prepares a directive to the loader, instructing it to store the address of the SIN subroutine in the blank memory location after the subroutine is loaded. We will illustrate this concept of **linking** a program with a subroutine with a specific example.

Let us assume that memory location 5 is selected by the assembler for the linking procedure. The assembler then translates the SAVE AND TRANSFER TO* SIN instruction as if it were SAVE AND TRANSFER TO* 5. If, when loaded, the SIN subroutine is stored in the memory starting at location 5627, then the address 5627 is stored in memory location 5 by the loader. When executed, the SAVE AND TRANSFER TO* 5 instruction is therefore equivalent to SAVE AND TRANSFER TO 5627 and so correctly transfers control to the SIN subroutine. Any number of subroutines in the library can be incorporated into a user's programs in this manner. A separate memory location is used for linking each subroutine, but every SAVE AND TRANSFER instruction which refers to a particular subroutine can be assigned the same linking address.

The operation of the computer is the same whether a subroutine is requested by an assembly language program or by a compiler language program. In a compiler language program, however, a statement such as Y=SIN(X) is used to indicate the requirement for a library subroutine. This type of statement is translated as if it were equivalent to

```
LOAD ACC, X
SAVE AND TRANSFER TO* SIN
STORE ACC, Y
```

The operation of the loader, as described above, stores the users' programs into fixed memory locations, but stores library subroutines, or **relocates** them, wherever there are a sufficient number of memory locations available. Some loaders are able to relocate the users' programs as well and are therefore called **relocatable** loaders. In order to relocate a program in the memory, memory references must be changed by the loader so that the new addresses conform to the new memory locations. This procedure consists of adding a fixed **relocation constant** to each absolute address during loading. In addition, in a computer which also uses page addressing, the page numbers in the SET PAGE instructions, whose use was described in Chapter 6, must also be changed. In a computer which uses relative addressing, rather than page addressing, no changes need be made to the relative address memory references; the relocated instructions are still stored in locations which bear the same relation to each other, regardless of where they are stored in the memory. In a machine which uses a relocatable loader, the translators include a short directive with each address to inform the loader whether the address should be relocated or not. Similarly, all references to page numbers are also identified for the loader so that they can be properly assigned during loading. In a time-sharing system using page addressing, the use of a relocatable loader is a prerequisite if a program is to be loaded into nonadjacent pages as described in Chapter 10.

The supervisory programs which we have described thus far are used to prepare the user's program for execution. The translator converts the program into machine language instructions, and the loader reads these instructions into the memory for execution. The **operating monitor**, which is described next and which includes the interrupt subroutines, is a set of supervisory programs which oversees the operation of the computer at all times.

11.4 THE OPERATING MONITOR

The loader and translator programs are stored in an auxiliary storage device and transferred into the computer when called for. The operating monitor, however, is loaded into the computer once, and thereafter remains in the memory throughout the operation of the machine, thereby enabling it to oversee every operation performed by the computer. Most of the programs in the monitor are activated by the interrupt subsystem. When an interrupt occurs, control is transferred to a subroutine in the monitor, which determines the cause of the interrupt request and services it. The details of the operation of the interrupt subroutines were presented in Chapter 9.

A monitor subroutine can also be activated by a suitable SAVE AND TRANSFER instruction which the user inserts into his program. This approach enables input–output transfers to be executed in a computer whose I/O instructions are privileged. Information which specifies the type of transfer, the

I/O device, and other pertinent details about the transfer is first stored by the user's program in several reserved memory locations whose addresses are known by the monitor. Control is then transferred to the monitor via the SAVE AND TRANSFER instruction. The input–output subroutine in the monitor examines the stored information; and if it determines that the requested transfer is legitimate, it proceeds to execute it. However, if the requested transfer is not legitimate because it may destroy useful information, execution of the user's program is terminated. An error message is provided by the monitor to inform the user that an illegal I/O transfer was attempted.

Another subroutine which is often provided in the monitor allows certain interrupts to be disabled. For example, a programmer may anticipate that an overflow could occur during the execution of his program. He can therefore request that the overflow interrupt be disabled by the monitor. Having done this, he must be certain to insert the necessary instructions in his program to test for the overflow condition. This procedure provides the programmer with the ability to take suitable corrective action in the event that an overflow occurs during the execution of his program. If the same program were executed in the usual manner, the overflow would produce an interrupt which would cause the monitor to terminate execution, and no corrective action would be attempted.

Computers can be designed in several different ways. In one commonly used **approach**, the operations which must be carried out to execute each instruction are built into the machine. In another approach, only the operations needed to execute a small basic set of instructions are built into the machine. The other instructions are built up from this basic instruction set by a technique known as **microprogramming**. The microprogrammed computer has several advantages over its conventional counterpart as we see in Chapter 12.

EXERCISES

11.1 What is the difference between machine language, assembly language, and compiler language?

11.2 What is a translator? What are the different types of translators called and what is each used for?

11.3 What is a loader?

11.4 How are library subroutines incorporated into a user's program?

11.5 What is a relocatable loader, and what advantages does it have over an absolute loader?

11.6 What is the operating monitor?

12

MICROPROGRAMMING

A subroutine, as we indicated in Chapter 2, is a self-contained program which can be executed by a user's program whenever it is needed. In most computers, subroutines are available for calculating functions such as square roots, sines, and arctangents. In some computers, subroutines are used to implement instructions for operations which are not built into the machine. In a fixed-point computer, for example, subroutines are often available for performing floating-point arithmetic. The difference between performing floating-point arithmetic on a fixed-point machine and on a floating-point machine lies only in how the machine is used; the numerical results obtained by either method should be the same. The reader will recall that a floating-point operation can be broken down into a set of fixed-point operations on the fraction and exponent parts of the number. In a floating-point computer, the operations for manipulating the parts of a floating-point number are built into the machine; in a fixed-point computer, they are programmed as instructions of a subroutine.

Some small fixed-point computers do not have built-in instructions for performing multiplication or division. In these machines, subroutines can be used to implement the MULTIPLY and DIVIDE instructions. The operations which are programmed as instructions in the multiplication and division subroutines are described in detail in Chapter 3.

Thus, even in a computer with an extremely limited set of instructions, very sophisticated programs can be executed as long as subroutines are written to implement the more elaborate operations. That even the most sophisticated computer need have only a minimal instruction set is the basis for the

microprogramming concept. Instead of using subroutines to implement more complex instructions, **microprograms** are used. In some computers, the microprograms cannot be altered during the operation of the machine; these are called **fixed microprogrammed** computers. However, in other computers, the microprograms can be changed during operation; these are called **dynamic microprogrammed** machines. In this chapter, we describe these two concepts in detail.

12.1 FIXED MICROPROGRAMMING

The block diagram of a fixed microprogrammed computer is shown in Figure 12-1. The basic computer contains an arithmetic unit, a main control unit, an input–output control, and a set of registers. It is capable of directly executing a very limited set of instructions called **micro-instructions.** Examples of the type of micro-instructions which are built into the basic machine are shown in Table 12-1. The **read-only memory** is a high-speed memory containing a fixed set of subroutinelike microprograms written in the micro-instruction language. The microprograms contained in the read-only memory cannot be changed by the computer as can the programs contained in the main memory. A complete microprogram consisting of a set of micro-instructions is read from the read-only memory and executed to implement each instruction of a program which is stored in the main memory.

TABLE 12-1. Examples of Micro-Instructions

ADD	READ MEMORY
SUBTRACT	WRITE MEMORY
COMPLEMENT	TEST
AND	SHIFT
OR	LOAD REGISTER

To illustrate how a microprogrammed computer operates, let us examine how the instruction ADD, n is executed. The ADD micro-instruction is simply a command which instructs the arithmetic unit to perform addition and so cannot be used directly. It is first necessary to obtain the operand from location n in the memory using the READ MEMORY micro-instruction. Thus, the execution of the ADD, n instruction requires that a microprogram be read from the read-only memory and executed. An example of a set of micro-instructions for the ADD, n microprogram is

```
LOAD REGISTER M FROM IRAD
READ MEMORY
ADD
```

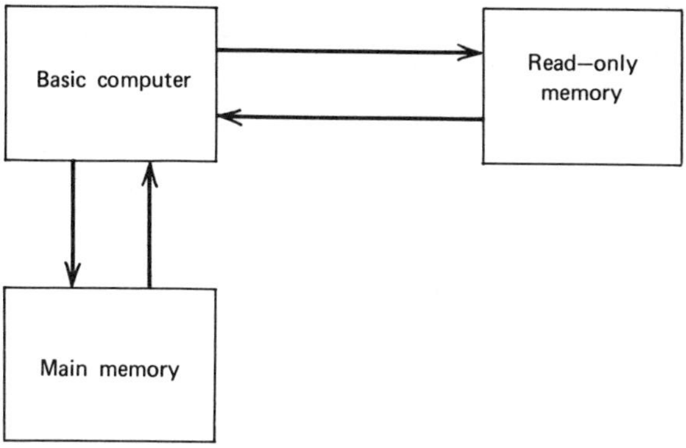

FIGURE 12-1. Block diagram of a fixed microprogrammed computer.

The LOAD REGISTER micro-instruction takes the address n from the address part AD of the instruction register IR and puts it into the memory address register M. the READ MEMORY instruction reads the contents of memory location n, as specified by the M register, and puts it into a buffer register. The ADD micro-instruction causes the operand to be added into the accumulator from the buffer register. For simplicity, the micro-instructions used for providing address modification such as indexing, have been omitted, as have the micro-instructions for causing the next instruction in the main memory to be read and executed.

Other instructions are implemented in a similar manner, although the microprograms are generally more complex. For example, to execute the MULTIPLY, n instruction, the following microprogram is executed from the read-only memory: The address n is loaded into the M register and the operand read from the memory into the buffer register. The signs of the multiplier in the accumulator and the multiplicand in the buffer register are tested, and if either number is negative, it is complemented. A sign indicator bit is set to ONE if only one of the two numbers is negative. Then a sequence of TEST, ADD, and SHIFT micro-instructions are executed. As a result, the most significant bit of the multiplier is tested. If it is a ONE, the multiplicand is added to the accumulator B register. The accumulator A and B registers are both shifted left by one bit position, and the process is repeated for each of the remaining bits of the multiplier to form the product. Finally, if the sign indicator bit is a ONE, the product is complemented. These steps were described in detail in Chapters 3 and 5.

Although the same steps are executed in a microprogrammed computer as in a conventional computer, the former machine is "designed" using programming techniques rather than logic design techniques. Thus, microprogramming allows the same basic computer to be used in machines with different instruction sets by simply supplying a different read-only memory with the computer. That is, one machine can be provided with a read-only memory containing floating-point microprograms, while another is provided with a read-only memory containing double-precision fixed-point microprograms in place of, or in addition to, the floating-point microprograms. The manufacturer of such a system has great flexibility, since he does not have to maintain a large inventory of different computers. He merely plugs the appropriate read-only memory into the basic machine before it is shipped to his customer.

The user of the fixed microprogrammed machine is unable to distinguish between this type of computer and the more conventional type in normal operation. However, if he should want to upgrade his machine to a model containing a more elaborate instruction set, the difference becomes apparent. In the conventional machine, modifications to upgrade its performance are extremely difficult to implement and may even require the computer to be shipped back to the manufacturer. The microprogrammed computer, on the other hand, can be modified by simply replacing the read-only memory with a different one. In practice, this can usually be accomplished in a relatively short time at the user's facility.

If the read-only memory is replaced by a high-speed read–write memory, then the microprograms can be changed during the operation of the computer. This type of microprogrammed machine is described next.

12.2 DYNAMIC MICROPROGRAMMING

As long as the microprograms in the high-speed read–write memory are not changed, the operation of a dynamic microprogrammed computer does not differ from its fixed microprogrammed counterpart. However, the potential advantages of dynamic microprogramming cannot be fully realized unless the ability to change the microprograms is exploited. As an example of how the dynamic microprogramming feature can be used, let us examine a system for which two sets of microprograms are available. One of the sets of microprograms is used for ordinary operation of the machine. It implements an extremely sophisticated set of instructions which takes full advantage of the potential of the hardware. Let us assume that the other set of microprograms implements the instruction set of another computer. Thus, programs which are written using the instruction set of the latter computer can be executed on the dynamic microprogrammed system. Because the dynamic microprogrammed computer can execute the programs written for another computer, the replacement of the latter computer with a dynamic microprogrammed system is simplified. Existing programs which were written for the machine being replaced can be executed on the new machine without being rewritten. Moreover, new programs can be written in the more sophisticated language for execution on the same machine. As a result, the changeover from one computer system to another can be accomplished smoothly, and the full potential of the new machine realized immediately.

When operating a system with two or more sets of microprograms, provision must be made for changing the microprograms in the high-speed memory. The most straightforward way of making this change is to do it manually; that is, whenever the microprograms are to be changed, the computer is halted and the operator initiates the required operations by actuating an appropriate sequence of switches. This action results in the transfer of the desired set of microprograms from an auxiliary storage device to the high-speed memory. In addition, the operating monitor which is stored in the main memory must also be changed because a monitor written in the instruction set of one machine cannot be used with any other set of instructions. The new monitor can be read into the main memory from an auxiliary storage device at the same time that the new microprograms are read in. The operator then restarts the machine, and it will operate in the correct manner.

Halting the machine to convert from one set of instructions to another is very inefficient from the standpoint of computer utilization. Therefore, special input—output instructions are provided so that a new set of microprograms can be read into the high-speed memory automatically. Each program which is to be executed by the computer contains a directive which the monitor uses to determine which language is needed for proper execution of the program. Whenever the monitor determines that the microprograms should be changed, it executes a subroutine which performs the required transfers. This subroutine must be compatible with both instruction sets so that the computer can continue to operate properly during the changeover. A potential dilemma exists during the changeover because the monitor must itself be changed under the control of its own subroutine. We cannot resolve this dilemma, since the details depend intimately upon both the machine itself and the languages being interchanged. Moreover, before the changeover can be initiated, all interrupts must be disabled and the machine brought to a state from which normal execution can be easily resumed. If an interrupt were allowed during the changeover, it might cause the computer to attempt to execute an interrupt subroutine written in one language at a time when the high-speed memory contains the microprograms for executing another language.

One advantage of the dynamic microprogrammed computer lies in its ability to implement the language of another machine. Programs written for the other system can be executed with relative ease and do not require expensive reprogramming. Another advantage lies in the ability of a user to write his own microprograms. Although writing the microprograms for a complete instruction set is not a recommended practice, there are occasions when modifications to a set of microprograms can be advantageous. For example, let us assume that the computer is used for performing a real-time task which, when it generates an interrupt, requires both rapid response by the machine and extensive computation. Although the computer may be capable of providing such action, it may tie up the system excessively while the subroutine servicing the real-time task is being executed. During the execution of the interrupt subroutine, each instruction of the subroutine is read from the main memory and causes a set of micro-instructions to be executed. If the equivalent set of micro-instructions were written into the high-speed memory so that they formed a single microprogram, the resulting microprogram would then be executed in response to a single instruction read from the main memory. Thus, the need to read and interpret a large number of conventional instructions from the relatively slow main memory is eliminated, and the real-time situation is thereby dealt with in a much more efficient manner. Special-purpose instructions, such as the one we have just described, can also be added to the read-only memory of a fixed microprogrammed machine, but extensive wiring changes to the read-only memory are required in this case. In the dynamic microprogrammed machine, however, the addition of a special-purpose instruction requires only that an additional microprogram be read into the high-speed memory.

The usefulness of a computer lies in the ability of the software to cause the computer to perform the tasks required of it for any given application. The software described in Chapter 11 is needed for the computer to function properly and to aid the user in writing and executing his programs. The users' programs are oriented toward solving problems for specific applications. In Chapter 13, we briefly examine some of the applications of computers.

EXERCISES

12.1 What is the difference between a subroutine and a microprogram?

12.2 Compare fixed microprogramming and dynamic microprogramming.

12.3 If a computing system is to be updated by the installation of a new computer, what benefits will the new system have if the new machine is a dynamic microprogrammed computer?

13

APPLICATIONS OF COMPUTERS

As we have seen, the digital computer can manipulate large quantities of information and can also perform logic and arithmetic at high speed. Thus, in addition to solving problems requiring a great deal of arithmetic capability, computers are used as controllers, in business applications, for simulation, as a design aid, and in the field of education. In this chapter, we present examples of how computers are used for each of these applications.

13.1 SCIENTIFIC CALCULATIONS

The ability to perform over a million arithmetic operations in one second makes the computer an indispensable tool in virtually every scientific discipline. The engineer uses it as a design aid and to perform extensive analysis tasks which would otherwise not be feasible. The physicist and chemist use computers to evaluate complex equations which lead to the verification of new theories. The statistician is able to compile accurate statistics using large volumes of data which would be impossible to process manually. A list of the types of computational problems for which computers can be used is endless. We will provide an example which illustrates the power of the computer for performing scientific calculations.

In the design of a large bridge, several thousand steel beams and other structural members are used. The engineer must not only compute the size and position of each member but also the stress it must withstand. A bridge can be subjected to a variety of loading conditions which depend on the traffic, wind, and temperature conditions. Thus, to achieve a good design, the stress in each beam must be checked for each of several extreme loading conditions. Evaluation of these stresses requires hundreds of calculations for each of the members or well over one million calculations. Thus, to verify the design of a bridge could take several man-years of effort. However, once a program is written to perform the necessary calculations, it can be executed in seconds. If a particular beam is found to be incorrectly designed, it can be modified and the new design verified in a very short time by the machine.

13.2 COMPUTER CONTROL

The digital computer is ideally suited for use as a controller. The computer generates commands by transferring data to the controlled system via suitable output devices such as the digital-to-analog converter, and monitors the operation of the system being controlled by examining input transfers from various sensors connected to the system. The external system can also be monitored by the interrupt subsystem using sensors which are preset to detect abnormal operating conditions. Using these control and monitoring capabilities, the computer can control such things as industrial processes, scientific experiments, automobile traffic flow, transportation systems, and space vehicles.

For the control of an industrial process, information generated by the computer initiates the process and provides the commands necessary to maintain it. For example, in the operation of a steel rolling mill, the thickness of the metal being rolled must be held within very close tolerances. The computer controls the temperature of the metal, the rolling speed, and the pressure exerted on the steel during the process. By monitoring the thickness of the metal being produced, the control variables can be rapidly adjusted by the computer to maintain the desired thickness and quality of the finished product.

When used to control a scientific experiment, the computer is often superior to the best research scientist. It can monitor an experiment in meticulous detail and is able to reproduce the experimental conditions as often as needed to verify the experiment. Unlike a human being, it does not introduce any idiosyncrasies into the experimental data. An example of an experiment which lends itself to computer control is found in the field of experimental psychology. To determine how human beings behave in a certain situation, the conditions of the desired situation are presented to many subjects, and their behavior is recorded. A computer can present a situation via suitable audiovisual aids connected as output devices and can also record and correlate the responses produced. This technique produces results which are unaffected by the expectations of the psychologist which might be significant were he to conduct the experiment directly.

Computers are used to control and coordinate automobile traffic flow in an increasing number of cities and towns. In most installations, the computer controls every traffic signal located in a complete population center. It is preprogrammed to coordinate the operation of the traffic signals with the anticipated traffic flow. For example, during the morning rush hour, traffic moving toward the business districts is expedited, whereas during the evening rush hour, traffic moving in the opposite direction is expedited. At other times, it is assumed that traffic moves equally in all directions, and the signals are set to operate accordingly.

In more sophisticated traffic control systems, the actual flow of traffic is measured and provided as input to the computer. Thus, in addition to the preset control patterns described above, the computer can provide special signal control patterns when necessitated by unusual traffic conditions.

Modern high-speed transportation systems, such as monorail and rapid transit systems, use sophisticated computer control systems for safe, reliable operation. Status information which provides the location of each vehicle in the system is fed into the computer. The computer in turn generates commands to control the acceleration and velocity of each vehicle. When a vehicle is loading and discharging passengers, a conductor, rather than the computer, has control of the doors. However, once he closes the doors, the computer takes over control of the vehicle, causing it to accelerate and proceed to the next station. Until it comes to a halt and the doors are again opened, the computer has complete control over the system. Since it is possible for an emergency, of which the computer is unaware, to occur, a conductor can stop his vehicle by using an emergency braking procedure which cannot be counteracted by the computer. In this way, completely fail-safe operation is obtained.

Computers are used during every phase of the operation of a manned spacecraft. During the prelaunch countdown, computers monitor all the launch rocket systems. During the launch itself, all systems are controlled by computers located on the ground and in the space vehicle. While in space, the on-board computer controls many of the spacecraft systems. For example, using data received from the ground, the spacecraft computer can control the vehicle during a course-correction maneuver to ensure that the maneuver is executed accurately. The same computer is also responsible for controlling many of the intricate maneuvers needed to land the vehicle on the moon and launch it from the moon's surface. Finally, to ensure a safe reentry into the earth's atmosphere, the computer is used to orient the spacecraft so that it enters at a precise angle and with a precise attitude. It is extremely difficult to perform these tasks without the aid of a highly sophisticated computer control system.

13.3 BUSINESS APPLICATIONS

The business computer is used primarily to process large amounts of data which require sorting and collating. Thus, a machine which is intended for business applications is often called a **data processor** or a **data processing system**. Data processors are widely used by manufacturers, merchants, banks, stockbrokers, insurance companies, and government agencies, to name a few. They are used for inventory control, account billing and maintenance, payroll preparation, verifying tax returns, and other applications.

When a data processor is used for inventory control, a running balance of each item stocked is stored in the memory or in an auxiliary storage device. For each transaction involving one of the inventoried items, the balance is adjusted accordingly, depending upon whether a sale was made or additional items were purchased or manufactured to maintain the inventory. The computer can be programmed to check the balance of an item whenever a transaction occurs; if this balance drops below a preset level, a purchase or manufacturing order is generated by the machine.

Credit purchasing of commodities and services by individuals and institutions necessitates that customer accounts be maintained and that these accounts be billed periodically. A file is set up for each account in an auxiliary storage device. As each purchase or payment is recorded, the current balance is updated in the file. At a specified interval, a bill is prepared showing each transaction since the last billing date and the customer's current balance. A similar scheme is used by banks to maintain checking and savings accounts.

The preparation of payroll checks requires many repetitious arithmetic operations which are simple for a computer to perform but tedious for the human being. The hourly wage is multiplied by the number of hours worked to compute both the regular and overtime wages, and the amounts are added together. Deductions are calculated for income tax, social security, and group insurance payments and are subtracted from gross wages to compute the employee's net wages. The machine then prints the employee's name and net wages on an output form which serves as his paycheck. Another output form is also provided which tabulates all wages and deductions for the employee. When the payroll preparation is completed, a summary is prepared for the employer, as well as for the Internal Revenue Service, the Social Security Administration, and the insurance company. The latter summaries show each employee's gross wages and the amount deducted for taxes, social security, and insurance, respectively.

Until recently, the Internal Revenue Service had no way of checking each income tax return for accuracy or possible omission of taxable income. With the recent installation of extensive data processing equipment in several tax centers throughout the United States, it is now possible to check the arithmetic for each return submitted. Additional checks are made to confirm that all taxable income is reported. Information supplied by employers, banks, and investment companies are correlated with all returns, and obvious omissions are noted so that the tax examiner can request an audit. The computers also check each deduction, and if one appears excessive when compared to income, it is reported to the examiner for further scrutiny. By using such techniques, it is possible for all individuals to receive equal treatment, and anyone suspected of making an error on his tax return can be checked further.

13.4 SIMULATION

To evaluate a scientific theory directly is often either very expensive or potentially disastrous. For example, let us assume that three designs are proposed for the wing structure of a new aircraft which is being developed. To build three prototypes, each incorporating one of the proposed wing designs, is extremely costly. Moreover, if the design of one of the structures is not sound, it could cost the life of a test pilot. Since the engineering equations governing aerodynamic behavior are well-established, it is possible to simulate the behavior of each of the proposed wing designs on a computer. The simulation experiments can be made to cover a large variety of conditions, and the behavior of the three structures can be compared for these conditions. Thus, the best wing design can be chosen before the first prototype aircraft is constructed.

The example of the design of a bridge presented earlier also serves as an example of a simulation problem. The loading conditions which the bridge must withstand are simulated as part of the design procedure, and the design is therefore verified before the bridge is built.

13.5 DESIGN AUTOMATION

We have provided an example of how the computer is used to help design a bridge. We have also shown that many tasks can be automated with the aid of a computer. If the design process itself is automated, we have indeed achieved a desirable goal. For this reason, the subject of **design automation** is currently receiving a great deal of attention.

Design automation has been applied to the general problem of template optimization which can be illustrated by an example from the clothing industry. In order to minimize the cost of a man's suit, for example, the manufacturer attempts to obtain the maximum number of suits from each bolt of cloth. The patterns for the different parts of the suit are laid onto the cloth and manipulated by a tailor until the amount of wasted cloth is minimized. To do this for every size and style of suit to be cut turns out to be a very tedious task. It is also likely that the end result is not the true optimum, since it is not possible to try every possibility in a relatively short time.

The computer, however, is capable of examining a greater number of possibilities and can manipulate patterns from a greater variety of sizes and styles for a single bolt of cloth. In addition, once it has found an optimum solution to the problem, the same computer can be used to automatically control the cutting machine which cuts the cloth into the desired pieces. Thus, the entire process, from the optimization of the patterns to the cutting of the cloth, can be completely automated.

13.6 EDUCATION

In the field of education, computers are used in a variety of ways. In most colleges and universities, computers are used routinely to solve complex research problems that only a decade or so ago would not have been attempted. Computers are used to run sample programs written by students who are being taught how to program them. They are also used to grade test papers and to maintain student records. However, one of the most interesting applications of a computer in the field of education is its use as a teaching machine.

Several types of computerized teaching machines are in use. In one common type, the student is presented the text material on a CRT in a manner similar to that used in a conventional textbook. As he completes each "page" of the text, he signals the machine, which provides the next "page." After each topic, he is interrogated by the machine to determine whether he has indeed learned the material presented. Multiple-choice questions are displayed on the CRT screen, and the student indicates his answers by activating suitable keys on a simple input device. In some machines, a record is kept of the student's responses, and he is permitted to continue. In other machines, he is informed of the correctness of each response and given the option of reviewing the troublesome passages or continuing on. In the more sophisticated machines, an incorrect response automatically initiates a new teaching sequence to reemphasize the textual material which is causing the confusion. In this type of machine, it is possible to vary the review sequence with each student so that the maximum teaching effectiveness is achieved. The student is allowed to proceed to new material only when he has completely mastered the preceding text. An "I GIVE UP" button is provided so that the student who is hopelessly lost can review the complete lesson at any time.

Most computers which are used as teaching machines are capable of instructing many students simultaneously. Each student is provided his own display device and input keyboard which are connected to the machine in a manner similar to the time-sharing terminals in Chapter 10. A computerized teaching machine enables each student to study completely different subject material and to proceed at a rate consistent with his own learning ability.

The **third-generation** computer organization which we have described has evolved over a period of about twenty years. What will future generations of computers be like? In the final chapter of this book, we describe several new designs currently being built and explore other potential designs for the computers of the future.

EXERCISES

13.1 In each section of this chapter, different applications of computers were described. Under each heading, describe an application with which you have had some contact. Elaborate on how you think the computer is used for each application described. [Hint: If you have difficulty getting started, note that several of the applications which were mentioned in the introduction to Chapter 1 were not discussed in this chapter and can be used.]

14

COMPUTERS OF THE FUTURE

The **first generation** of electronic digital computers was introduced in the early nineteen fifties and used vacuum tube technology. These machines were very slow, compared to current computers, being capable of performing no more than several hundred arithmetic operations per second. Input—output was performed by relatively unsophisticated paper-tape and punched-card readers, and the computer itself had to wait while each character was being transferred into or out of the machine.

The **second-generation** computer used solid-state transistor technology rather than vacuum tubes. These machines were physically smaller and computationally faster than the older computers, being capable of executing over 50,000 arithmetic operations per second. Many of the input—output devices described in Chapters 7 and 8 were developed for the second-generation machine, and an early form of input—output channel was used to speed up overall operation.

The current **third-generation** computer is characterized by solid-state integrated-circuit technology, input—output control systems using multiple I/O channels and memory sharing, and an interrupt system. Size has again decreased, whereas speed has increased to over one million arithmetic operations per second.

It is extremely difficult to increase the speed of operation of a single computer beyond ten million arithmetic operations per second. Therefore, the **fourth-generation** computers now being contemplated and under construction use some form of multiprocessing structure to achieve higher speeds. One type of fourth-generation machine which will be capable of executing over two hundred million arithmetic operations per second is called a **parallel computer** and is described next.

14.1 PARALLEL COMPUTERS

In a multiprocessing system, each computer operates autonomously, sharing at most a common memory and several input–output and auxiliary storage devices. In this type of system, a tenfold increase in operating speed requires nearly a tenfold increase in size and cost. In a parallel computer, more systems are shared, so that a much higher speed is achieved for a given cost, as compared to an ordinary multiprocessing system.

A simplified block diagram illustrating the organization of a parallel computer is shown in Figure 14-1. Although the number of arithmetic units is left unspecified as N in the figure, typical values for N lie between 32 and 256. The arithmetic units are controlled by a single main control unit which executes a program stored in the main memory. Each of the arithmetic units therefore performs the same operation at the same time using different data, since each arithmetic unit uses operands which are stored in its corresponding memory module. Thus, the main control and its associated hardware, such as the index register and main memory, are not duplicated for each arithmetic unit as in a conventional multiprocessor.

The parallel computer is best suited for solving a specialized type of problem which involves the manipulation of **arrays** of numbers. An example of such an array is the **vector** $(a_1, a_2, \ldots, a_N)$. To add two vectors together, the corresponding elements of each vector are added together. Thus,

$$(a_1, a_2, \ldots, a_N) + (b_1, b_2, \ldots, b_N) = (a_1 + b_1, a_2 + b_2, \ldots, a_N + b_N)$$

As a specific example, the sum of the two five-element vectors (5, 7, 3, 6, 4) and (8, 0, −3, 8, −10) is (13, 7, 0, 14, −6). To add together twenty N-element vectors in a conventional computer requires N times as long as to add twenty numbers together, since the loop to add the numbers together must be executed N times. Using a parallel computer, the addition of twenty vectors takes as long as the addition of twenty numbers. To set up the problem, the first element of each vector is stored in memory module 1, the second, in memory module 2, and so on. While the first arithmetic unit is adding together the first elements of each vector, each of the other arithmetic units is simultaneously adding the other corresponding elements together. Therefore, the complete sum vector is produced during the execution of a single loop of instructions by the computer.

It is possible for an arithmetic unit to use an operand or result from another memory module. This type of operation is necessary for operations on **matrices**, which are **two-dimensional** arrays of numbers. The organizational details for this

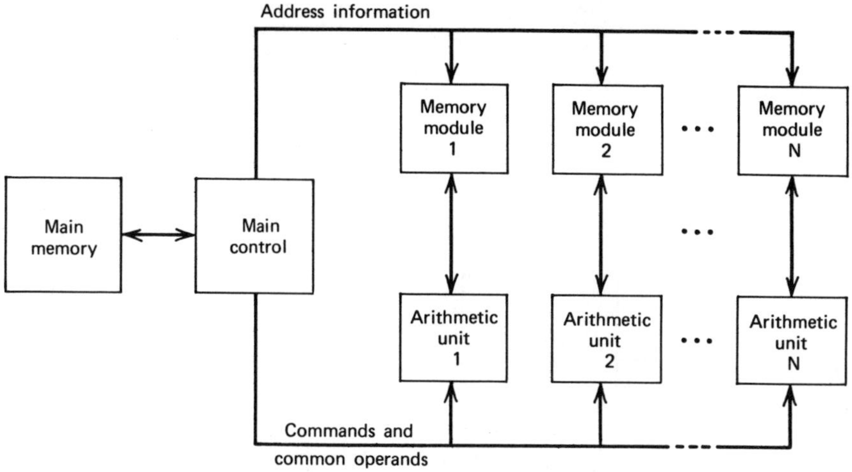

FIGURE 14-1. Block diagram of the organization of a parallel computer.

type of operation are not shown in Figure 14-1, since they are beyond the scope of this discussion.

Another computer which is well-suited for solving problems involving the manipulation of arrays is called the **pipeline computer.** In the pipeline computer, operands are manipulated in parallel in a set of **pipelines**, which replace the arithmetic units of the multiprocessor and parallel computers. We examine the operation of the pipeline computer next.

14.2 THE PIPELINE COMPUTER

Both the pipeline and parallel computers are capable of executing over two hundred million arithmetic operations per second. The pipeline computer, however, manipulates numbers in a completely different manner than does the parallel machine. The organization of the pipeline computer is illustrated in block diagram form in Figure 14-2. As shown in the figure, N pipelines are connected directly to a single memory. Operands are transmitted from the memory to each pipeline, and computed results are returned to the memory from the pipelines. Each pipeline performs a single predetermined operation on the operands transmitted to it. For example, for each pair of operands sent to an ADD pipeline, the sum of the two operands is computed. Similarly, a MULTIPLY pipeline computes the product of each pair of operands sent to it, and so forth. A typical pipeline computer consists of several ADD and MULTIPLY pipelines as well as a number of pipelines for computing special functions such as square roots.

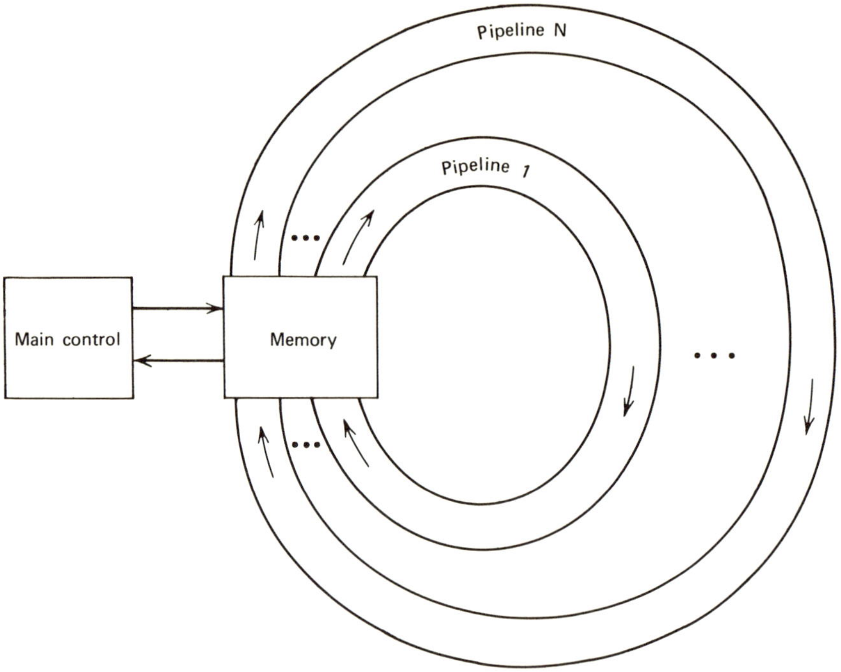

FIGURE 14-2. Block diagram of the organization of a pipeline computer.

Each pipeline operates in a manner similar to an assembly line, with several steps of an arithmetic operation being executed at each station along the line. For example, a typical station in a MULTIPLY pipeline implements the following processing steps: test the next multiplier bit; add the multiplicand to the partial product sum if the tested bit is a ONE; shift the partial product sum one bit position to the left. Because of the nature of the multiplication algorithm, it is necessary to provide k identical stations which implement these steps, where k is the number of bits in the multiplier. Each pipeline, therefore, consists of as many stations as is necessary to perform the respective arithmetic operation. The operation of a pipeline is further illustrated in Figure 14-3.

Assume that initially the illustrated pipeline is inactive and that the first set of operands A_1 and B_1 of arrays A and B are just being transmitted to it, as shown in Figure 14-3(a). After the operands have passed through one processing station, the pipeline appears as shown in Fig. 14-3(b). Note that the second set of operands A_2 and B_2 are just entering the pipeline at this time. Figure 14-3(c) illustrates the state of the pipeline after the operands have passed through another station. Note that while A_1 and B_1 were passing through station 2, A_2 and B_2 were passing through station 1. Operands A_3 and B_3 are just entering the pipeline at this time. This procedure is repeated, and in Figure 14-3(d) we show the state of the pipeline after A_1 and B_1 have passed through the last station, M, and the computed result C_1 is being transmitted to the memory to be stored in array C. At this time, A_2 and B_2 have passed through station M-1, A_3 and B_3 have passed through station M-2, and so on; A_M and B_M have passed through station 1, and A_{M+1} and B_{M+1} are just entering the pipeline. From this point on, until arrays A and B are completely processed, computed results will be transmitted to the memory and stored in array C at a rate determined only by the time that an operand spends in a single processing station. The total time that the operands spend in the pipeline does not influence the computation speed.

In order for the complete system to function properly, it is necessary that the memory be capable of transmitting data to and from the pipelines in a highly efficient manner. Efficient operation is ensured if pipeline data is stored in the memory in arrays which are then transferred to and from the pipelines in the same manner that memory blocks are transferred to and from input–output devices through I/O channels, as described in Section 6.2. In the example given above, the transfers of arrays A and B from the memory to the input of the pipeline, and the transfer of computed results into array C in the memory, are initiated by the main control and thereafter take place without its further intervention until they are completed. Thus, several pipelines can operate simultaneously, each obtaining operands from and transmitting computed results to the memory. Caution is necessary on the part of the programmer, however, to ensure that the computation of a particular array is complete before an attempt is made to use it as an input array for another pipeline.

We have assumed in the description of the pipeline computer that the memory operates rapidly enough to keep up with the pipelines. In practice, it is difficult to achieve the required speed in a single memory. However, by using a multiple memory organization, as described in Section 6.3, the required memory speed can be obtained.

The use of a parallel or pipeline computer to solve conventional problems is very inefficient, since a single arithmetic unit is sufficient for this purpose. However, there are many scientific problems, such as those encountered in the field of atomic physics, which require the manipulation of large arrays. The parallel and pipeline computers are far more suitable for solving problems of this type at high speed.

A picture such as an aerial photograph can be represented by a two-dimensional array of numbers wherein each number corresponds to the image density at a particular point. An aerial photograph can therefore be processed by a computer to reduce it to a line drawing or a map and to locate objects such as buildings, rivers, lakes, and automobiles on the map. The use of a conventional computer for this purpose is not very efficient, since arrays are manipulated more easily by a parallel machine. However, a parallel computer which is

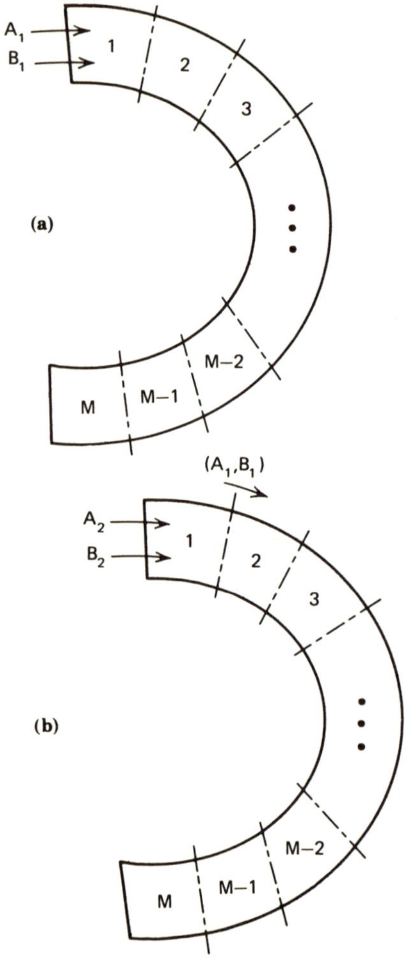

FIGURE 14-3. Details of the operation of a pipeline. (a) Initial state of the pipeline. (b) State of the pipeline after operands have passed through one station.

intended primarily for picture processing is organized differently from the parallel machine we described in Section 14.1. In Section 14.3, we describe the **picture processor** and how it operates.

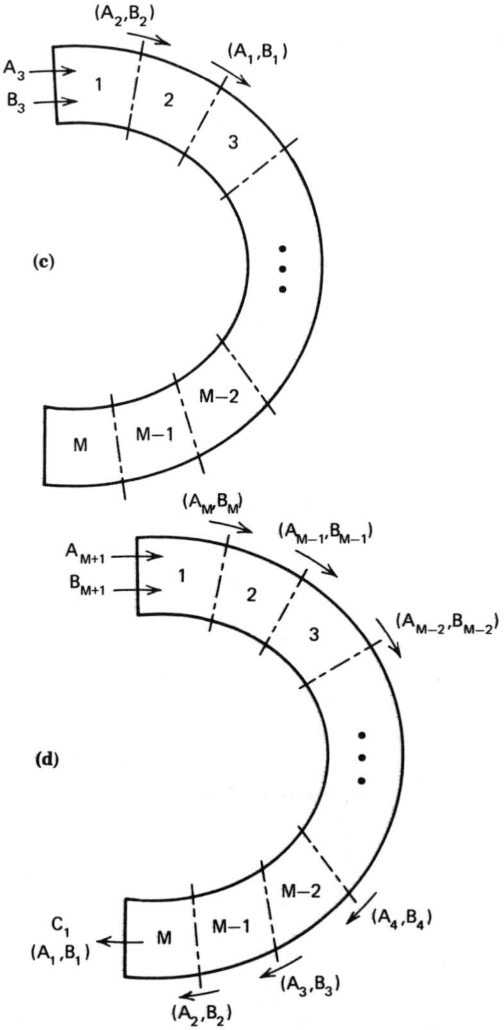

FIGURE 14-3. (c) State of the pipeline after operands have passed through two stations. (d) State of the pipeline after operands have passed through M stations.

14.3 PICTURE PROCESSORS

A parallel processor consists of an array of between 32 and 256 arithmetic units, each of which is capable of performing arithmetic and logic. In a picture processor, the arithmetic capability is unnecessary, and only very elementary

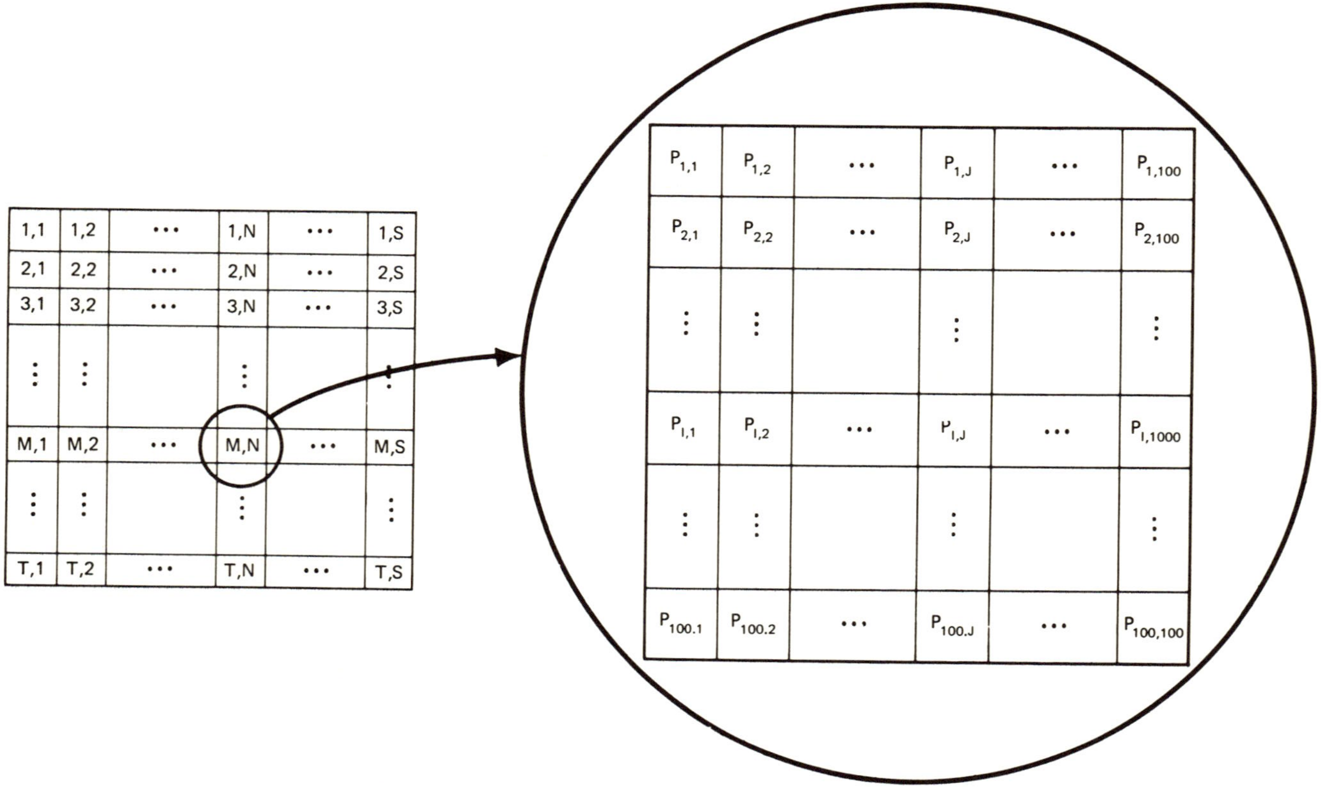

FIGURE 14-4. Illustration of how a picture is divided into S x T segments for processing by the picture processor. The inset shows how a segment (M,N) is further divided into 10,000 picture elements.

logic operations are required. Thus, the arithmetic units are replaced by a much larger number of less complex **processing units**. The ideal picture processor should contain a sufficient number of processing units so that a complete picture, down to the most minute detail, can be processed at one time. For a typical picture, such a machine would require at least one million processing units, which would make its cost prohibitive. Since a picture processing computer consisting of 1000–10,000 processing units is more realistic, each picture is initially subdivided into segments, and a single segment is processed by the machine at one time. Figure 14-4 illustrates how a picture is divided into segments and how each segment (M,N) is further divided into 10,000 picture elements $P_{I,J}$ for processing. Each processing unit is uniquely associated with one of the 10,000 picture elements and has available to it picture information from its associated picture element and the eight neighboring elements. For illustration, Figure 14-5 shows picture element $P_{I,J}$ and its eight neighbors, all of which are available to processing unit I,J. For simplicity, we will assume that each dark picture element is represented by a single ZERO, while each light element is represented by a ONE.

In operation, the picture processor extracts geometrical **features** such as edges, line endings, corners, and circles and processes these features to determine what objects are present in the picture. As an example, we will show how a line ending can be detected. Figure 14-6 illustrates how a line ending appears to one of the processing units. To detect this feature, each processing unit whose corresponding central element $P_{I,J}$ is a ZERO is instructed to count the ZERO's present in the eight neighboring elements. If only one of these neighboring elements is ZERO, the processing element responds that it has found a dark line ending. Note that the orientation of the line ending is not considered nor is any restriction placed on how many dark line endings can be detected in a single picture. Every processing element finding a dark line element responds, and its output is recorded in the memory. Other geometrical features are similarly detected. As an example of how features can be interpreted as objects, let us examine the features present in the dark rectangle shown in Figure 14-7. If, after detecting the appropriate edges and corners, further processing verifies that the eight features are oriented as shown in the figure, then it is noted that a dark

$P_{I-1,J-1}$	$P_{I,J-1}$	$P_{I+1,J-1}$
$P_{I-1,J}$	$P_{I,J}$	$P_{I+1,J}$
$P_{I-1,J+1}$	$P_{I,J+1}$	$P_{I+1,J+1}$

FIGURE 14-5. Illustration of picture element $P_{I,J}$ and its eight neighboring elements.

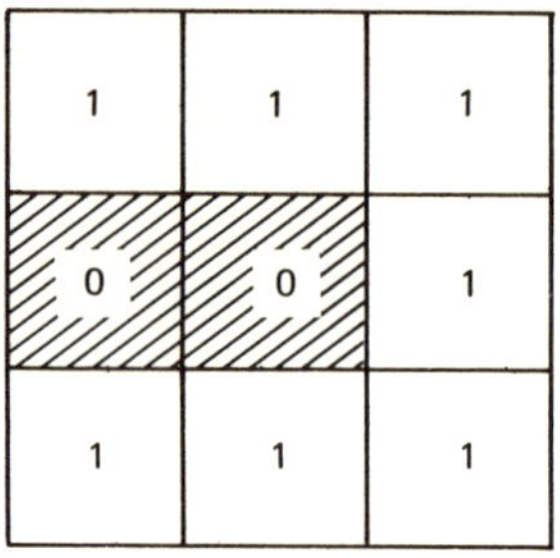

FIGURE 14-6. Example of a dark line ending (0 – dark elements, 1 – light elements).

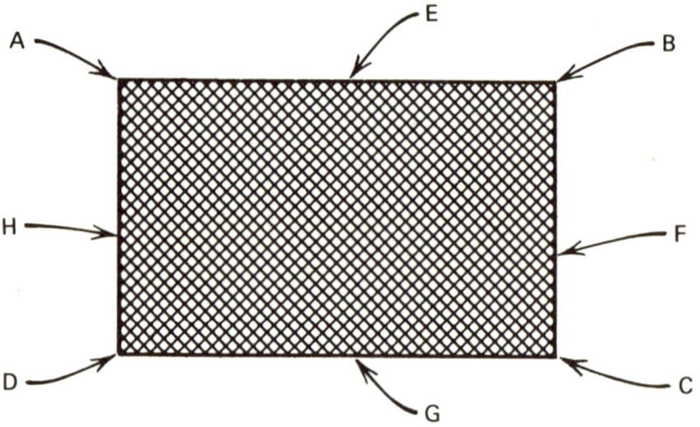

FIGURE 14-7. Illustration showing features present in a rectangle: A, upper left corner; B, upper right corner; C, lower right corner; D, lower left corner; E, upper edge; F, right edge; G, lower edge; H, left edge.

rectangle has been found. The location of the rectangle in the picture and its size can be determined from the location of the features.

The picture processor can be used to process many different types of pictures, since it can be programmed to look for different combinations of features for different applications. For example, the processor can be used to interpret aerial photographs obtained during military reconnaissance missions and provide maps which can be used by the armed forces. It can also be used to evaluate bubble chamber and spark chamber photographs obtained from experiments in nuclear physics. During these experiments, thousands of pictures are taken, but only a few show any significant results. The processor can quickly evaluate each photograph and thereby eliminate most of the extraneous ones. In the field of medicine, the picture processor can be used to interpret photographs of many types of microscope slides for the physician. There is reason to expect that the machine will be more consistent in its evaluation of these pictures than either the physician or the laboratory technician. In these and other applications, the capability of the picture processor is just being discovered, and it will be many years before it is properly exploited.

Another type of parallel computer is the **associative processor.** It differs from the third-generation computer because data can be retrieved from the memory using **stored information** as an alternative to using an address. We describe how the associative processor operates and what its potential uses are in Section 14.4.

14.4 ASSOCIATIVE PROCESSORS

Just as in a conventional computer, each location in the memory of an associative processor is assigned an address. The memory can therefore be used in the manner described primarily in Chapters 1 and 6. In addition, each piece of stored data is assigned a **label** which is stored along with the data in the memory. When used in the associative mode, the label, and not the address, determines which of the data is to be read from the memory. In operation, a label is sent to the memory and the memory is instructed to read the data from every location whose label is identical to the one sent. Data can therefore be read from many memory locations simultaneously. To see how this data is used and to point out the advantages of this type of machine, we present an example illustrating the use of the associative processor for information retrieval.

Let us assume that we wish to use the associative processor to perform a literature search of books written about computers. Each book is assigned a data code; each major topic, such as fixed-point numbers, time-sharing, parallel computation, and so on, is assigned a label code. For each major topic contained in a book, a location in the memory contains both the corresponding label and data codes. In Figure 14-8, we have shown the contents of several memory locations for illustration. Books A and B are assigned data codes 563 and 879, respectively. Thus, book A includes topics on fixed-point numbers (001), floating-point numbers (056), and parallel computation (102), while book B includes topics on floating-point numbers and time-sharing (083). Information can be read out by specifying an address, such as 1055, which yields label code 102 and data code 563. However, if the memory is requested to read the data from all locations containing label 056, data codes 563 and 879 will be among the codes read. If the codes are interpreted and listed, the list indicates that both books A and B contain topics on floating-point numbers. If label 001 is specified, data code 563 will be among the codes read. In order to perform this type of search on an ordinary third-generation computer, it is necessary to sequentially read the contents of each memory location and test it to see if it contains the correct label. The associative processor performs all of the required logic in a single step and is therefore much more efficient for this application.

Complex labels can also be specified when an associative processor is used.

Memory location	Contents	
	Label	Data
1053	001	563
1054	056	563
1055	102	563
1056	056	879
1057	083	879

001	Fixed-point numbers
056	Floating-point numbers
083	Time-sharing
102	Parallel computation

563	Book A
879	Book B

FIGURE 14-8. Example showing contents of several memory locations in an associative processor used for performing a literature search of computer books.

For example, two labels can be specified simultaneously, and then only data which is associated with both labels is read out. In our example, if labels 001 and 056 are both specified, data code 563, but not 879, is read out. This information indicates to the user that book A has topics on both fixed-point and floating-point numbers, whereas book B does not. As before, the associative processor performs all the required logic in a single step, whereas an ordinary machine would examine each memory location individually.

The computers described above operate more rapidly than the sequential machines because of their parallel organization. However, in either a sequential or a parallel computer, if a circuit does not operate properly, the whole machine is subject to malfunction. A computer worth over a million dollars and capable of executing millions of operations per second can therefore be totally disabled for hours while a serviceman tries to locate the malfunction. For this reason, it is desirable to build a computer which can continue to operate correctly despite the presence of a malfunctioning circuit. Such a machine is called a **fault-tolerant** computer. Several ways that fault-tolerant computers can be built are described in Section 14.5.

14.5 FAULT-TOLERANT MACHINES

The first requirement of a fault-tolerant computer is that it have the ability to detect computing errors when they occur. One way of building an error-detecting machine is to provide complete redundancy. For example, two identical arithmetic units can be used and the same data and instructions supplied to both. Then, the system is known to be operating correctly as long as the same results are computed by both units at all times. When an error occurs, there is no way of determining which of the two results is correct. By using three arithmetic units, the system can be made fault-tolerant. In the latter case, if the results computed by two of the units agree, the common result is used. An occasional disagreement by one of the arithmetic units can be ignored; however, if one of the units repeatedly disagrees with the other two, it is assumed to be malfunctioning and repairs are initiated. While repairs are being made, the system can still be used, as long as both of the remaining arithmetic units always compute identical results. Thus, the machine can continue to operate properly as long as two of the three arithmetic units are functioning properly. Although we have used the arithmetic unit for illustration, the same type of redundancy can be used for any subsystem of the computer.

Unfortunately, providing the degree of redundancy described above increases the cost of a computer substantially. A more economical fault-tolerant computer utilizes only partial redundancy. To each number being manipulated, several additional bits called **error-correcting** bits are appended. The values of the error-correcting bits depend upon the other bits of the number in a manner which allows errors to be detected and corrected. After each arithmetic operation, the error-correcting bits are examined to determine whether an error has occurred. If an error is detected, the result of the arithmetic operation is automatically corrected by the machine. The user of the machine is therefore supplied with correct results and need not be informed that an error has taken place.

Other methods for providing fault-tolerant operation include providing redundancy on the circuit level and using fail-safe circuits which can continue to operate with faulty components. Much work remains to be done before a reasonably priced fault-tolerant computer is introduced on the commercial market. However, such machines are currently being used in military and space applications where errors cannot be tolerated.

Other types of new machines will undoubtedly be introduced in the future. Many of the principles described in this book will be used in these systems. Just as with the parallel and fault-tolerant computers, many future generations of computers will be extensions of the third-generation machine which we have described.

EXERCISES

14.1 What is a parallel computer?

14.2 Compare a parallel computer with a multiprocessor.

14.3 For what types of problems is a parallel computer best suited?

14.4 How does the pipeline computer differ from a parallel computer?

14.5 What is a picture processor?

14.6 How does the picture processor differ from the "conventional" parallel computer?

14.7 What is an associative processor?

14.8 How does an associative processor differ from a parallel computer? How does it differ from a conventional computer?

14.9 What is a fault-tolerant computer?

14.10 What advantages does a fault-tolerant computer have over other types of computers?

BIBLIOGRAPHY

HISTORY OF COMPUTERS

Babbage, C., et al. Charles Babbage and His Calculating Engines, P. Morrison and E. Morrison, eds. New York: Dover, 1961.

COMPUTING PRINCIPLES

Bartee, T. C. Digital Computer Fundamentals, 2nd ed. New York: McGraw-Hill, 1966.

Calingaert, P. Principles of Computation. Reading, Mass.: Addison-Wesley, 1965.

Hellerman, H. Digital Computer System Principles. New York: McGraw-Hill, 1967.

Hull, T. E. Introduction to Computing. Englewood Cliffs, N.J.: Prentice-Hall, 1966.

Weinstein, S. M., and A. Keim. Fundamentals of Digital Computers. New York: Holt, Rinehart, & Winston, 1965.

COMPUTER ORGANIZATION

Flores, I. Computer Organization. Englewood Cliffs, N.J.: Prentice-Hall, 1969.

Gear, C. W. Computer Organization and Programming. New York: McGraw-Hill, 1969.

PROGRAMMING

Cutler, D. I. Introduction to Computer Programming. Englewood Cliffs, N.J.: Prentice-Hall, 1964.

Galler, B. A. The Language of Computers. New York: McGraw-Hill, 1962.

Ledley, R. S. Programming and Utilizing Digital Computers. New York: McGraw-Hill, 1962.

PROGRAMMING – ASSEMBLY LANGUAGE

Stabley, D. H. System 360 Assembler Language. New York: John Wiley & Sons, 1967.

Wimmert, R. J. Computer Programming Principles, Vol. 1, Machine/Assembly Language. New York: Holt, Rinehart, & Winston, 1968.

COMPUTER ARITHMETIC

Flores, I. Logic of Computer Arithmetic. Englewood Cliffs, N.J.: Prentice-Hall, 1963.

Richards, R. K. Arithmetic Operations in Digital Computers. New York: Van Nostrand Reinhold, 1955.

COMPUTER DESIGN

Chu, Y. Digital Computer Design Fundamentals. New York: McGraw-Hill, 1962.

Flores, I. Computer Design. Englewood Cliffs, N.J.: Prentice-Hall, 1967.

Foster, C. C. Computer Architecture. New York: Van Nostrand Reinhold, 1970.

MEMORY SYSTEMS

Renwick, W. Digital Storage Systems. New York: Barnes & Noble, 1964.

Yovits, M. C., ed. Large-Capacity Memory Techniques for Computing Systems. New York: Macmillan, 1962.

INPUT–OUTPUT

Hoagland, A. S. Digital Magnetic Recording. New York: John Wiley & Sons, 1963.

Hoeschele, D. F. Analog to Digital: Digital to Analog Conversion Techniques. New York: John Wiley & Sons, 1968.

Wilson, R. A. Optical Page Reading Devices. New York: Van Nostrand Reinhold, 1966.

TIME-SHARING SYSTEMS

Orr, W. D. Conversational Computers. New York: John Wiley & Sons, 1968.

Wilkes, M. V. Time-Sharing Computer Systems. New York: American Elsevier, 1968.

REAL-TIME SYSTEMS

Desmonde, W. H. Real-Time Data Processing Systems: Introductory Concepts. Englewood Cliffs, N.J.: Prentice-Hall, 1964.

Rothstein, M. F. Guide to the Design of Real-Time Systems. New York: John Wiley & Sons, 1970.

PROGRAMMING – FORTRAN AND OTHER COMPILER LANGUAGES

Bauer, C. R., P. P. Anthony, and D. A. Gomberg. Basic PL/I Programming. Reading, Mass.: Addison-Wesley, 1968.

Iverson, K. E. A Programming Language (APL). New York: John Wiley & Sons, 1962.

Kemeny, J. G., and T. E. Kurtz. BASIC Programming. New York: John Wiley & Sons, 1967.

Ledley, R. S. FORTRAN IV Programming. New York: McGraw-Hill, 1966.

McCracken, D. D. A Guide to ALGOL Programming. New York: John Wiley & Sons, 1962.

McCracken, D. D. A Guide to COBOL Programming. New York: John Wiley & Sons, 1963.

Organick, E. I. FORTRAN IV Primer. Reading, Mass.: Addision-Wesley, 1966.

Randell, B., and L. J. Russell. ALGOL 60 Implementation. New York: Academic Press, 1964.

Spencer, D. D. A Guide to BASIC Programming: A Time-Sharing Language. Reading, Mass.: Addison-Wesley, 1970.

Weinberg, G. M. PL/I Programming Primer. New York: McGraw-Hill, 1966.

Wendel, T. M., and W. H. Williams. Introduction to Data Processing and COBOL. New York: McGraw-Hill, 1969.

SYSTEM PROGRAMMING

Barron, D. W. Assemblers and Loaders. New York: American Elsevier, 1970.

Hopgood, F. R. Compiling Techniques. New York: American Elsevier, 1969.

Rosen, S. Programming Systems and Languages. New York: McGraw-Hill, 1967.

Wegner, P., ed. Introduction to System Programming. New York: Academic Press, 1964.

MICROPROGRAMMING

Husson, S. S. Microprogramming: Principles and Practices. Englewood Cliffs, N.J.: Prentice-Hall, 1970.

NUMERICAL ANALYSIS

Carnahan, B., H. A. Luther, and J. O. Wilkes. Applied Numerical Methods. New York: John Wiley & Sons, 1969.

Pennington, R. H. Introductory Computer Methods and Numerical Analysis, 2nd ed. New York: Macmillan, 1969.

Ralston, A. First Course in Numerical Analysis. New York: McGraw-Hill, 1965.

Stanton, R. G. Numerical Methods for Science and Engineering. Englewood Cliffs, N.J.: Prentice-Hall, 1961.

APPLICATIONS

Borko, H., ed. Computer Applications in the Behavioral Sciences. Englewood Cliffs, N.J.: Prentice-Hall, 1962.

Evans, G., et al. Simulation Using Digital Computers. Englewood Cliffs, N.J.: Prentice-Hall, 1967.

Favret, A. G. Introduction to Digital Computer Applications. New York: Van Nostrand Reinhold, 1965.

Fry, E. B. Teaching Machines and Programmed Instruction. New York: McGraw-Hill, 1963.

Martin, F. F. Computer Modeling and Simulation. New York: John Wiley & Sons, 1968.

Salton, G. Automatic Information Organization and Retrieval. New York: McGraw-Hill, 1968.

Savas, E. S. Computer Control of Industrial Processes. New York: McGraw-Hill, 1965.

PARALLEL COMPUTERS

Hobbs, L. C., ed. Parallel Processor Systems, Technologies, and Applications. New York: Spartan Books, 1970.

FAULT-TOLERANT COMPUTERS

Lin, S. An Introduction to Error-Correcting Codes. Englewood Cliffs, N.J.: Prentice-Hall, 1970.

Pierce, W. Failure-Tolerant Computer Design. New York: Academic Press, 1965.

Sellers, F. F., L. W. Bearnson, and M. Y. Hsiao. Error-Detecting Logic for Digital Computers. New York: McGraw-Hill, 1968.

INDEX